Praise for All the Power

"Mark loves to dance with words. He finds struggle in right as well as wrong, all the while keeping time with a cadence of thoughts and approaches. He is a free-agent believer open to possibility. His decision to reflect on his personal journey through what he refers to as 'revolution' may lull the reader with the packaging, as the written word is often mistaken for the truth. The fact that questions in a written form can at times resemble answers is a danger for most activist writers, as well as writing activists. Be that as it may, it is Mark's content; the inexhaustible work ethic, and boundless hope for the better, that serves as the true ballast of his conviction."

—Ian MacKaye

"By naming some of the difficult, unanswered questions from past movements, *All the Power* opens up exciting conversations about how to proceed in today's world. This fascinating examination of activism over the past fifty years is a must-read for anyone wanting to contribute effectively to movements for change."

—Cathy Wilkerson, Students for a Democratic Society and the Weather Underground

"Mark's decency and vision are both appealing and effective in suggesting practical strategies to make systemic change. *All the Power* is an incisive and important look at past and present North American radicalism that can help us build a better world."

—Heather Booth, Student Nonviolent Coordinating Committee, cofounder of "Jane" collective and Midwest Academy

"Does organized rebellion need its own Martha Stewart? Relax, this isn't it. In your grasp is a heartfelt, brick-by-brick guide from a committed veteran activist on heart, soul, music, his own life's surprises, and how we can all bring ongoing change to our own communities." —Jello Biafra

ALL THE POWER

REVOLUTION WITHOUT ILLUSION

MARK ANDERSEN

PUNK PLANET BOOKS
CHICAGO

Published by Punk Planet Books/Akashic Books
©2004 Mark Andersen

Punk Planet Books is a division of Independents' Day Media

Book design by Pirate Signal International

ISBN: 1-888451-72-6
Library of Congress Control Number: 2004106234
Printed in Canada
First printing

Akashic Books
PO Box 1456
New York, NY 10009
Akashic7@aol.com
www.akashicbooks.com

Punk Planet Books
4229 N. Honore
Chicago, IL 60613
books@punkplanet.com
www.punkplanetbooks.com

In memory of Sandra Foster, John Wiebenson, Buster Crohn, John Farrell, Sita Paulickpulle, and Joe Strummer.

Thanks first and foremost to my parents and Craig O'Hara (without whom this book would not exist); Johnny Temple, Dan Sinker, and Johanna Ingalls at Akashic/Punk Planet; my beloved Tulin for patience, love, and support; to my other mother, Lucy Stokes, and my other family, the Emmaus community (while not forgetting the Tischmaks of Reserve, MT!), especially Diane Amussen and Sally Matthews; Brendan for nurturing my raggedy old computer; Ian for beyond-maximum inspiration and friendship; my brother Dale and his wife Cindy, my sister Barbara and nieces Rachel, Tanya, Gracie and nephews Royce, Beau, and Christian, and cousins Jon and June with loving memory of my sister Judy and sister-in-law Debbie; the Demolition Cat (with love to Mothra); Ramsey at AK Press; Mark Jenkins, Robin Diener, and their beautiful, feisty felines; all my comrades at Emmaus Services for the Aging, Positive Force DC (especially my book discussion group pals Scott, Katja, Ellen, Sunny, DeeDee, Cassandra, and Asantewaa, as well as Christina, Wade, and Ryan), and all who have worked on building the Flemming Center; my political allies (and enemies) down the years for all the challenge and education; Barbara Hill, Mary and Sylvester Judd, Alice Jones, Lillian Mickens, Mary Hall, Marilyn Davis, Augustine Black, and Alverta Munlyn for sustaining St. Aloysius Parish over the years, and to all my other inspiring friends there; Jennifer Baumgardner, fellow radical refugee from the Great Plains; Heather Booth, Elaine Brown, Cathy Wilkerson, and Jello Biafra for the gifts of courage and vision; Sean Knight, Marie Theimer, Lynne Owens, Frank Smyth, Donna Rich, Alexandra Escudero, Maja, Anoop, Stephen Maley and Alice Stanley, Piero Gleijeses, Diane Monash, Riordan Roett, Robert Rydell, Marvin Shaw, Ken Weaver, Anne Williams, Lynda Sexson, Jerry Calvert, Barbara Honeyman, Greg Carr, Sherm Janke, Don Clark, and my all other catalytic compatriots at MSU and SAIS; Charlie Parker, Katherine Wertheim, Kevin Mattson, Jenny Toomey, Brad Sigal, Anna, and Sandino; Benji and Joel Madden, as well as Nick; Justin, Pat, Anne of the Anti-Flag family; to the kids growing up at Sursum Corda and anyone else feeling forgotten, forsaken, and alone; and finally to all of my extended family and the other people of Sheridan County, Montana, that harsh, unforgiving, but beautiful land: thanks for giving me life.

TABLE OF CONTENTS

PREFACE
BY JENNIFER BAUMGARDNER

I was eighteen years old and happily ensconced in a small, progressive, mid-western college by the time I could be proudly radical. That is, through my feminist group and my guerrilla theater troupe, I finally had a band of like-minded friends who supported my values and enabled me to feel like I "belonged," rather than being a weird, crazy, bitter outsider.

I also belonged in ways other than being radical. I remember learning sophomore year about intersecting oppressions of class, race, education, gender, sexuality, appearance, religion, etc., and feeling very grateful to be a woman. I hadn't ever had any overt sense of being ripped off by Mother Nature or the world at large, but suddenly, at college in 1988, I realized that by dint of being a woman, I was oppressed.

This was actually a relief because, as I said, I was learning about hierarchy and the cruel and unjust use of authority and feeling a bit awkward to be at the top of the food chain, as it were: you know, white, middle class, Protestant, straight (at the time), educated, thin-ish. (Granted, I was from North Dakota, but I didn't realize that might qualify me as oppressed—or at least deprived—until I moved to New York.)

Still, why be relieved? Why identify as oppressed? Well, at the time, I was learning about power in a new way and the overarching message I had absorbed was that power ("the ability to do, act, or affect strongly") was negative. *Power corrupts. Power requires the disempowerment of others. Power might be an aphrodisiac, missy, but the kind that will make you wake up next to Henry Kissinger!*

Being oppressed made me feel, paradoxically, *powerful* as a radical. I wasn't one of those nasty oppressors. I was automatically, as of birth, part of the innocent club. My oppression gave me permission to speak in left-wing settings. *Those white guys,* I thought at the time, *they've had their time to talk—they don't have permission here. No oppression, no dice.* Of course, this kind of philosophy inevitably hoisted me by my own petard, since in a diverse group of women I might be the equivalent of the white middle-class guy, too privileged to have any credence in a radical setting. (*But wait,* I'd think, *I'm also bisexual! Does that count for anything?*)

I wasn't always so confused about power. In fact, four years before college, I had an experience that I now recognize as my formative activist click. I was fifteen and living in Fargo. My sister was sixteen and also happened to be sixteen weeks pregnant. She didn't want to tell my parents, even though they were pro-choice and certainly would have paid for her procedure and supported her, so she turned to me. I remember feeling a thrill when she laid down the problem and the deadline: We needed to raise $200 in just a few days or she wouldn't be able to get an abortion in North Dakota and would have to travel to get a more expensive procedure in Minneapolis, four hours away.

I hopped into action, phoning my one acquaintance that I thought might have $200 and not tell on us. His name was K., a senior in high school who had portrayed Danny Zuko in our recent school production of *Grease.* (I was Cha-Cha.) K. had to pay for his own college the next year and I guessed, correctly, that he had savings. Long story short, he helped me. When I steered my bike into the parking lot of the Fargo Women's Health Clinic, ten twenties bulging in the back pocket of my Benetton jeans, and then handed off the dough to the receptionist, I never felt so good. It was a mix of success, relief, righteousness, and power. I felt like I had the ability to have an impact on the world, my community, my sister's dire situation, and my own life. I was *powerful.*

Power is a tricky thing; one that is integral to the life of a social-justice activist. This is something I know but at times have forgotten or misunderstood in my journey. My feelings of relief to be called powerless (by virtue of being female) in college reflected a fear of being seen as inferior in radical terms because of my other privileges. Was I really interested in transforming the world? Or did I simply want to feel superior?

In Mark Andersen's *All the Power: Revolution Without Illusion,* he asks exactly that crucial question of us radicals and idealists, as well as so many other challenging queries. He writes about real power in all of its potential. He examines the power of radicals—the ones that want nothing to do with the existing system, who don't go to church or drive SUVs. And he talks about the power of—hmmm, shall we call them the regular folks?—the ones that have lawns or respect the police, but who are nevertheless invested in a socially just world.

There is an inherent tension between the radicals and the "milder" visionaries, but Mark points out the illusions that we radicals sometimes drape ourselves in that can keep us from really making change or truly connecting to the communities we purport to want to help. He describes, for instance, the hopelessness of simply hating America, and invites a vision of patriotism for us lefties. It's our country, too. And furthermore, if America is as powerful (and oppressive) as we activists think it is, we *have* to be part of this country; shaping it, not just running from it so its taint doesn't besmirch our pure idea of ourselves. (*I might be American but I'm not part of the problem,* this ideology seems to say, *I hate McDonald's and I'm wearing hemp!* As if America is only its corporate brand names and not the millions who work in the fast-food dives or live in shelters or teach in the high schools.) As Mark asks, "If we give up on any possible redemption of this country, what is our alternative?"

Mark's alternative is to believe in the country, to believe in the flawed middle class, and to believe in the radical punk rock scene that gave him his most profound arena in which to be an activist. A call to reclaim power in all its possibility is one of the gifts of this anti-manifesto.

This book is also the very instructive memoir of a man who has devoted decades to radical movements, including ones we often think of as politically retrograde—like Mark's devotion to his Catholic Church. It's the story of an idealist's struggle to create a separate margin that would be much better—more utopian, more egalitarian—than the mainstream, *and* it is the story of his acknowledgment of the elitism those margins can unwittingly contain. Mark's message is that we *can* have revolution, but we must do it with our eyes wide open, honestly, and with acknowledgment that the mainstream has a power that we must connect to as well. After all, by definition, the mainstream has the power of sheer numbers—and if we assume no possible redemption for or value in that huge populace, then where is our revolution?

In *All the Power,* Mark talks a lot about reasons to join radical move-ments that have to do with personal gain—such as needing to fit in or to find a venue in which we can easily become leaders and earn big reputations. Without overly judging these personal, perfectly human reasons that people are drawn to alternative movements, Mark nudges us to an authentic understanding of revolution as the common good: social justice for all. When we try to "be the change we want to see in the world," as Gandhi said, we must understand power, understand our part in it and believe that we are powerful.

For my part, I no longer secretly say to myself, "I'm so relieved I'm oppressed as a woman." I have realized that the missing sentiment embroidered in that relief was, "I'm not responsible." *All the Power* says that we *are* responsible—and, moreover, it says that we can change the world.

Jennifer Baumgardner
New York City, June 1, 2004

"All the power is in the hands
Of people rich enough to buy it
While we walk the streets
Too chicken to even try it."
—The Clash

"The purpose of the artist is to inoculate the world with disillusion."
—Henry Miller

"We must speak with all the humility that is appropriate to our
limited vision, but we must speak."
—Martin Luther King, Jr.

INTRO:THE BURNING SKY

"When you're young
Have no illusion
And no disillusion."
　　　—The Alarm

A certain amount of arrogance is probably necessary in order to write any book.

After all, the action assumes that the writer thinks to have a story—and the skill sufficient to convey it—worth killing trees over! This is perhaps especially true of a book like this, claiming to offer advice about a topic as lofty as "revolution."

Ironically, these pages are intended as a loving corrective to a familiar arrogance: the hubris that would-be activists/radicals/revolutionaries (choose your term) tend to have about topics like "the system," "the people," and so on.

The shortcomings of so much "radical" activity became painfully obvious to me in the process of writing *Dance of Days*, a narrative history of the D.C. punk underground. Never mind anyone else's arrogance; I saw all too clearly my own blindness.

So often I/we seemed to think that simply screaming about the world's injustices, seeking a transcendent moment, or cutting ourselves off from mainstream society would somehow magically change the system. This can be an appealingly romantic notion, but it is not likely to succeed.

Legendary community organizer Saul Alinksy perhaps said it best in 1971 in *Rules for Radicals: A Pragmatic Primer for Realistic Radicals*, speaking of then-fiery '60s activists: "Today's young revolutionaries have no illusions about the system, but plenty of illusions about the way to change our world."

To accept the wisdom of these words is not to somehow disavow the power of punk, or the value of college activism, or even the importance of some '60s-era experiments Alinksy so rightly skewered. Many of those stands were a place to start from, not an ending.

Of course, the potential in any human or community is never completely realized; all cry out for continued growth. A central, inspirational part of the D.C. punk story was its effort to stretch past narrow, even elitist, subcultural radicalism. In *Dance of Days*, I urged punks to persist in this process, to take the idealism and DIY creativity nourished in our narrow terrain into a broader community.

I still believe in this. In some ways, my own life is a testament to this endeavor. Punk has been my main inspiration for almost thirty years. In 1985, I helped cofound Positive Force DC, a punk activist collective. I lived in the PF communal house from 1987 to 2000, participating in an often chaotic yet deeply rewarding experiment in intentional living and radical democracy. Two decades later, I still remain active in the all-volunteer group, having organized literally dozens of benefit or free concerts, protests, and educational events, as well as the *State of the Union* benefit compilation CD with Dischord Records.

From the very beginning, however, punk pushed me past narrow bounds toward a broader engagement. I have participated in a multitude of campus, community, and, more recently, church groups on issues ranging from union organizing, U.S. foreign policy in Central America, South Africa, and the Middle East, the nuclear arms race, abortion, sexual assault, human rights, affordable housing, racial justice, the environment, homelessness, and animal rights.

I have worked on local and national election campaigns, while also engaging in civil disobedience and direct action. I have served meals to homeless people, tutored inner-city kids, assembled safe needle kits for intravenous drug users, distributed condoms to street sex workers, and volunteered extensively with a free clinic. I have been employed by a U.S. Senator, the Montana State University Women's Resource Center and Political Science Department, the Washington Peace Center, the

Arlington Food Cooperative, and People for the Ethical Treatment of Animals. Beyond this, I have served on the board of directors of the Washington Free Clinic, Helping Individual Prostitutes Survive, Student Action Corps for Animals, Punk Voter, and Pax Christi Metro D.C., as well as with the parish council and the justice & service committee of St. Aloysius Church.

Ironically enough, however—given my punk proclivities—my main work has been with senior citizens. Since 1989, I have done outreach, advocacy, and community organizing with Emmaus Services for the Aging, a small nonprofit in a low-income, largely African-American neighborhood called Shaw. In the process, I have scrubbed toilets; battled landlords, cockroaches, and bureaucrats; brought seniors to medical appointments, holiday parties, and protests; delivered groceries and hot meals; coordinated volunteers and oral history projects; moved furniture; installed air conditioners; fixed vacuum cleaners; and much, much more.

In addition, I have drawn Positive Force deeply into this direct work with low-income, inner-city elderly, building bridges between two extremely disparate communities. This partnership, in turn, has helped to create the Arthur S. Flemming Center, a cooperative project of Emmaus, Positive Force, and about ten other diverse nonprofit organizations.

This center includes a radical infoshop, an independent media center, a domestic violence prevention group, a religious anarchist bookstore and furniture exchange, a senior activist network, an interfaith alliance, a peace center, a computer resource provider, a books-to-prisoners project, an art gallery, a community library, and a performance/meeting space. This wildly eclectic mix of direct service, arts, education, and organizing is indicative of the cross-cultural, multi-issue approach I endorse.

"No more ghettoes," howled the Texas punk group Really Red back in the early 1980s, and I took them at their word. We cannot afford to stand apart, or to be aloof. Somehow radicals must reach out, to learn and to teach, to protest and to serve. Balance, not purity, is the standard to which we should aspire. We must engage the world, not hide from it or scorn it; all while not unduly compromising ourselves— often the hardest part of the equation.

Indeed, the difficulty in carrying through this open-ended challenge seems part of why we often prefer the safety and satisfaction of our illusions more than actual growth. I know this tendency as much as anyone; it is surely as human as the drive toward idealism or self-seeking.

On its own, this wouldn't tend to bother me much, certainly not enough to try to write a book about it. However, I fear that our illusions tend to prevent us from achieving the very thing we say that we want: a more just and equal world.

This is tragic. After all, tens of thousands of people—mostly children—die needlessly every day from simple want of sufficient nutrition or the most basic of medicines; all in a world of plenty where others nearly drown in consumer excess. This gap between the rich and the poor in our world grows daily.

At the same time, our own nation has become the hyper-power, the undisputed Rome of our day. The dangers of this immense might have become evermore apparent with angry cries for vengeance after the terrorist attacks of September 11, 2001. While such attacks were perhaps predictable, they have shocked a North American public once secure in its seeming invulnerability.

In some ways, this trauma represented a "teachable moment" for the United States. So far this possibility seems mostly unrealized. Instead, as worrisome ripples have spread through our collective psyche, the selected-not-elected George W. Bush has made a power grab. Using the grief of our often shortsighted, self-centered nation, he is threatening not just our civil liberties, but the stability of the entire world with his imperiously unilateral search for "security."

Under the convenient banner of a "war on terror," Bush is drowning cries for food, shelter, medicine, jobs, and education under an avalanche of *Top Gun* posturing, tax cuts for the rich, and macho military might. His astonishing arms build-up is the nuclear-armed tip of a global iceberg: an arms race that steals food from the mouths of the hungry as surely as any thief, killing even in moments when the bombs are not falling.

As our national arrogance wastes global sympathy felt after the brutal attacks—and, no doubt, breeds more terrorism—we lose sight of a more insidious threat all around us: our environment being consumed in a mad, mass rush for commodities and fossil fuels.

The California-based punk band Bad Religion has put it well: *"I see my ancestors spend with careless abandon, assuming eternal supply."* Humanity's reach may well exceed its grasp, as the steady spread of genetic engineering, nuclear power and weaponry, cloning, and other disturbing technology suggest.

Beyond this, the extinction of this planet's species is running at a frightening and unprecedented rate, as the rain forests shrink under human onslaught. Meanwhile, the population continues to boom.

The burning sky is no longer simply some metaphor that UK punk pioneers the Jam thought up to symbolize the money-hungry, ideal-disdaining "real world." Now it is physical reality as global warming seemingly ratchets up the temperature, promising massive new disloca-tion and suffering. According to a 2004 study done for the journal *Nature*, more than a million species may be extinguished in the near future, the largest single burst of extinction in recorded history.

Worries have spread to unexpected corners of North American society. A secret inquiry commissioned by the Pentagon has suggested that a worst case scenario of global catastrophe costing millions of lives in wars and natural disasters is possible within twenty years. The London *Observer* reported on February 22, 2004 that, according to the study, "Abrupt climate change could bring the planet to the edge of anarchy as countries develop nuclear [weapons] to defend and secure dwindling food, water, and energy supplies." This threat to global stability could vastly eclipse that of terrorism, some experts argue.

Revolution, then, is not a luxury. No, a fundamental change in our world's values, structures, and relationships, reaching to the roots of the system—thus, "radical" in the sense suggested by civil rights icon Ella Baker—is essential.

The only other option, really, is to simply accept the carnage described above as inevitable. Maybe some folks can do that. But while fully aware of all my human frailty, I can't, not without dying myself in some very real way.

In order to live, I need to be a part of the solution. This is some-thing I have known about myself ever since first hearing bands like the Clash, MC5, Avengers, and X-Ray Spex in the late '70s. At the risk of sounding arrogant or blinkered, for me it really is just that simple.

At the same time, I can't settle for an illusion. This means I need the courage to keep testing my beliefs to be sure that I am staying true to my aim. Sometimes illusions can have the power to exalt. After all, had I not been a bit deluded about the amount of work involved in Positive Force, *Dance of Days*, the Flemming Center, or any of my other many projects through the years, I might well have never started them.

More often, however, I see illusions as the would-be revolutionary's worst enemy. Most common is the mirage that change will come quickly. We believe fervently, naïvely; as if our mere belief could make it so!

When "the revolution" fails to appear on schedule, we often turn cynical, even fatalistic, dismissing any attempt toward change as doomed. More quietly, we may accept compromises that make a lie of our original intent. Or, perhaps most sadly of all, our stance can become a security blanket—not so different than any of the religious faiths that we might disdain—sustaining us but offering no real benefit to the world in need.

This is why I think the warnings that precede this chapter from Henry Miller and the Alarm are so crucial, for illusion is the parent of disillusion, the deadly enemy of change. It generates the cellophane coating of irony that is spread across so many of our supposedly alternative communities. Beyond this, disillusion nourishes the fatalism that infects so much of our society—often the very sectors that could be incubators for the seeds of transformation.

As noted earlier, I am no stranger to illusion. To some degree, this book was written for me. Standing at what might reasonably be the midpoint of my life, with "youth activism" behind me, but hopefully decades of engagement to come, I am writing in part to reflect on my past.

With an acute awareness of how swiftly our lives flee from us, I am straining for lessons to guide me in the time remaining, to fuel and direct my future work, that it may be more effective. However small a contribution any of us make, I want mine to be as significant as I can muster; thus the need to learn from the past in order to move into the possible.

My only real qualification as author of this book is my own life. I have drawn on more than two decades of activism in punk and student communities; on Native American reservations and in the inner-city; in secular and church circles; with teen prostitutes and African-American elderly; in centers of power (Capitol Hill, Embassy Row) and on the margins (Central America, the Middle East).

In the end, working on this book has helped me find clues on how to live, how we might create a world where all can flourish. For me, therefore, it is already a success.

I also hope that these words might prove useful for you, the reader. At its best, this book can be part of a vital, ongoing conversation that might bring us closer to some truths.

Of course, the punk skeptic in me knows that possibly everything that I have just told you is wrong. After all, my own activism has coincided with a dramatic shift to the right in this country, from the Carter years through the long, disheartening Reagan/Bush era to our current imperial moment of King George II.

What right, then, do I have to speak? I'm not sure. Do I really know anything with real certainty? No, but I try to do the best I can with what I've got. In the end, like Martin Luther King, Jr., I do believe we each must speak—the time demands no less of us.

One result of stepping to meet this challenge is the "anti-manifesto" which you now hold in your hands, created out of an odd mix of urgency and contradiction. Turning off the road well-traveled, it begins with the hard questions, the doubts. Sometimes it seems like radicals escape one matrix of half-truths and self-deception simply to embed ourselves in another. This is why I sometimes put quotation marks around words like "revolution" or "the system." These markers are there simply to encourage a certain critical distance. While they can represent something profoundly important, such words also can be used so loosely as to prevent genuine thought; as to be almost meaningless, maybe *worse* than meaningless.

There is no better way to turn people off to one's message than using rabid rhetoric. Such empty words are an unparalleled medium for spreading what I would call "radical illusions," the lazy, self-serving chimeras that discredit our movements and prevent us from achieving our goals.

Still, what may seem to be simple jargon or rhetoric can also carry essential meaning. Maybe these terms are not to be abandoned, just used more sparingly, with greater precision, given more clear definition. In a way, this is part of why I have written this book—to define and reclaim such words. In so doing, I hope to advance the struggle to make these ideals real.

As already mentioned, in certain ways this book picks up where *Dance of Days* left off. Much of it addresses how inherently narrow subcultural forms of activism (punk, student, and beyond) might grow to connect with other communities to build a movement for broad, fundamental social transformation.

To accomplish this, we need to affirm and build on our existing strengths. At the same time, we must challenge assumptions rampant in radical communities that tend to keep us self-satisfied but often ineffectual.

In *Silent Takeover: Global Capitalism and the Death of Democracy* (Free Press, 2001), author Noreena Hertz notes a sharp decline in belief in traditional party politics and elections among the nations of the industrialized West. The United States stands as a prime example of this phenomenon. Given the subservience of even the supposed "party of the people"—the Democrats—to corporate financing and their agendas, growing voter apathy is understandable.

But if the Democratic Party seems to have sold its soul for campaign donations, while failing to adequately reach out to those in need, let us not complain too loudly. How often are we North American radicals really stretching ourselves toward the dispossessed of this nation? We seem all too caught up in our subcultural tribalism, our rhetorical radicalism, our glamorous causes. I fear that the common people of this country are as much strangers to us as to any politician.

Our generation of radicals is hardly alone in this. "To revolutionaries, the idea of 'the people' is more important than the people themselves. The compassionate ideas of our common heritage are really masks of hostility and contempt. We . . . are the enemies of the very people we claim to defend. Our promise of liberation is only a warrant for . . . more terrible oppression. It is the reality of ordinary humanity that necessitates the totalitarian measures."

These contentious, unsettling words come from two of the more reviled defectors from '60s radicalism: Peter Collier and David Horowitz. Once integral members of the movement as editors of *Ramparts*, a key New Left journal of the time, Horowitz and Collier shocked and horrified their peers by becoming vocal supporters of Ronald Reagan in the mid-'80s.

Their 1989 book, *Destructive Generation: Second Thoughts About the '60s* (Free Press), attempts to justify their right-ward journey. While the book has been widely derided within progressive circles, some of their analysis and history rings true, more than most of us on the left would like to admit. Most uncomfortable of all for the more secularly minded among us must be their critique of radicalism as a quasi-religious faith. After quoting early Church father Tertullian's motto *"credo quia impossibile"* (I believe because it is impossible), Collier and Horowitz charge, "If self-righteousness is the moral oxygen of the radical creed, self-deception is the marrow of its immune system. *Credo quia impossibile*; because what he [sic] believes is impossible, the radical believes because it is *necessary* to believe."

Such assertions can hardly be proven, only tested by our own experiences. Mine suggest that there is actually some truth in this analysis. Sometimes it does seem as if radical politics mostly serve the ego and identity needs of activists, not the "wretched of the earth." In fact, the left can seem awfully willing to excuse savagery, even genocide, in the name of revolution.

"Radical" can sometimes mean the loudest mouth in the crowd, with the crudest (rather than deepest or most sensitive) analysis, backed by the largest degree of macho bluster. We can fall into a kind of "if it feels good, do it" politics, justified by the exhilaration of certain kinds of actions. Less dramatic forms of dissent seem boring and lack instant gratification by comparison.

In another way, activism can become just another one of the many lifestyles out there, with its own consumption creed to separate the righteous from the unclean. Given such obsessive attention to consumer detail and/or identity, it is small wonder that we have so much trouble working together.

It is also no surprise that our dissident cultures can be alienating to the average person; more elitist than populist. We often disdain religion and patriotism, which for many people are defining verities in their value systems. Our activist-speak itself can be off-putting, as if we expect others to meet us where we are, rather than the other way around.

Self-righteousness may be seductive, but it is self-defeating, as it hurts any effort to change minds. We have to be inviting, not judgmental. Sometimes listening well is more important than speaking boldly; at least if we are here to learn as well as teach. If we think to have all the answers, we are wrong.

None of this, of course, justifies the extremity of Collier and Horowitz's turnabout. If the moral of *Destructive Generation* is presented as a foregone conclusion—"the radical future is an illusion"—it remains highly debatable. Collier and Horowitz's own words have the stink of disillusion born out of illusion. Horowitz rose from a "red diaper baby" milieu, steeped since birth in an insular radical left subculture, closely linked to the Communist Party U.S.A. This narrow background was not unique to him, but hardly typical for much of the '60s movement. It is certainly alien to my own upbringing, and may have predisposed Horowitz toward a naïve faith that was the natural precursor to his subsequent neo-conservative disaffection.

I still believe that another, radically more just world is possible. However, if our visions are to be realized, we must come to grips with illusions like those hinted at above. Most fundamentally, we must move past righteousness and self-deception to a more grounded, self-demanding stance.

In early 2004, I bought a fascinating new anthology—*We Are Everywhere: The Irresistible Rise of Global Anticapitalism* (Verso, 2003)—at Left Bank Books in Seattle. A full decade and a half after the supposed victory of free-market capitalism and Collier and Horowitz's obituary for the left, this book offered a starkly different vista. With its upbeat title and foreword by Naomi Klein, renowned critic of corporate globalization, this handsome, compact tome is at once a celebration of a new movement and a call to expanded action.

"This isn't a book, it's a brick with which to shatter cynicism," wrote one commentator on the back cover, and he isn't wrong. Edited by a British and North American collective out of reports from across the globe, the book documents the rising resistance to neo-liberal economics and the institutions that enforce them from Seattle to South Africa to Thailand and beyond.

But for all that is beautiful and hopeful in *We Are Everywhere*, it is hardly free of illusions. In the book's "Opening Salvo," the legacy of 17th-century Briton Gerrard Winstanley is evoked. Like the others in the Digger movement, Winstanley argued that "the Earth is a common treasury for all." This simple assertion provides the missing link between ancient millennial Jewish and Christian traditions, modern communism and anarchism, as well as the current movement against corporate globalization.

Acting on these beliefs, the Diggers led hungry, landless peasants in a takeover of an unused commons on St. George's Hill in Surrey. Shortly before the brutal suppression of this prophetic if doomed endeavor in 1649, Winstanley wrote, "Thoughts and words ran in me that words and writing were all nothing, and must die, for action is the life of all, and if thou dost not act, thou dost nothing."

This is an appropriate epigraph for *We Are Everywhere*, for *action*—and that of a very specific kind—is the watchword for the kaleidoscopic global mosaic of images and dispatches collected in this anthology.

Photos of dramatic street protests are everywhere. In page after page, we witness masked rebels in tear-gas-heavy confrontations with riot police; demonstrators scaling fences, breaking down walls, spraying graffiti; a shouting protester with a clenched fist, carrying his skateboard emblazoned with a "fuck war" slogan; a broken store window in Spain; radical cheerleaders outside of Niketown.

This imagery can be—and often is—very stirring. But how real is it? Will our new world be built mainly in the streets, fighting the police? Is this revolution? Is it even democracy? Is "anti-capitalism" a sufficient basis for collective action? Can we hope to realize a vision based simply out of what we are against? Is there any kind of unity over what we are for, how to achieve it? Given immense differences in class, culture, race, and nationality, is there even truly a "we"?

These are urgent questions. While I desperately want to believe in a reasonably unified global "we," I am not sure that such exists, at least not yet. *We Are Everywhere* may not aid this process as much as it would like, for in its desire to celebrate what it optimistically describes as "an irresistible global uprising," the book can seem to blithely equate the theatrical street protests of the West with grassroots movements of the less privileged world.

To me, an action to "reclaim the streets" by the children of relative privilege in a vague quest to recover public space dominated by cars and other corporate culture seems awfully esoteric. If some link to the Diggers—or more recent movements like Sem Terra in Brazil—can be made, an illegal street party, however "radical," surely does not carry the same value or meaning as landless peasants risking their lives to squat unused land and feed their families.

Again, the two struggles are not entirely unconnected. But they are hardly equivalent, and it is dangerously illusory to suggest otherwise, as this book sometimes seems to do.

My mission here is to mix what is best in both the brutal self-criticism of *Destructive Generation* and the heady, hopeful spirit of *We Are Everywhere*. In a way, this book also aims for the same target as Alinsky's—although I could never title something as presumptuously as *Rules for Radicals*. Instead, I hope that this is rendered with some genuine humility, as well as passion.

This book rises out of the necessity to act, yes; however, it also exists to challenge actions taken without deep reflection. It seeks to query the motivation of the radical, the activist, to ask disturbing questions: What role does self-interest play in our activism? How much do we really believe in and value people? Does radicalism sometimes provide a cover for self-affirmation, even elitism? How often do we assess our activism on its results, not its intentions?

My answers to such questions will not always be reassuring. This book is a paradox, at once a manifesto that poses questions and an anti-manifesto that suggests that while words are never enough, neither are actions.

The following chapters will, in turn, suggest the limitations of tribal and subcultural approaches to change, while examining the left's tendency toward elitist, insular politics, divorced from organic engagement with a broad mass of people and their concerns. Ideas we often disdain—religion, patriotism—may not only be routes to hearts and minds, but sources of revolutionary potential. Unbalanced emphasis on identity or lifestyle can divide us, shredding our possible power. Hypothetical arguments "for" or "against" violence are rarely useful, as naked force is a weapon relevant only in certain, very narrow contexts. In the end, our search for a fundamentally different planet must be rooted in the world as it is and people as they are, not as we would wish it/them to be. To do otherwise is to squander our dreams, to sacrifice them on the altar of radical illusion.

This book seeks not to be a brick, but a horsefly, nipping at the reader (and writer) as to rouse us from the complacence of what too often passes for radicalism. It is a book that critiques revolution without abandoning its pursuit.

Perhaps this is just as it should be. We find ourselves in an odd, ominous, yet exhilarating time where hopes engendered by a rising global-justice movement collide with the reality of immense and still growing corporate power, aided immeasurably by reactionary regimes in Washington, D.C. and elsewhere.

The triumph of capitalism and resultant "end of history" is no longer taken for granted. To some, it seems that there are sparks in the global air that could catch fire, opening a whole new era for humanity, for the Earth itself.

But will this mean the rise of a definitive corporate hegemony—or a return to some romanticized yet benighted past? Either is possible. If our world is locked in a battle between "McWorld and Jihad," as scholar Benjamin Barber has suggested, with one aggressive, authoritarian force feeding the other, is there another way? Could our sparks ignite a quantum leap toward real democracy, both economic and political; in other words, a revolution?

The stakes are high, and the outcome uncertain. Still, the call to courageous, thoughtful engagement is inescapable. Our actions will help write the next chapter in this drama, so we must make them as intelligent and effective as possible. Belief is needed, but absolute commitment to truth seeking and self-examination must be the foundation of this work. To put it plainly, we cannot afford to fool ourselves—too much is hanging in the balance.

In this energizing, scary moment, then, this is my "inoculation" and my rallying cry; a book not about purity or certainty, but about balance and possibility. The entire aim of the pages to come is simply this: *to help us claim all the power we could have, together; so that we might build the world of our dreams, the world we so desperately want and need.*

I offer up these words in hopes that you find something of value here, even if it is to show what not to do. May they serve, if only in the smallest way, to keep the viruses of fatalism, cynicism, and self-delusion from infecting our souls, even as they push us persistently toward the light of a new—and better—day dawning.

ONE: HERE COMES THE ARGUMENT

Crude wooden crosses stood in the place of gravestones, stretching across this lonely patch of Central American earth. There were no names, only a series of Xs, painted unsteadily on the wood. Here lay the remains of *"los desconocidos,"* unknown people. Their bodies had been found by the side of the road, mutilated beyond any recognition.

In acts of grace and courage, local townspeople had buried these nameless ones, trying to restore a shred of the dignity stripped from them in their last hours. The people did so knowing full well that this act of common decency might now mark them as well for disappearance, torture, and agonizing death.

This was the simple reality of Guatemala, where tens of thousands had been murdered over the first half of the 1980s by a government facing a guerrilla war. Beyond such graves, I had witnessed many heartbreaking sights in my travels there: posters on the campus of the national university memorializing students killed by death squads; murals of church workers, unionists, and peasants cut down; a mutilated body dumped by police behind the National Cathedral; relatives of the disappeared pleading for the return of their loved ones.

I had also seen a baby shriveling, near death from malnutrition and parasites, one of many in a makeshift clinic in the Indian highlands. In city streets, desperate, dirty kids scrambled to survive. Such might swarm an incautious tourist, scrawny arms reaching out for life itself, as much as for any treat.

Meanwhile, some of the most fertile farm land in the world was planted with crops like coffee and cotton, intended for rich people who lived far away. This bountiful vista contrasted with tiny, eroded plots of corn, struggling to grow on steep hillsides, the only land left for the common people.

One day, while walking down a street, my heart and mind cracked wide open. On one side, a mother cooked food over an open fire in a ragged tin shack with a dirt floor, a runny-nosed baby on her back. On the other, a high wall stood, topped with jagged broken bottles. Beyond this lay a massive, manicured lawn that led up to a huge white-walled mansion, shaded by tall, lush trees.

This is not just Guatemala, I thought, *this is our world*. Life is cheap; some people have everything, most have nothing. Armies exist to keep it that way, yes, but mostly the machine rolls on unchallenged. Little wonder that even the immense cost in overt carnage—from death squads, army massacres, more—ultimately paled before the insidious, invisible violence of poverty.

The death toll seems beyond comprehension, as does the breadth of the injustice. Imagine our world of 2004, all six billion—plus souls, shrunk to one hundred people in a classroom or a basement punk show, on a soccer field or in a village. Of these hundred, roughly sixty-one would be Asians, thirteen Africans, twelve Europeans, and eight Latin Americans. Only five would be from the U.S. and Canada; yet those five would use over thirty percent of the resources expended each year. Meanwhile, the poorest twenty would receive just one percent. Overall, six people would own nearly sixty percent of the whole community's wealth. There is no shortage of food, yet sixty of the hundred are always hungry; twenty-six are severely undernourished, existing in need so dire as to die prematurely of hunger or related diseases. Only twenty-four always have enough food to eat. Around seven people would have a college education, and eight would own a computer.

I have chosen to begin this book—all about, in some sense, activism—with this little exercise, for reasons that are probably apparent. Who can look at this heartbreaking reality and wonder why one might choose to be an activist? Isn't this horrific status quo inherently radicalizing? Once one is aware of such incredible disparity and injustice, how can one not act?

Statistics, of course, can be twisted to prove almost anything. Some argue, for example, that the mere existence of a record—and swiftly growing—world population suggests immense progress. Quite simply, our advances have reduced death rates while birth rates remain high; thus, our exploding numbers, and related inequities, are an imbalance which will begin to correct itself as development spreads.

There is some truth in this view, especially over the longer term; yet millions live and die in the short term. Less upbeat observers would note that there are many more poor people now than at any other time in history. Indeed, 2.8 billion people are forced to try to live on less than two dollars a day.

The material distance between different groups of people can be staggering. Columbia University economist Jeffrey Sachs has reported that "the world is more unequal than at any time in world history . . . the gap can be one hundred to one, in some cases, maybe a gap of $30,000 per person [in one country] and $300 per person [in another]."

In the face of this, influential observers like the editors of the *Economist* magazine have shrugged and asked: *"Does Inequality Matter?"* (Their eventual, grudging answer: maybe, but mostly because people think it does.)

Viewed on the PBS documentary series, *Commanding Heights: The Struggle for the World Economy*, Sachs seems a bit unsure. While admitting that it is "absolutely astounding to be on the same planet and have that extreme a variance in material well-being," Sachs also notes that "two hundred years ago, almost everyone was poor . . . The difference now is that a relatively small percentage of the world's population has experienced what economists call 'modern economic growth'"—in the process, leaving most of humanity behind.

Whatever the theoretical complexity, the issue is clear enough: The fruits of the Earth are being shared in an obscenely unequal way. As a result, tens of thousands of people die needlessly every day.

Numbers, however, can only go so far to touch us, to awaken consciences. It has helped me to have direct experience with the bone-crushing poverty that is the lot of billions. There, the fate of the all-too-unknown ones become real.

I may have grown up more sheltered than most, raised in rural Montana. I was heartbroken simply to see the poverty festering amidst power and privilege upon moving to Washington, D.C. in 1984. Raised with small-town politeness, I was shocked by the way pedestrians stepped right over seemingly lifeless bodies in the streets or coldly ignored pleas for money or food.

Imagine how shattering it was, then, when I visited Central America the following summer and encountered their reality! In Guatemala City, I found my way into "La Barranca," a stinking slum built illegally on the side of a ravine in the midst of the city. This was very dangerous terrain, terribly vulnerable to earthquake or mudslide. However, it was the only land available, and it was home to thousands.

I was a curiosity there, a tall, young, white man with blond hair, walking unaccompanied amidst houses pieced together out of scraps of cardboard, corrugated tin, and lumber. The structures seemed less luxurious than our cattle sheds back in Montana. Near-naked children played with mangy, bone-thin dogs next to open trenches of raw sewage, in muddy twisting streets. The children's dulled eyes betrayed insidious, growth-stunting malnutrition.

Back home, I was a bohemian, a student radical. Here, I was a rich man, wealthy beyond these people's wildest dreams; the kind of person the residents of La Barranca might only hear about, but never meet. Not surprisingly, groups of curious kids began to follow me after a few minutes. Noting my ancient box camera, they begged me to take their picture. As I paused to do so, a few teenage girls came close and, no doubt hoping for a way out this place, shyly enquired if I had a *novia*, i.e., a girlfriend or fiancée.

While the children crowded around me and I snapped their pictures, an older man named Efraim approached. Friendly but grim-faced, he warned that I was not safe there, that I must leave before the street gangs in the area found me. As Efraim walked me out of the community, we continued to chat. Conscious of a much-ballyhooed presidential election then underway, I asked if the government helped at all. He frowned, spat on the ground, and told me bitterly: "They come and promise many things, but then they go. Here we wait and eat promises . . . The poor are always forgotten."

Efraim's terse words carried the unwelcome ring of truth. Since then I have been to other such slums, in San Salvador, in Managua, the Gaza Strip . . . enough to know that they are far more widespread than the sparkling, cookie-cutter suburban subdivisions of this country.

Indeed, entire communities exist on the garbage dumps in places like Mexico City and Manila. There, the desperately poor abide amidst the stench, competing with seagulls, vultures, rats, and other creatures, hoping to scratch a living from others' cast-offs, sifting through the mountains of trash for sellable odds'n'ends.

Tears of rage well in my eyes even now, across the span of nearly twenty years, thinking of these lives—just as precious as any of ours—being casually thrown away, day after day, as if they mattered not at all.

There are, of course, many ways that the privileged (like me or probably you, dear reader) can dodge our responsibility to these "disposable people." We all know them: "This is just how it is, the masses of humanity will always have to suffer; it's terrible, but how will giving up what I have help the needy; besides, it is partly their fault anyway, if they didn't just have so many children/weren't so corrupt/didn't have such odd traditions/embraced the free market; I am just one person, what difference could I make; besides, isn't this what the United Way or Catholic Charities or [fill in the blank] is supposed to take care of . . ."

So it goes, the merry-go-round of denial that keeps our world a playground for some and a living hell for billions of others. Exactly *what* we must do to change this is not an easy question to answer. Still, to pretend that the world doesn't cry out for fundamental transformation is, at its base, ridiculous.

At the same time, anyone who has been around activist circles knows that they are hardly unblemished bastions of peace, love, and under-standing. Indeed, the same ego trips, petty power politics, personality conflicts, and back-stabbing infest even the most apparently idealistic and elevated of enterprises.

Often ideology seems to matter more than people. Supporters of electoral politics butt heads with direct-action advocates; human rights proponents wrangle with animal liberationists; secular activists disdain faith-based ones and vice versa; the communists fight the socialists who fight the anarchists who all fight each other . . . and on and on.

It is hardly a surprise that the title "activist" will be greeted with almost the same ambivalence as the more threatening "radical" by the average onlooker. People can (and often do) ask if those who claim to be speaking/working for those in need are really involved in anything more than the same old human contests for power and recognition, mixed with a simple desire to make a living.

It will be tempting for those of us who embrace labels like "activist," "radical," or "revolutionary" to dismiss such critique as motivated by the desire to evade responsibility already noted. This is understandable, yes; perhaps even easy—but also foolhardy, at least if we really wish to transform our world.

So I ask once again: Why be an activist? In my own case, the reasons are multiple and, in some ways, a bit hard to distinguish from my own self-seeking. In part, I have surely been motivated by the aching injustice outlined above. However, I was only vaguely aware of this suffering when I began on the road to activism; clearly, this was not just an intellectual commitment.

In fact, I find that our politics are often very personal. My own experience of having been regularly roughed up by two older boys on my rural school bus surely prepared me for sympathy with the underdog—although, admittedly, it could have just as easily encouraged me to be a bully myself later in life.

But whatever the reason I took one path and not the other, my very first attempt at organizing dates from those terror-filled bus rides. Aware that alone I was powerless to stop the older boys, I tried to rally the other kids on the bus to stand up together against the abusers. The effort failed when the key element of our would-be coalition—a peer of the older boys—decided it wasn't in his self-interest to get involved.

On or off the bus, I felt out of step with my world. I was deeply lonely, living outside the popular crowd in my tiny public high school, isolated on a farm that was more than twenty miles (over dirt roads) from Medicine Lake, Montana, where I attended classes. I was bored by the manual labor that filled my non-classroom hours, suspicious of working-class manhood, scared that this was all that life had to offer, not sure it was worth the pain of living.

For me, there is no activism—maybe no life itself—without the glimpse into other possibilities that rock music (first, '60s-related artists like the Doors, Janis Joplin, Jefferson Airplane, and Jimi Hendrix; then, punk like Patti Smith, Sex Pistols, the Dils, and Stiff Little Fingers) helped to provide. It was through this vision and validation that I found the courage to live, to learn (especially about radical politics and culture), to speak out, and, finally, to begin to act in small but at least personally significant ways.

"To those who buried me alive/I will survive/Attack/ATTACK," sneered Johnny (Rotten) Lydon on the first Public Image Ltd. album. That became my motto; my activism, then, began with a big mouth. As musician/activist Steve Earle has said, "My mouth wrote a check that ultimately my ass had to cash." Eventually I had to do something to back up my big talk, or look like a fool.

Our lives turn on moments, most often when we least expect it. For years, my punk journey was largely internal. Then, one day in early 1980, while out walking between classes, I impulsively joined a picket line during a strike at our campus in Bozeman, Montana.

While other students were providing "scab" labor, filling vacated jobs to make a buck, I joined a group supporting the striking janitors. The official student newspaper snidely dismissed us as "'60s-wannabes." My delicate punk sensibilities offended by this, I wrote my second letter to the editor, the first with a clearly political agenda. (Perhaps not surprisingly, the earlier one, written a few months before, had been about rock: a critique of the inaccuracies in Hollywood biopic *The Buddy Holly Story*.)

Initially, I was a bit disgruntled about the disruption that meetings, pickets, and protests caused in my routine of hiding out in my room, eating, reading, and listening to music. I recall looking forward to getting back to my old life once the strike was over. Unbeknownst to me, however, I had stepped into a whole new way of being. Once out of my self-imposed closet of isolation, out into that wider world, I could never go back.

What I found in those days was precious beyond the power of words to express: a reason to live, a glimpse of who I was meant to be. This sense of purpose and identity is one of the major emotional/psycho-logical paybacks of activism. No longer mere consumers of the life handed to us by parents, teachers, ministers, or other authority figures, we feel powerful. We cease being spectators and become actors; creators, at least in some small way, of our own destiny. It is as if the locked shutters of life have suddenly opened, offering windows into a universe of possibilities. For this "straight edge" kid (i.e., I didn't drink alcohol or use other drugs), it was pretty damn intoxicating.

We often become active for reasons largely disconnected, at least in part, from objectively helping to address injustice. *We may become activists, in other words, because it helps us feel better about ourselves.*

In addition, we may remain activists because it draws attention to us, or helps us to find meaning in an otherwise chaotic, overwhelming world. Sometimes we may even get the chance to write books or be featured in newspapers, TV, radio, or film—all nice ego boosts, to be sure.

This is not necessarily a bad thing. Still, if we are to really contribute to change, much less revolution, we must distinguish between the "subjective" (internal: seeking personal identity, meaning, purpose) and the "objective" (external: actually helping to change power relations, structures, and values that uphold oppression of the many by the few) aspects of our activism.

Let me be very clear here: I am *not* saying that one is important and the other is not. Both the subjective and the objective are critical, at different times and in different ways. They are even interconnected— i.e., I begin to feel personal power, which enables me to take actions that might help striking workers get better pay and working conditions or, more fundamentally, help to build power to alter social structures. *However, the two are not the same.*

Can radicalism sometimes be simply about feeling better than other people? Yes, I think so, sad to say. That fact, however human, is a betrayal, the kind of self-defeating illusion that this book exists to challenge. This troubling self-aggrandizement-in-do-gooder-clothing psychology will be probed more deeply later in this journey. For now, suffice it to say that frank examination of our own motives—a subjective aspect of our activism—is always necessary.

An Earth Liberation Front (ELF) press release publicizing the sabotage of a Wal-Mart construction site in Martinsville, Indiana illustrates this point perfectly. The communiqué was reprinted in the Winter 2004 issue of *Green Anarchy*, whose editors described the event as "the 11th known [ELF] action of 2003."

The sabotage itself was effective, but fairly run-of-the-mill: survey stakes pulled up, windows broken, buildings and machines spray-painted, sand poured into fuel tanks, with tires, engine hoses, and tubes slashed on the construction equipment. The anonymous statement claiming responsibility for the action is anything but typical, however. Well-written and provocative, the Green Anarchy Collective described it as "one of the best ELF communiqués ever released." It is also notable for its unusual candor.

After detailing the damage done, the essay offered a stinging critique of the corporate consumer culture that inspired it:

> We are overwhelmed by the amount of shit society has to offer us. We look around us and see our lives displayed in neon lighting. In one city block there is a McDonald's, a Chevron, a couple of banks, and a new Taco Bell. Two massive car dealerships glow in the distance, the new SUVs proudly displayed in front. We can even see the old Wal-Mart which apparently wasn't large enough or new enough to satiate a growing population of consumers . . . and there is nothing unique about this location. This is life in North America. This is becoming everywhere . . .
>
> Most people are content with this but we are not . . . We know that the places we live can offer us much more than Wal-Marts and McDonald's and Chevrons . . . because we have experienced a break with this reality and know that other possibilities exist.

This sentiment resonates recognizably to anyone who has grown—as I did—in an anti-corporate, DIY subculture like punk.

The next leap is telling, for the anonymous authors ask what, for me, is this book's key question: "And how can things change really?" They offer no answer, but simply a candid admission: "For us, sabotage may not be a means to change any world but our own, as an expression of our feelings toward this society. We strike for ourselves, out of our own frustrations, and rage and despair . . . as a means of therapy and adventure."

Rarely are we radicals so frank in our analysis. Here the authors have straightforwardly admitted that their action was really aimed at addressing subjective concerns: their own emotional need to express their "discontent." The saboteurs implicitly acknowledge that their actions may have no objective impact (save possibly a negative one) on the outlook of the larger population, people for whom they seem to hold only righteous disdain. Likewise, how this action might practically help to stem the relentless onward march of corporate monoculture is unclear. Pragmatic aspects of activism seem to have little appeal for these intrepid souls in search of adventure and therapy.

I don't mean to be unduly critical here, for these activists are hardly alone in this emphasis. In fact, I find their honesty refreshing. Their willingness to openly admit their self-oriented motivations starkly illuminates my argument here. Above all, this anecdote reflects the importance of the distinction between the subjective and the objective. However much radicals might dislike the choices of other people, the importance of engaging them in an inviting way remains.

This becomes apparent when we assess how change, even revolution, might actually happen. This involves an unavoidable analysis of power: who has most of it, who doesn't, how they keep it that way, and how we might alter this equation.

In the simplest terms imaginable, I would argue that the rich of the world have the vast majority of the money and the guns, two key sources of power. The less fortunate and their allies are hard-pressed to challenge this near-monopoly. We must, in general terms, depend largely on two counterbalances: our numbers and our creativity.

On the face of it, the scenario of inequity outlined above is hopeful, at least in one sense. It suggests that a credible movement to tilt the distribution of resources in the direction of equality has the potential for massive support from among the world's impoverished majority.

In order to win this struggle, we have to organize creatively across boundaries to build on our strengths, assembling powerful, flexible, multi-issue coalitions. Conversely, we need to avoid dogmatic stances that would tend to marginalize ourselves from the mass of people here and abroad—*and we must begin the work right where we are.* We cannot afford to blithely dismiss the concerns and feelings of "most people," even here in our relatively privileged context.

This might not seem very easy; in practice, it is even harder than it sounds. What this calls us to is work that is determined by the demands of the process, not so much by our own preferences. To explain this challenge more clearly, I'll revisit my own story for a moment. Recall my solitary past and how I began to feel power by speaking out, acting, and finally, by joining with others, beginning with the strike support group. All of this change was real. At the same time, I had been an isolated, rebellious loner for most of twenty years. Now circumstances demanded that I somehow learn to work well with others, to be part of a team. This was fine when the others agreed with me; but was not nearly so much fun when they did not. Practically, my love for punk, its style, and its individualist rhetoric tended to keep me on the margins of the support group. Simply, it was something the others did not share at all and, in fact, were possibly even alienated by.

Yet, we needed to have unity in order to achieve our objectives. How much did I stretch myself to serve our common goal? Often not very far. Perhaps it was no surprise that I mostly went my own way after the strike ended, initiating other projects that I could more clearly direct, that were more "owned" by me.

This was not necessarily misguided. In this case, it may have even been healthy, since I did grow as the result of the experience. Nonetheless, note the tension here: Doing things the way that felt good for me did not necessarily jibe with what the rest of the group wanted, or even what might help achieve our goals. And this was within a relatively homogeneous group on age, racial, cultural, and class levels.

Diversity can generate a creative tension, where different perspectives lead us to stretch ourselves, to innovate. It can lead us to develop new approaches, wedges that may force their way into tiny crevices in society's walls and crack them open, at least a bit. It can also be profoundly destructive, causing groups to descend into bitter, internecine strife and ultimate dissolution—hence, the attraction of sticking with "our own kind."

Realistically, however, if we are to truly triumph against long odds, *we need each other.* Striking the proper balance, embracing diversity—so that it might become what writer/activist Audre Lorde has called "our greatest strength"—must be one of the critical goals of our activism.

This is, of course, only one of the challenges that can arise when we step into engagement with the world and its problems. Activist groups can also fail if they don't succeed in matching appropriate strategies to their desired ends.

Let me use another example, this time from my experience with the spirited, intentionally disruptive "No Business As Usual"–style street demonstrations in the mid-'80s. NBAU (as we then knew it) was a loose coalition of punks, anarchists, communists, and other assorted dissidents and malcontents. In the face of Reagan's frightening military buildup and resulting Cold War face-off with the Soviet Union, NBAU employed the creative, mobile tactics first glimpsed in the demonstrations against the 1984 Democratic and Republican conventions. We brandished one simple slogan: *"Stop World War III, no matter what it takes!"*

While the hyperbole was a bit troubling (stop World War III no matter if it means killing everyone who believes in the two-party system?), this was an audacious and worthy aim. Sadly, as any experienced activist might guess, the group—national in some sense, but tiny and marginalized from the get-go by its tactics and rhetoric—was simply not equipped to accomplish this mission.

In retrospect, we desperately needed a lesson in the difference between strategy and tactics. While we will revisit this in depth later, the former is the overall plan of how to accomplish your aim; the latter is the series of small actions you take on the way to realizing your strategy.

Put plainly, we were all tactics, no strategy. While No Business As Usual Day (April 29, 1985) was surely empowering for some of the political neophytes who mustered the courage to race about blocking streets, staging "die-ins" in government buildings, banks, and other corporate institutions—while handing out the occasional flier—it made no noticeable dent on business-as-usual. In D.C., despite months of advance publicity, the march attracted fewer than one hundred participants, escorted around town by a roughly equivalent number of police.

Today, it is hard to argue with the downbeat assessment of UK Subhumans' singer, Dick Lucas, interviewed in May 1985 by Krishna Dorney (a key early Positive Force DC member later to gain notoriety as Felix Von Havoc of Profane Existence). Friendly but frank, Lucas—a veteran of the "Stop the City" demos that drew thousands to disrupt the financial district of London and helped inspire NBAU—gingerly responded to news of the slender turnout by saying, "Sounds like a bit of a disaster."

To be fair, the action did help set the stage for the creation of Positive Force six weeks later, and, as such, it was a valuable beginning. But we didn't have much of a sense of where to go with the energy being generated.

Just how clueless early PF was became obvious when one of our members, Travis Keller, suggested an ambitious direct-action blockade, called "Stop D.C." This idea was again inspired largely by the Stop the City actions and grew logically out of NBAU. In order to have the slightest chance of shutting down the Pentagon (the target floated for the action, if memory serves), we needed thousands of committed, trained activists.

The question of how to get anything close to such numbers left us stumped. Travis had the best suggestion, which was to invite legendary UK anarcho-punk band Crass—who had never performed in the U.S.A.—to play a free concert in D.C. With effective publicity, this would attract hundreds, perhaps thousands, of sympathetic souls to the D.C. area. In principle, these folks could then be mobilized to carry out the blockade.

At best, this was a bit of a stretch, with numerous apparent logistical hurdles. When it was discovered that Crass had disbanded, we were left entirely at a loss. We had no real idea how to organize to build such a coalition without falling back on our music community contacts. We had little idea how to mobilize even our own subculture, much less a broader public.

When a notion somewhat similar to Stop D.C.—the N30 actions in Seattle—succeeded in shutting down the World Trade Organization sessions fourteen years later, it was because some people had found an unglamorous but effective answer to this dilemma. The success of those actions was the result of years of patient, committed grassroots organizing that cut across boundaries; building bridges, for example, between labor and the environmental movement.

In the case of PF, the failed Stop D.C. idea was just one of a series of overly ambitious endeavors that ultimately left many in the group disillusioned. As key activists dropped out in droves, PF nearly died. Although the group ultimately reorganized and survived, it nearly became a victim of its own illusions.

• • •

There are many challenges before us. I would argue, however, that we make a huge step in the right direction when we build a strong foundation for our efforts by being realistic (in some sense) from the get-go. We need to be as free of illusions as possible, even while reaching toward that which has never existed, but that ultimately *must* be: a world where everyone is free.

This may seem to be rather odd advice: Be ruthlessly practical so that you can accomplish, bit by bit, that most impractical of enterprises— revolution. Mistakes are unavoidable, but not to be feared. In fact, our errors can be our best friend, in that they can help us to grow, to learn what might work.

Perhaps most important to grasp at the very outset is that there is no one victory, no single point at which this process is over, where heart and mind can be disengaged from one another. Punk taught me to question, yes, but not to disavow any belief, or even faith. Faith is fine; it just has to be tested, regularly and rigorously.

In a 1977 issue of the fanzine *Search and Destroy*, Tony Kinman of the Dils put it this way:

> In the U.S., it's easy to be lulled into a false sense of being comfortable. You have to keep searching—continue to suspect. To be aware of what the revolution encompasses, it is impor- tant to remain in touch with life on a gut level. Thomas Jefferson said there should be a revolution every fifty years. Of course, they have intellectualized that he meant an "intellec- tual" revolution or a revolution "in spirit," but that is a bunch of shit because he didn't mean that! All great revolutionaries— and, whether we like it or not, Jefferson was one—are conscious of the fact that *the revolution never ends* [emphasis in original].

It may be true, then, that as Bad Religion claims, *"The searching never ends/It goes on and on and on for eternity."* To say that much in life is a mystery is not to say that there can be no answers at all. It is to insist that humility, as well as fervent belief, must be the constant companion of anyone who aspires to help make life more just, in however small a way. This is even truer for anyone audacious enough to try to be a revolutionary.

The small bit matters, just as the big one does; indeed, one is built from the other. Even so, we will not succeed without grounding our efforts in this simple understanding: Ultimately we need the numbers, in order to get the power to change the structures, values, and rela- tionships. I know there is no "one-person revolution"—yet, as Kathleen Hanna of Bikini Kill/Le Tigre once wrote, I also believe that revolution can begin, right now, with you.

This paradox is real, and filled with unexpected power. To grasp that potential and move toward this horizon, we must organize in ways that strike the balance between skeptic and seeker, individual and collective. Even as we affirm our own unique selves, we must also stretch to do the same for others, to be able to learn (especially from the less privileged) and to build together.

This does not mean that every approach is as valid as the next. What must be emphasized at any given moment depends upon *context*. While we all each exist in numerous contexts at once, cautious generalization, at least about the readership for this book, may be possible. I suspect those who read this will tend to come from the educated North American context, a place of relative privilege. Most will also have some connection to punk, college activism, or some other form of counter- or subcultural community.

This is also, largely, the context I spring from. These backgrounds, I will argue, tend to exalt the individual, even if only as a ploy to sell consumer commodities. This book is intended to especially challenge that perspective, to turn it toward a critical examination of our motives and a resulting deeper engagement with the common good.

Again, this is about restoring balance, not seeking some illusory purity, much less some correct party line. And maybe this approach makes no sense at all, even seems contradictory. Perhaps this is so. Still, I am not here to make it easy for you, for me, for anybody.

Nor am I afraid of apparent contradiction, for it can spark new, unexpected insights, even breakthroughs. While critical of much of the way Marxism has been utilized (and horrified by the terrible skill of Leninism, Maoism, and the like in generating new forms of oppression), I believe that one of Marx's ideas is powerful and appropriate to mention here: the dialectic.

Put simply, this is a theory (originally found in the writings of German philosopher Hegel) that history is driven forward by the clash of opposing ideas. Another way to say this may be that in every era, the key paradoxes of life collide, contend, and finally merge. The result is a new creation, a synthesis that takes us a step further along the road toward fundamental transformation.

To me, the key to an authentic life is being able to live in the paradox; that rich, real, demanding, and rewarding place. For example, I believe in the Situationist "revolution of everyday life." Nonetheless, much of what I have to say here will critique it and other individualist stances that can seem to turn revolution into a radical art statement rather than concrete improvements in poor people's lives.

Speaking from my present context, the most important point of this chapter is to suggest that we must look past the subjective aspects of our revolutionary impulse to engage more seriously with the objective, lest we betray the very causes we claim to be upholding.

So "all power to the imagination," yes; but grounded in the under-standing that "to be truly human is to work for the common good." The tension between these two, adjusted for our own contexts, might be a creative one, leading us closer to achieving what I think we want: a world where all can flourish.

This is my argument. These ideas may seem extremely simplistic, perhaps even verging on platitudes. Once applied in concrete ways, I hope that they will not still seem so.

In any case, for me, it has been a necessary starting point, a hope-fully solid foundation. Everything I write from here will be based in these fundamental assumptions. How punk or student activism can be affirmed—and challenged—by this set of ideas is the question to which we will now turn.

I'm not sure what I expected when I picked up my first copy of *Riot Grrrl*, but I'm sure I didn't expect to be overly impressed. It ...airly humble-looking (...l/4 page), xeroxed, ...ered mini-zine, the ...p, flip through, set ...about, all in about

...ne wasn't like the ...l inside was a deli- ...to the bonehead ...dictability or cyni- ...nates much of our ..." Brimming with ...naked emotion, ...us thought, *Riot* ...of fresh air in the ...DC's "Victory"

...iot Grrrl ("grrrl" ...latable as "angry ...ory of friendship ..." network that ...ington, DC to ...Though two of ...tors of *Riot* ...nna and Molly ...t portions ...its sub- ...ington ...came ...oice ...s. In ...Mt. ...a DC ...t zone, ...g for "a girl ...C scene. ...old. Molly, ...returned to ...with their ...Bratmobile—

Riot Grrrl was the result. It's very much about punk rock, its power...and its failures. Punk initially gained its fame and adherents by venting its rather considerable spleen at idiocy and injustice in society. But, as time passed, punk came to reflect more than reject society. This was hardly surprising—as Allison notes, "How can we be totally free of our socialization?" Molly agreed, adding "We all come into punk with our own histories." Still, "for women to come into the alternative scene and feel excluded...or silenced...is really fucked up," says Kathleen. It was time, once again, for a change—a revolution.

Revolution is what *Riot Grrrl* preaches, but not exact-ly the grim, grey "male" version that might first come to mind. The rev-olution "grrrl-style" is a very open and human one, imbued with the iconoclastic spir-it of Emma Goldman (her credo: "If I can't dance, I don't want to be part of your revolu-tion") and more than a little bit of humor. A list of "revolutionary advice" in RG #3 ranges from "be a dork, tell your friends how you really feel" and "cry in public" to "selectively

similarly sly and sassy but ...stantive. "Feminist rhetor... really alienating," admit... "especially for punk girls"... departs from the feminist ... with its reclamation of ... "girl," a deviation they ... both more fun and more ... than the... "woman... by old... nists.

Inclu... very ... the...

inclusi... tionally ... groups such ... Since such in ... course, is not l... "happen" on its ...

...ion of the Riot Gr...

...could be. ...d in equal ...er and the ...the West ...their

ignore all oppressive laws" and "make amendments to this list and think about why you don'... with...

announced "an all-girl... about the ways to encou... ...male scene input, w... ...ch other learn to p... ...ents," and to, above ...port and help to bre... those

THE NEW ...VE ROCK ...PLOSION

...os ...ons MUSIC

THE MUSIC'S NOT A THREAT

SK8TREES: ...ah Lerner/POBox 6778/ ...New York 10128/

chumbawamba

Chumbawamba

...OSIT... F...

...rking for f... ...cial change... ...vement. W... ...efit and free... ...rations and ... ...do direct w... those

...turday at 1... ...gs are open... ...for more in... ...eforcedc.c...

TWO: OUR LITTLE TRIBE HAS ALWAYS BEEN

"Do you wanna live this teenage dream
The punk white privilege scene?"
—Heavens to Betsy

The rally for affordable housing was small but spirited; righteous and raucous, with a rainbow of races, ages, and cultures represented. But something important seemed to be missing.

It was a typical D.C. summer day, with any comforting shreds of morning's cool burned away by the blistering sun. Yet even as a senior friend and I suffered in the heat, the power of the protest outside the Cavalier Apartments was palpable.

Like many complexes built or renovated in D.C. after the 1968 riots, the Cavalier was now in danger of losing its "Section 8" status and thus becoming no longer affordable to those of low-to-moderate income. The event, organized by the Cavalier Tenants Association, Washington Inner-City Self-Help (WISH), and the National Alliance of Housing and Urban Development Tenants (NAHT), was intended to put the building's owners on notice. The message was clear: These tenants would not go, not without a fight.

Squinting in the searing sun, dripping with sweat, I found myself deeply moved as speaker after speaker came to the mic, vowing to fight for their homes.

Sometimes the fiery talk led into rowdy chanting. One elderly African-American woman rested on her cane, standing with other seniors. Together, they leaned into round after vigorous round of a rather inelegant chant: *"We tenants are tired of getting screwed/We'll fight back, that's what we'll do!"* The sight brought both a smile and a tear.

We were black, brown, and white; female and male; old and young, together, united in struggle for a basic human right: the right to housing. In its way, the morning was a glimpse of the larger movement we would need to truly change this city, country, and world. But why was I so troubled?

As it happens, the Cavalier stands within sight of a number of past and present punk rock group houses, nestled at the edge of two bohemian-heavy neighborhoods, Mount Pleasant and Columbia Heights. Yet I recognized only one other person from the punk community, Michelle Lee of the National Coalition for the Homeless, later joined by another punk friend. We made up a mere trio amidst the couple hundred in attendance.

Beyond our little knot, this rally was virtually punk-free. Perhaps it was simply due to the early hour (10 a.m. on a Monday morning) or lack of publicity, but the striking absence of punks left a nagging twinge in my heart. When Parisa Norouzi, a gifted young organizer for WISH, asked about "the book you are writing"—this book—I tried to explain its intent. I did so a bit sadly, knowing that in some ways this event exemplified why I was writing it.

Coming only a couple of hours before I began work on this chapter, the moment jolted me into a renewed awareness of the urgency of its main question. How do punk and other subcultural phenomena tie into a larger picture of possible transformation, for good or for ill?

At the outset, one thing absolutely *must* be said. For me, punk has been a profoundly liberating and empowering force. If it were not for punk, I would never have written these words, this book would not exist. I might well not even be alive today, given the desperate hopelessness I felt as a teenager.

This is one of the magical aspects of art. Somehow, some way, art can cut through the walls that society—or we ourselves—have built around our hearts. In so doing, it can touch and motivate us, planting the seeds of transformation. Whenever anyone expresses skepticism about the power of music or other art to truly change anything, I have a ready answer: *I know it can, simply because it has changed me.*

It is true that the route was a bit roundabout. For example, virtually all of my initial rebellion was focused on my issues, my "oppression." It had little connection to anyone else, except that my incipient social critique in some sense might apply to others also under the grip of the "system" I was fighting.

In retrospect, my initial politics (if you can call them that) were almost entirely focused on my personal freedom. Much of this was about the creation of my own identity, affirming that I might not be crazy after all, that perhaps there was something wrong in the expectations and preoccupations of the larger world. I didn't feel much responsibility to anyone else; indeed, much of my fight was to avoid the responsibilities that others tried to force upon me.

This streak of stubborn antiauthoritarianism runs deep. My mother recalls a time when, as a child, I was lost in play, unaware of my father's repeated requests to do something. Finally, he lost his temper and yelled to get my attention. Apparently I responded by turning squarely to face him, puffing myself up, and simply, sternly retorting: "Don't speak to me that way!"

Given that this was the four-year-old Mark, you can guess what fun lay ahead for my unfortunate parents. At base, I did not like anyone telling me what to do—and still don't. Punk was a perfect match for me, because all of it, in one way or another, was saying "fuck you" to the larger world.

"I'm not like everybody else!" proclaimed the Kinks, in one of my key early anthems. This proto-punk rallying cry burned with a liberating truth, one that I was barely willing to acknowledge in the deepest recesses of my heart: This life I have been given is not for me, CAN'T be for me. Maybe it works for others, but for me it is a living death.

The next step was natural: I won't pretend to belong here, will not conform myself to this, not any longer.

The mere act of saying no, of yelling this out loud—bouncing along to the song alone in my room, dime-store stereo turned up high—was empowering beyond words. I was affirming myself, just as I was; as good as the others, maybe even better. Bit by bit, such songs (taken to the highest level by the British and American punk that came soon after) helped me to build an identity. I was able to affirm myself as worthy, even if others seemed to not agree.

My initial vision was inevitably self-centered. *"Don't dictate to me!"* was the rousing cry of Penetration's Pauline Murray; *"I wanna be me!"* screamed the Sex Pistols. Each anthem took the Kinks' stance one explicit step further; self-determination became my goal.

Soon, groups like the Clash, X-Ray Spex, Dead Kennedys, and Stiff

Little Fingers helped me begin to contemplate broader social concerns. A statement by the hammer-and-sickle-wearing Dils, encountered in a 1977 *Creem* magazine trashing of West Coast punk, became my credo: "[Punk] is a rebirth, a change in values . . . We are anti—rock'n'roll, anti-drug, anti-booze, anti-groupie, anti-star."

Even though *Creem* dismissed them as "urine-stained communists," the Dils' idea of punk—stated elsewhere by singer/bassist Tony Kinman as "a regeneration of [personal] integrity"—made a lot of sense to me, sickened as I was by the state of modern rock and trapped between the twin tyrannies of church and bar, the "temples" of my rural working-class culture.

Such statements, together with songs like "White Riot" by the Clash and "We Are the One" by the Avengers, began to give me a dim sense of how my struggles might connect to larger, barely understood challenges. Nonetheless, punk was pretty much focused on "to thine own self be true," no matter what the consequences. At the outset, it was all about being real, not buying into the bullshit seemingly all around, unmasking society's illusions and lies.

This was a limited but essential foundation for what could come next. The key was to keep growing, to keep expanding my awareness, and—most difficult of all—to keep applying what I learned to my own life and choices.

This challenge is not to be taken lightly. At the time, I was heavily influenced by the heartfelt "existential politics" of writers like Lester Bangs. In a powerful 1977 piece on the Clash in the *Village Voice*, Bangs identified (somewhat self-consciously, self-critically, and in best beat-poet-stream-of-consciousness-style) the crisis of the moment as, "Blah blah blah depersonalization blah blab no one wants to have any emotions anymore blab blip the human heart an endangered species blah blare cultural fascism . . ."

All of which was to say that real emotion was hard to find amidst the cookie-cutter commodification/mechanization of life, including art. This malaise of the modern age was targeted in songs like Graham Parker's "Passion Is No Ordinary Word" and Elvis Costello's "Radio Radio." And, conversely, Bangs loved the Clash largely because of the passionate heartbeat pulsing beneath their political stances.

This makes a whole lot of sense—emotionally, intellectually, spiritually. On the other hand, while there is undoubtedly a connection between the authentic "me" and the revolutionary "we," there is also a certain inescapable tension.

For example, this pursuit of "authenticity" could just as easily lead one to allegiance to the capitalism-loving, individual-exalting theories of Ayn Rand as to Karl Marx, bell hooks, or Murray Bookchin. Indeed, some versions of punk anarchism seem about as self-obsessed as Rand's *Atlas Shrugged*, or as American (in the negative sense) as John Wayne's cinematic "rugged individualism."

It is as if we seek to defy "God and Master" only to elevate "the enlightened individual" to the role of God and Master. This heroic view of the individual can only lead to an elitist position, sometimes bordering on fascism. We, the living (privileged), earn our position on merit, despite the jealous obstruction of the lesser folk, the herd—or so the story goes.

Much of the power of punk (and, consequently, the activism rising out of it) is tied not just to an "us vs. them" vibe, but to a "me"-centric, sometimes even "better than them" outlook. However appealing in subjective, emotional terms, this stance is anything but revolutionary.

No one has been guiltier of this than me, at least in punk's early years. I say this with some real affection for the wounded, confused kid I was—and still remain, in so many ways. Coming from a place where I experienced others seeming to imply that they were better than me, songs that helped me to gain personal affirmation were, in that difficult moment, truly healing and hopeful. Listening to them even now—Stiff Little Fingers' "Alternative Ulster," X-Ray Spex's "Identity," Patti Smith's "Gloria," Elvis Costello's "Big Boys," Graham Parker's "Fools' Gold," the Avengers' "White Nigger," Generation X's "Promises," and more—is like walking through the awkwardness, idealism, and anguish of adolescence all over again. In this desert, my thirst was relieved only by these friends; friends who were often just sounds on vinyl, pictures in magazines, or printed words of interviews on lifeless pages.

It was while reading *Rock Scene*, and later *Slash* and *Search and Destroy*, that I first began to believe in the possibility of another community—a "misfits club," if you will—one where I wasn't so alone. Transsexual Wayne County as *Rock Scene*'s advice columnist made total sense to me then. After all, why should only the "straights" have a forum in which to share, sympathize, and sort out their issues?

Even if I really wasn't like anybody else even there, still we were held together by the mere fact that none of us fit in elsewhere. In a way, we were what Bob Marley called "the rejected of society" in "Punky Reggae Party," his 1978 tribute to the Clash and the associated punk scene then erupting. Together we helped each other to breathe, to believe, to *be*.

That this "misfits club" existed hundreds, even thousands of miles away from my isolated existence in Montana seemed to matter little to me. Just knowing that they were out there gave me courage to stand up for myself, to believe in myself . . . just to go on living. Even without being in the physical presence of these kindred spirits, their mere existence interrupted "business as usual" for me, opened up a little space where alternative possibilities could flourish.

This insight points to a larger and more crucial point: The punk scene can and does function as a "free space," a "temporary autonomous zone." This is a context in which the control of society is weakened enough, in whatever way, to allow for seeds to be planted, to germinate, and begin to grow, even blossom.

The importance of such spaces should never be underestimated. In *Free Spaces: The Sources of Democratic Change in America* (Harper and Row, 1986), Sara Evans and Harry Boyte note, for example, that "black history, like the history of other dispossessed and powerless peoples, demonstrates with particular power the way in which oppressed and powerless people can discover and use subversive themes hidden in dominant ideas as resources for self-affirmation, resistance, and struggle."

In other words, cracks and crevices discovered within an oppressive system are critical. However small, those vulnerable spots can be the refuge where efforts to envision and build another, better world can take root. As Evans and Boyte explain, "For such alternative cultures to emerge and survive, people need community places that they own themselves, voluntary associations where they can think and talk and socialize, removed from the scrutiny of those who hold power over their lives . . . Free spaces, then, are the places in which the pieties we learn in school or hear in Fourth of July speeches take on living substance and meaning."

Punk is hardly the only place where this can happen. For some, college has also provided this, especially through certain classes, activities, or student groups—a theme we will explore in depth in the next chapter.

Evans and Boyte go on to argue that "the black church has especially played a role as a free space in black history." This reality—affirmed by other key observers like Bernice Johnson Reagon of the Student

Nonviolent Coordinating Committee's "Freedom Singers" and, later, the all-female a cappella group Sweet Honey in the Rock—challenges punk's often narrow view of religion as inevitably a "pacifier of the masses," a simple tool of oppression.

This is not to suggest that religion (like the punk or college scenes) does not function in some regressive ways, for surely it can. My point here is not to be blind to imperfection or contradiction, but to be aware of and open to common ground. This flexible stance is crucial, for it is in this place of shared concern and spirit that we might be able to construct a true alternative.

We will revisit this later, but for now the key point here is simply that "free space" is an essential precondition for transformation. Or, put in more punk rock terms (a mid-'80s Chumbawamba lyric adopted by Positive Force DC via *Maximum Rocknroll*), *"Isolation is the biggest barrier to change."* When Positive Force started out, the mere fact that we were together, in the same room, having the courage to speak the dreams of our hearts out loud, made all else possible.

In principle, then, punk can tie into larger struggles in a positive way. A growing sense of personal identity can lead to solidarity with other misfits, and to a consistent stance supporting the underdog, with a healthy insistence on individual liberty. To briefly leap ahead a bit, this is what I would call a truly revolutionary politics.

Punk should readily lend itself to such a stance. In fact, the very name suggests identification with the outcasts, the untouchables, the throwaways of the world. Originally, "punk" was Old English for "prostitute," appearing, among other places, in Shakespeare's writings. Since then, the term has come to signify, in turn, a young male partner of a homosexual (catamite); a hoodlum; poor in quality; an inexperienced youth; a weakling. Most recently, it has come to be a gay slur in African-American urban culture, and, finally, to refer to the victim of homosexual rape in prison slang.

The common thread here should be obvious. All of these refer to "something or someone worthless or unimportant," as noted by the *Random House Compact Unabridged Dictionary*.

Punk, therefore, at its root, can be seen as a potentially inclusive and empowering term. Once reclaimed (à la "queer" by gay, lesbian, bi-, and trans- activists), the word can affirm the value of those deemed worthless by society. To see the world from the "punk" point of view, from the underside of life and history, could be a truly fundamental, even revolutionary shift in consciousness.

That is, it *could* be, in principle. Sadly, punks often don't get to this larger view. Instead, punk (as it actually exists, not in possibility) has tended to become attached to a politics of self-affirmation and independence in a narrow, self-focused way that leads us to glorify ourselves and our movement (largely white, male, middle-to-upper class). Unfortunately, wrestling with and overcoming personal desperation does not necessarily translate into progressive, much less revolutionary, politics.

I, for one, have had to learn this the hard way. To understand how this can play out, let's step back and look at Nirvana's "Smells Like Teen Spirit" and the controversy it helped to unleash.

"Smells Like Teen Spirit" is a rarity: a musical benchmark, delineating the end of one era of mainstream rock and inaugurating another, for better or worse. Its impact was genuinely revolutionary in cultural terms. Whether this was truly progressive or not depends largely on one's point of view.

For many of my friends who weren't part of the punk underground, the song and associated album, *Nevermind,* marked a turning point. For Stephanie Olson, cofounder of the Empower Program (a visionary project to reduce gender violence), *Nevermind* was "the beginning of something hopeful, progressive out of the Reagan/Bush years . . . It was like our generation was finally starting to fight back, to create something of its own."

Seen from within the underground, the view was a bit different. Stated in the most stark and unforgiving terms, Nirvana was the Benedict Arnold of underground punk, opening it to plunder and pillage by the corporate powers-that-be. To such observers, after "Smells Like Teen Spirit," everything in the scene began to "smell" as well; to stink with the rank aroma of greed.

Whether this is a fair assessment or not, one thing is clear: After "Smells Like Teen Spirit," punk would never feel quite the same. While the underground not only survived, but even thrived (sometimes cleverly taking advantage of corporate resources), never again did it exist as before Nirvana blew the roof off the place, OUR place. Now, underground punk will always stand in an uneasy, blurry tension with a more mainstream variant. This makes the situation all the more complex; it also fills punk with more possibility.

"Smells Like Teen Spirit" was unusually well-equipped both for its role as cultural breakthrough and benchmark dividing one punk era from another. First of all, the song itself was wrestling with the question that the burgeoning punk underground had begun to beg: Just how far can this go?

Nirvana biographer Michael Azerrad has cannily suggested that the song was both a dismissal *and* an affirmation of the revolutionary power of punk. As Kurt Cobain told Azerrad not long after the song radically altered the terms of pop discourse, "The whole song is made up of contradictory ideas. It's just making fun of the idea of having a revolution. But it is a nice thought."

If this double-edged exegesis seems shot through with the safe irony all too vogue in "alternative rock" circles, the power and passion of the song made it clear that much more was at stake. As Cobain elaborated: "[Nirvana] was in a position where it was expected to fight in a revolutionary way toward the major corporate machine. A lot of people just told me flat out, 'You can use this as a tool . . . something that will really change the world.' I just thought, how dare you put that kind of pressure on me. It's stupid. *And I feel stupid and contagious*" [emphasis in original].

The radical intent of the band was surely telegraphed by the album's cover, a slightly slicker descendent of punk artists like Winston Smith and Raymond Pettibon, creators of many of the Dead Kennedys and Black Flag graphics, respectively. An entire social critique was elegantly and subversively communicated in one simple image: a newborn baby swimming after the almighty dollar, the bait on society's hook.

This cover set an immediate tone for interpreting "Smells Like Teen Spirit," but its usefulness in this regard only went so far. Arriving without a full lyric sheet, the song's words were so distorted and slurred as to defy understanding, much less clear interpretation. As a result, the "Smells Like Teen Spirit" video—allegedly inspired by teen-insurrection flick *Over the Edge*—provided the subtext. The clip is one of the rare occasions where a video added depth to a song, rather than damaging it.

As this might suggest, I am a confirmed follower of the "Total Rejection Line"; indeed, I find the whole music-video genre to be a generally banal and depressing affair. Most often, music video debases what it claims to exalt. Rarely is it more inspired than the commercial advertising tripe it so clearly has influenced; all in all, a sad waste of talent and resources.

Even so, I find enough of my own past dreams for punk encapsulated in the four-minute mini-drama of the "Teen Spirit" clip—conceptualized by the band and crafted by Samuel Bayer, matched exquisitely to the song itself—to still choke me up more than a decade after its debut.

From the sight of a Converse All-Star sneaker in the opening shot, to the subversion of that most hated high school institution—the pep rally—by the smashing of regimented roles (cheerleaders breaking ranks, sprouting tattoos and anarchy symbols; the blurring of the band into the crowd, with audience members taking the instruments), the video gets a lot of what is most precious in my experience of punk just right.

As fate would have it, the song soon took the teenage rebel dream common to the underground and blasted into the mainstream, pushing the social impact of punk far beyond the basements that theretofore had been its bastions. Suddenly the idea of "revolution" seemed both more likely (so many people being touched by the message) and further away (the radical method and message of punk being turned into corporate consumer commodity).

Viewed from the present moment where punk has been an "alternative rock" product in the mainstream for more than a decade—an entire new generation of punks having grown up with that as a primary point of reference—the conflict that erupted within the scene in the '90s seems almost incomprehensible. However, viewed from the context of that time, it seems almost inevitable.

With the dizzying ascent of Nirvana, followed closely by other punk-related acts, lines began to be drawn, often in the most stark, simplistic terms. In the deal-making frenzy and subsequent backlash, compromise bore the bitter fruit of purist counterreaction. Once flush with the free air of creativity, the scene now swirled in a confused, poisonous haze. Old friends turned on each other with frightening regularity, their splits sometimes played out in the gutter press.

"Insanity" is a strong word, but it actually seems applicable here. How else can you describe a situation where a major national 'zine (*Maximum Rocknroll*) published a fake interview making Nirvana look like homophobic, sexist, redneck rocker-dudes? Or *MRR*—despite its left-wing politics—putting a (bad) joke band like the Dwarves on their cover, while refusing to even review groups such as politicized DIY punks Rain

Like the Sound of Trains, all because their music wasn't "fast and loud" enough to be punk?

Matters only got worse when a powerful new magazine, *Heart Attack*, started up in response to such self-destructive purism, only to then refuse to review indie stalwart Fugazi. Why? Simply because of Fugazi's use of a UPC symbol (not included in the band's artwork, just as a sticker, a glorified price tag), thus suggesting they were somehow complicit in the corporate evil.

At the same time, a genuine grassroots phenomenon like punk-feminist Riot Grrrl was getting gushing praise (even if often inaccurate and condescending) in the mainstream press, while regularly being attacked in underground contexts. Soon, under immense pressure, Riot Grrrl began to turn on itself and its allies, shredding community in an orgy of ruthless critique that left no one involved unscarred.

Many more examples of the conflict then ripping the underground apart could be given. This was a profoundly challenging time, where the punk world was literally turned upside down. As such, insanity might be a reasonable response to an insane world. Faced with situations few of us had ever expected in our wildest dreams, we all struggled to do the best we could.

Often, that wasn't very good. My own response was far from flawless: arrogantly trashing key friendships and then descending into a near-fatal self-destructive spiral when I was targeted, in turn, by equally self-righteous purists.

The destructive power of illusions was painfully on display during this punk "civil war." For me, the biggest chimera of all soon became apparent: my belief that the underground punk scene could be some sort of revolutionary "vanguard," just by staying true to its independent path.

While I still believe in building flexible, inclusive counterinstitutions to the corporate mainstream, now I see the "major vs. indie" argument in a more complex light. Although this debate is important, it can distract from larger issues. Moreover, it can feed a purism and elitism that keep us talking only to ourselves, locked in subcultural ghettoes.

At base, the question is quite simple: Is punk meant to be "populist" (for the masses) or "elitist" (for the enlightened few)? This tension has been present since the beginning, since our "tribe," like all others, finds some of its power in the exclusion of others, in the sense that we are somehow different. Thus does the "misfits club," once successful, tend toward becoming "for only the chosen few."

This is deeply ironic, since many of us came to punk out of a feeling of rejection or exclusion. We wanted to find a place where we belonged, where we were affirmed, where we found community. This, in itself, is surely a healthy impulse; yet a sanctuary for self-affirmation can quickly turn to the denigration of others, into a ghetto of arrogance and self-righteousness.

What I am suggesting is that the punk ideal of "independence" is a misguided, even dangerous illusion, at least if taken too far. The DIY ideal is a powerful, positive affirmation of untapped human possibility when interpreted as "doing what you can with whatever you've got wherever you are right now." Taken as "I won't ally with you for fear of appearing to compromise myself," a more retrogressive, anti-revolutionary approach is hard to imagine.

What I am challenging is the idea of independence as the highest political good, as contrasted with *interdependence*, the idea that people are tied together in a multitude of ways, that we need each other. While this is true on the most basic human level, it is even more so once we try to objectively assess how to build the power to challenge or even fundamentally alter the system.

The "subjective" appeal of finding sanctuary in underground communities removed from the taint of compromised modern life is real. After the shock and horror of my time in Central America, having the subterranean realms of punk was a necessary balm. In that context, the Make-Up's mid-'90s cry of "*Death to traitors!*" about those who seemed to be selling out our community for personal gain rang true to me.

It is surely true that the small, intimate scale of punk shows (as opposed to "stadium rock") and affiliated culture is not meant as an elite stance. For many punks, it is more than a statement about life within a mass consumer society; it is a concrete act of rebellion against it.

As '60s countercultural historian Kirkpatrick Sale has argued, the seeking of human scale can be a radical political position in this society. Far beyond any political theory, for many punks, those tiny, intimate contexts ushered in personal transformation. Perhaps for the first time, we felt ourselves there as actors in life, not as mere spectators or consumers.

How, then, can punk (which has historically drawn so much of its power from this intimate, DIY scale) translate in any meaningful way to a mass audience? Some of the mainstream punk surely acts as a bridge, helping to bring fans to a less commodified, underground experience of the community. Commercially successful punk can also bring radical ideas into the mainstream, as Rage Against The Machine, Pearl Jam, Chumbawamba, Good Charlotte, Red Hot Chili Peppers, Beastie Boys, and Jane's Addiction have sometimes tried to do.

At the same time, the selling of punk via these corporate channels can help disarm its subversive power, by making punk a simple product. Which tendency ultimately wins out? Hard to say. In the end, there is no easy answer here.

However, this much I do know: If we simply stay in our sheltered underground, it can become an odd mix of would-be "utopia" and prison; a place where we live, still in relative privilege, proud of our marginality, able to ignore the life-or-death struggles of the mass of humanity, while claiming to somehow share them.

This brings us back around to "Smells Like Teen Spirit." The affirmation and accusation implicit in the key line, *"Our little group has always been/And always will be/Until the end,"* contains a rich and painful paradox. On one hand, the line—often sung by Cobain in concert as *"Our little tribe has always been"*—is an affirmation of the human spirit to stand against conformity, to persist in a vision of another, better world. At the same time, it carries a certain resignation, as if the dream is forever doomed to be just that: an illusion, held tightly to by a tiny minority, secure in its righteous failure.

This elite notion has little place in genuine revolutionary theory or practice, as the possibility of radical transformation is ultimately for *everyone*—not just the chosen, lucky few—or it is not real. Indeed, this contradiction was made explicit by Cobain: "Everyone seems to be striving for utopia in the underground scene, but there are so many factions and they're so segregated that it's impossible. If you can't get the underground movement to band together and stop bickering about unnecessary little things, then how the fuck do you expect to have an effect on the mass level?"

This points back toward the basic tension at the heart of any punk/revolution equation. If it is true that punk tends to start from an emotional place of *"I'm not like everybody else,"* how do we find common cause, even among ourselves, much less the broader world? Some of this challenge is hardly unique to punk. As suggested above, we might speak of punk as "tribal" in a loose sense, as "a class or set of persons, especially one with strong common traits or interests" (*Random House Compact Unabridged Dictionary*, 1996).

The punk subculture has many of the hallmarks of a tribe, including signifiers borrowed—some might say stolen—from traditional tribal communities: piercings, tattoos, more. These markers, also including hairstyle, dress, music form, even slang, help to demark the boundaries of the group, to set it off from the larger populace. In this way, appearance can even be a form of dissent, a strikingly visual way to say, "I am not a part of your corrupt world."

This makes sense in tribal terms, helping to build group solidarity—but exists in tension with any revolution based in trying to motivate masses or change minds. After all, why would the larger world even listen to us if our message seems to begin with the statement, "We think you are stupid and wrong"?

As (quasi-)tribes go, punk is probably one of the more fractious, lacking the typically tight-knit, often hierarchical internal structure. Still, even the most coherent of such communities have clear shortcomings on this level. While their structures (whether formal or informal) can result in a great degree of autonomy, they also make broader alliances difficult.

If this assumption is correct, then such approaches are problematic for building resistance. For example, North American Indians—already on the losing end of the guns-and-money portion of our "power" analysis—were made more vulnerable to white aggression due to dissension among the various tribes. As canny European settlers recognized, the relatively small and diverse nature of their social units made it possible for Native Americans to be turned against each other, or left to be picked off one by one. It is no accident that the most powerful and effective resistance occurred when Native groups allied themselves against white initiatives.

This is not merely an American phenomenon. Over the past several centuries, tribes have been decimated by the onslaught of the modern nation-state. They were simply not equipped to face such a monolithic juggernaut, armed with modern weaponry and advertising technology, driven by the fierce hungers of nascent global capitalism.

Interestingly enough, contemporary observers like Benjamin Barber, author of *Jihad vs. McWorld: How Globalism and Tribalism Are Reshaping the World* (Ballantine, 1996), argue that the reverse is now developing, to the detriment of dreams of human freedom and democracy. While for some, Barber may seem too beholden to classic concepts of representative democracy, his thesis is worth reviewing:

> Impartial judiciaries and deliberative assemblies play no part in the roving "killer bands" that speak on behalf of newly liberated "peoples" and such democratic institutions have only at best a marginal influence on the roving multinational corporations that speak on behalf of newly liberated markets. Jihad pursues a bloody politics of identity, McWorld a bloodless economics of profit. Belonging by default to McWorld, everyone is consumer; seeking a repository for identity, everyone belongs to some tribe. But no one is a citizen . . . What ends as Jihad may begin as a simple search for a local identity; some set of common personal attributes to hold out against the numbing, neutering uniformities of industrial modernization and the colonizing culture of McWorld.

This analysis neatly accounts for the rise of Islamic fundamentalism abroad, as well as the appeal of subcultures like punk here at home—quite simply, people crave an identity beyond the cookie-cutter/corporate/consumer culture. As Barber makes clear, it is hard to believe that "the clash of Jihad and McWorld will issue in some overriding good. The result seems more likely to subvert than to nurture human liberty." All of this is to suggest the painful limitations of a tribal (or quasi-tribal) approach in our present context. We will extend and deepen this theme in our discussion of identity politics in Chapter Four.

• • •

Punk grew out of a nucleus of "cult" bands like the Velvet Underground, the MC5, the Stooges, New York Dolls, Big Star, and the Modern Lovers. None developed a mass following; indeed, most were failures in commercial terms. Instead, these bands had a small, intensely devoted following to whom they spoke powerfully.

I know just how transformative such connections between artist and audience can be. I know, too, that part of the power comes from the fact that these bands seem to be "yours," much more than the more popular music of the day, diluted and homogenized for mass appeal. To begin to appreciate something on your own terms, for how it touches you, not because everybody else likes it, is, in itself, a crucial step, personally as well as politically. The discovery of this internal compass and the related development of a critical consciousness toward the world (a.k.a., your "bullshit detector") is all-important, an essential precondition for joining any true revolution.

Sadly, there is a less liberating side to this as well. If we confuse the idea that something doesn't have to be popular to be good with "anything that is popular is bad," we are doomed to nurture an elitist community. I have seen this at play in the punk community many times, leading to the trashing of artists from Nirvana to Tori Amos to even Fugazi, simply because they had become too popular to somehow not have "sold out."

Sometimes this plays out along class lines. One example is when close D.C. punk friends dismissed Bruce Springsteen and John Mellencamp in the mid-'80s for being patriotic or writing boring, insincere "heartland rock." I understood the critique, especially given how enmeshed in the "money-make machine" both artists were. Still, their music spoke powerfully and sincerely to me and my family's working-class experiences, hopes, and fears. Moreover, they also seemed to articulate a progressive vision for this country not so far from what the D.C. punk community supposedly embraced.

Why didn't my otherwise smart, sensitive friends see this? Hard to say, but I would guess mostly due to the fact that they had grown up in a middle-to-upper-class urban professional community. What Springsteen and Mellencamp sang about was not their experience—but it was part of mine. This was hardly the only time I found non-comprehension around issues of class. To some degree, this was reflected profoundly in our attitudes toward mainstream success.

Did punks want to take over and remake the mainstream? If so, under what circumstances, and at what cost in compromises? Or did we wish to simply stay outside of "the system"? Was our essential aim to be pure or to reach people; to (objectively) change things or to (subjectively) feel superior? While granting that human motives are always mixed and mysterious to some degree, I still believe this is an essential question with which to wrestle.

Fortunately, there is another position that exists between the obvious extremes of "corporate sellout" and "underground elitist." This stance—which I would tend to describe as "independent populist"—suggests that an artist needn't sign on with the corporate powers-that-be nor hide in an underground where, somehow, success seems to be failure.

I have seen this approach most compellingly lived out by Fugazi, although Sleater-Kinney, Ani DiFranco, Dar Williams, and others both within and beyond the punk community have also shone in this regard. As the Web makes it increasingly possible to cut out corporate middlemen, more and more artists seem to be moving in this direction.

I can't speak for Fugazi, nor do I wish to unduly single them out for praise. Still, my experience with them as friends, and through Positive Force DC, while sometimes challenging, has been very inspirational. That a band made up of four extremely independent individuals would choose to ally themselves with a political group like Positive Force reveals the breadth and seriousness of their intent. It also points to how well they have been able to balance issues of independence and interdependence, freedom and responsibility. For example, they have sought to retain their creative and commercial freedom (putting out their material on Dischord Records, managing themselves, not doing song videos, etc.), but with the goal of making their work reasonably accessible to anyone.

Inclusion, not exclusion, was the aim. How large their audience might become was not predetermined, except perhaps to the degree that keeping away from the star-making machinery of MTV, major labels, and the like has tended to reduce the likelihood of a visit to the Top Ten. The band has nonetheless prospered, even though their performances in the U.S. rarely cost more than six dollars, and their CDs are priced inexpensively. In addition, the band sells no merchandise (i.e., T-shirts, baseball caps), generally one of the most lucrative parts of the biz for successful bands.

At the same time, by making all their D.C.-area gigs (since 1989) benefits of one stripe or another, they have helped to take resources from within privileged contexts to redistribute into places of need. Even as money was raised, the shows also fulfilled another function: raising awareness and activating people into community-justice work. A palpable sense of a larger community with values at odds with the dominant ones also arose, suggesting that Fugazi shows opened up "free spaces" for many.

Positive Force and Fugazi have shared an emphasis on watering the grassroots. Aware that the amount of money our events could generate was not immense—usually no more than several thousand dollars at a time, from five-dollar tickets—we have focused on directing it to small, lesser-known groups that are working on the front lines, where it might have the most impact. Such groups are often the most innovative, using creativity and hard work to make their money stretch to serve the largest number possible. We have also tried to hold the shows in community venues (church basements, union halls, community centers) where even rental fees could help struggling neighborhoods rather than fill a club owner's pocket.

Overall, this has worked well enough to silence all but the most tenacious of Fugazi's naysayers. Of course, this certainly doesn't mean that the band, like Positive Force, has never made mistakes, for both surely have. Nonetheless, I learned from even the most egregious of these errors. In the process, I have hopefully grown to be more effective in both my activist and artistic work.

One of the lessons I relearned from Fugazi—especially from singer-guitarist Ian MacKaye—during punk's fractious post-*Nevermind* era was simple but saving: *Keep your focus on your own side of the street.* The idea of checking out your own actions, letting them stand as your message, while largely refraining from critiquing others, suggested how punk might find its way past either sellout or self-destruction.

This experience has also pointed toward the most significant of our challenges in the punk community: How can we build an inclusive, flexible, populist underground with thriving counter-institutions that is also open to (in fact, seeking out) coalitions with other communities and networks, including those who may have chosen a more mainstream path?

This brings us back around to Nirvana's "Smells Like Teen Spirit." Even as the song extended the realm of punk, it also showed the subculture's limitations. The most obvious way, of course, is how punk itself—even that of self-described "redneck Situationists" like Nirvana—became part of the "society of the spectacle," a product to be consumed, profiting multinational corporations.

The persistence of the underground more than a decade past the "grunge" era suggests that punk remains more than simple commerce, however. As Naomi Klein notes in *No Logo: Taking Aim at the Brand Bullies* (St.

Martin's Press, 1999), "If, even after being singled out as the latest fad, [a movement] continues as if nothing happened, it's a good bet that it is a real movement."

But if punk is undeniably real, it remains hardly an all-encompassing entity. An obvious and troubling narrowness of the North American independent-music underground was on display in the "Teen Spirit" video. Examine the composition of the crowd, not so different from the average punk concert: young, largely white and male, reasonably affluent, rebelling against an authority that inevitably ends; i.e., high school. While the video does suggest female empowerment and (arguably) hints at some sort of cross-racial (a T-shirt for Bad Brains, trailblazing African-American punk band, is repeatedly glimpsed) or cross-class (the janitor sympathetic to the kids but not to the principal who is left bound and gagged at the end) coalition, the clip mostly evokes a slender slice of humanity.

The reality underlying this portrayal should be sobering to any punk looking toward a larger transformation. Olympia, Washington–based Riot Grrrl band Heavens to Betsy put it like this in "Axemen," a song that plays like a sarcastic rebuttal to "Smells Like Teen Spirit": *"Do you wanna live this teenage dream/The punk white privilege scene?"* This is perhaps the key question for anyone who was first spurred to activism by punk, only to eventually chafe against its boundaries.

Sharing "Teen Spirit's" soft/loud dynamics, "Axemen" conveys a desperate search for identity not predicated on oppression of others. Singer-guitarist Corin Tucker first looks around the pep rally/punk show, saddened to see *"so much white."* Casting about, she reaches within herself (to *"cut off my privilege inside of me"*), only to realize that even *"this is too easy/There is work I have to do."* Offering no easy answers, but suggesting a passionate engagement with the issues, "Axemen" is just as stirring as its more famous counterpart, and ultimately more hopeful.

As powerful and transformative as the punk scene has been for many of us, in order to truly "revolutionize," we need to step beyond. This does not mean necessarily leaving that community. However, we must at least continue to reinvent punk in ways that venture further out into the daylight, if you will.

While I prefer to work within an underground context, the broader possibilities created by punk's penetration of the mainstream must not be dismissed. For example, the "Rock Against Reagan" tours of the '80s reached tens of thousands. Now the Rock Against Bush CD and tour (and associated Punk Voter campaign), driven by Mike Burkett of NOFX and Fat Wreck Chords, can reach millions. This important initiative is a worthy counterpart to similar efforts coordinated by the likes of Russell Simmons in the hip hop community.

At the same time, we must not lose sight of the activism needed every day, not just on Election Day. Back in the mid-'90s, I worked with ex–Dead Kennedys frontman Jello Biafra to help realize his dream of creating the FSU Foundation. This entity—sadly short-circuited by legal troubles with Biafra's former bandmates—briefly channeled resources from popular punk bands like the Offspring and Green Day into creative grassroots activism around the country.

If FSU slipped away, another casualty of landmines left over from the early-'90s punk strife, its spirit lives on. For Punk Voter to be truly "punk" in the sense I hold dear, it must grow toward becoming "Punk Activist." If we are wise, alliances formed over the course of this campaign can be utilized to develop a national network of punk activist groups, perhaps with a small central coordinating office. Resources from bands, individuals, and institutions—especially those who have benefited from the post–"Smells Like Teen Spirit" explosion, as in the FSU idea—could be channeled into this endeavor.

The aim would be not only to build active community within punk, but bridges to other communities as well. In the end, we punks must get to know and bond with others, especially the marginalized; to embody the solidarity implicit in the name itself. Together we might help to build power rising (in the best punk fashion) from the grassroots—the power we need to change the overall system.

This brings us back to the downbeat vignette recounted at this chapter's beginning: the strikingly punk-free affordable-housing rally. As I wrestled with doubts about punk's possible irrelevance, a young woman (one of the few white people at the event) walked up and introduced herself. Her name was Anne, and she was a tenant organizer in Brooklyn, New York—and a former D.C. punk.

As it happened, she was a friend of my old PF compatriots John Pat and Julie and knew me from PF shows. She thanked me for past inspiration—but without knowing it, she gave me at least as much in return on that hot, sticky D.C. day.

Somehow, for Anne, as for many others, punk had come to mean something far beyond subcultural sanctuary. I took her words, just like the song "Axemen," as a hopeful sign that punks might be able to leave behind high school dramas, petty, elitist tribes, and grow to a deeper, broader application of their ideals.

This activist brew of empowerment, mixed liberally with privilege and elitism, is hardly unique to punk. As we shall see, that post-'60s cliché—*student radicalism*—also shares this tendency.

THREE: BACK TO SCHOOL DAYS

*"They told me that
It was like a film out here
But it's a real horror show . . .
I'm going back to school days
To put them right . . ."*
—Graham Parker

My first memory of campus protest is seared indelibly into my mind. I was perhaps ten years old, sitting in the living room of my family's home. Transfixed and disgusted, I watched grainy images of Vietnam War protests from the evening news on a black-and-white TV. Rocks flew, billy clubs swung, and tear gas swirled as students and police clashed. The exact date is unclear—some time after the Tet Offensive of January 1968, yet before the U.S. invasion of Cambodia in May 1970—but my feeling of disdain was palpable. *What spoiled brats!* I thought.

It is not surprising that I felt this way at the time, since virtually everybody else did where I grew up in rural Montana. Ours was a community where backbreaking manual labor and "love it or leave it" patriotism were the norms. In this context, the chance to go to college was not taken for granted. Many of my Sheridan County peers never continued on academically after high school, or did so only briefly before returning home to do farm or ranch work.

In my parents' generation, the situation was even starker. Very few had attended college, with some—like my father—leaving high school early to go to work. Many of those with higher education got it thanks to the GI Bill that aided the returning veterans of World War II.

This history helped to create a bond in many working-class communities like ours. The U.S. military was referred to simply as "the service," a way to defend our country and perhaps to get ahead just a bit.

My father and mother slaved tirelessly to give me and my siblings a better life, the chance to do more than just work with our hands. This background no doubt contributed to our sense of Vietnam War–era campus radicals—many attending elite institutions that felt hopelessly beyond our reach—as ungrateful, lazy, treasonous, and spoiled.

These students had so much, were so lucky. What did they have to be so upset about? This assessment was burned into my young psyche. While I would largely abandon this position within a few years, some genuine insights persist that give me an appreciation of both the strengths and limitations of college-based activism as a catalyst for broad social change.

For the present generation, college can often be seen as a rite of passage, nearly as necessary as high school in order to get a decent job. One's privilege often still determines whether and where one is able to attend.

Although only a small minority of students, even in the 1960s, were ever full-fledged activists, an image persists of college as a time of unbridled idealism, even radicalism; a last gasp of irresponsibility before settling into the "real world" of adult matters like career and family.

"Anyone who is twenty and conservative has no heart; anyone who is thirty and liberal has no brain," an older acquaintance back in Montana once told me. His own journey was more extreme than most—from McGovernite peacenik in 1972 to Reagan supporter and "security consultant" to the bloody Guatemalan oligarchy in the 1980s—yet his point of view has been echoed by many.

Of course, this path is not predestined, as proven by numerous counter-examples. The question is this: Are there ways that the college experience, even campus activism, sets us up to edge into compromise, to fade into business-as-usual? Or are there ways to sustain that idealism, to make it a beginning rather than an end to engagement? Beneath this is an even more basic query: Are there ways that college activism, despite its limitations, might contribute to a fundamental transformation?

Given my upbringing, it is certainly ironic that I ended up being one of those much-despised "campus radicals," albeit of another generation. Most of my peers certainly did not. Why me and not the others? In retrospect, my activism was largely an outgrowth of punk;

indeed, its inspiration was the reason why I even went to college in the first place, given my class background.

All of this was quite unlike many of my current D.C. punk friends. Most are from affluent, liberal, urban professional families—including some who have past student activists for parents. For them, college was an expected, even enforced part of their journey to successful adulthood. Not surprisingly, they often rebelled against it. By contrast, I came to view college as a way out of a "no future" life of manual labor, church, and barroom.

Thus, for reasons that went far beyond the eruption of punk, 1977 was cause for celebration. That was the year I began to attend Montana State University (MSU), nestled in the small Rocky Mountain town of Bozeman. At 30,000 residents—including some 10,000 students—Bozeman seemed like a big city to me. The change in locale was exciting, even liberating. Not only was I away from parental authority for the first time, but now I could (sometimes) actually buy records by the artists I was reading about.

Even in this somewhat more urban environment, punk was a very solitary pursuit. My oft-repeated joke—that there were perhaps a half-dozen punks in the entire state of Montana at the time—may well have been true. In the absence of such a music or social scene, it eventually became obvious that my ideals would need to be expressed in other ways. Given my intense bond to punk—music rooted in raw protest—student activism was a logical outcome.

That I would become a radical while at MSU was hardly inevitable, however. To put it mildly, MSU was no Berkeley. In Sheridan County, the school was seen as a "people's university," but in a very different sense. Founded in 1893, not long after Montana became a state, MSU's motto was the far-from-romantic *"Education for Efficiency."* While a fair number of its students did come from outside the state (including ski bums who spent more time on the slopes than in class), MSU catered primarily to its own. Its relatively low in-state tuition was affordable to children of the rural/small-town working-to-middle class. As a result, it was often where folk like me went—to find a mate, to have fun, to have a break before returning home to work.

This accessibility had its downside for some; indeed, MSU was nicknamed "Moo U" by its detractors. MSU was quite distinct from places like hippie-experiment-turned-punk-haven Evergreen State College in Olympia, or an elite institution like the Johns Hopkins School of Advanced International Studies (SAIS) on Embassy Row in Washington, D.C. which I later attended.

Being an activist at MSU took some commitment. In the absence of any "liberal" (much less radical) consensus, it also took some fairly serious thought and study to be a credible left-wing voice. Certainly '60s-era ideas of students as an oppressed class would have been laughed off the campus.

By accident, this became particularly true for me, as my first-year roommate, Larry Sweet, turned out to be a former president of MSU's ultra-right Young Americans for Freedom chapter, a college debate champion, a senior, and a connoisseur of Broadway show tunes. Quite a match for me, a freshman rural malcontent infatuated with the Sex Pistols, the Ramones, and radical left politics!

We were a hilarious "Odd Couple" pairing, to be sure, but it was a gift in disguise. Larry and I didn't agree a lot—in fact, looking back, the year seems like one long argument—but I did learn a whole bunch in the process. This is more than just a quaint story. I think it points to a key insight, one clearly lost on many of us: If we radicals are to be effective in arguing our points, much less in building a "new world," we can't just hang out with the already converted. We need to do a lot more than fiercely (or lazily) spout rhetorical left-wing clichés, denigrating or dismissing those who disagree with us.

In the face of de facto (if sometimes self-imposed) segregation, we must engage other communities, persistently and sensitively, listening as well as speaking. Other perspectives are not to be feared. Rather, they can help us to deepen our understanding, as well as to build relation-ships across boundaries. Both of these are essential aspects of sustaining—and realizing—our ideals.

If this story suggests how college can help bring different people together, the broader utility of college activism is nonetheless limited by at least two factors. The first is that it costs a lot to go to school. Simply having the chance to get a university degree put me in a certain lofty group in our world; recall that perhaps ninety percent of the world's population is not so lucky. By their very nature, student activists will therefore tend to be operating within a narrow context—a significant limitation. While this can allow some access of radical ideas into elite circles, the "system" (if you will) is set up to effectively contain this threat.

The second is that (despite the best efforts of some of us to prolong our time there indefinitely) college does end, either with graduation or simple dropout. It is a transient community, hard to organize. Indeed, many seem to view it simply as an extended pit stop/party on the race toward the adult world. The aim is often simply to make it through, to get a piece of paper that will help to secure a job that will pay the bills.

As this suggests, universities are not altruistic havens of humanism existing simply to serve the common good through the pursuit of knowledge and justice. They are gigantic institutions that, to varying degrees, are shaping their students to be cooperative cogs in the established economic machine. In certain cases—most obviously the so-called Ivy League in this country—schools are also gatekeepers for the ruling class. A vastly disproportionate segment of our country's top economic and political decision-makers come from that relatively tiny pool of East Coast graduates.

Back in Sheridan County, we knew this almost instinctively. From when I was very young, a message came through loud and clear: We are not masters of our fate. Our lives are determined by powerful people—mostly on the East Coast—who we will never meet, who disdain us even though we help to grow their food. We resented this bitterly, viscerally; well aware that virtually no one we knew would ever be included in those prestigious Ivy League ranks.

This class bias in higher education is hardly surprising, as most colleges depend on the rich for their funding, with their priorities set and agendas limited by that reality. In addition, they will tend to respond to the institutional imperatives typical of any large corporate entity: self-preservation, profit, endless growth, and aggrandizement.

It has become hard to say where the corporation ends and academia begins. As Liza Featherstone points out in *Students Against Sweatshops* (Verso, 2002), "Just about every aspect of collegiate life can be leased for corporate profit these days. Increasingly universities outsource services they used to provide themselves; on campuses nationwide, big capital's irresistible cartoonish logos are becoming ubiquitous as backpacks. Barnes & Noble has taken over the university bookstores, and Starbucks has set up shop in the student union."

Featherstone goes on to note, "It's not unusual for a university to lease the rights to its own brand name." As Naomi Klein shows in *No Logo*, sometimes these arrangements have included a "non-disparagement" requirement, as with the University of Kentucky and Nike, or the University of Wisconsin at Madison and Reebok. Such clauses have been used to try to muzzle campus critics of these corporations' labor or business practices.

Klein admits that such are "extreme examples of how corporate sponsorship deals re-engineer some of fundamental values of public universities." Beyond these, she argues, there are more subtle but equally disturbing effects: "The more campuses act and look like malls, the more students act like consumers." Indeed, some of the more candid administrators themselves have begun to speak of the university as if it were simply another corporation.

Much of this is driven, of course, by the need for money, especially in an era of cutbacks in public funding. This trend is nonetheless simply a more obvious manifestation of a current that has always been present. Such realities are why the idea of students being central in revolutionary transformation—another notion popular in the 1960s— proved largely illusory.

The Vietnam-era antagonism between college protesters and blue-collar "hard hats," and the refusal of trade unionists to fully ally with students during the Paris uprising of 1968, are but two examples of a larger problem. Quite simply, there will tend to be quite a lot of mistrust between working-class elements and student groups carrying, as they almost invariably do, the stink of privilege and self-interest, often speaking a language alien to those they would convert.

In some ways, then, college might be just as limited as punk as a vehicle for social transformation. At the same time, a reasonable rule of thumb for organizing is *to begin wherever you are*. Simple membership in a community provides inherent credibility, a decided advantage in organizing efforts. Any community—be that punk, college, high school, whatever—can be a place to start. As we will see in the next chapter, this kind of approach can be essential, especially when dealing with issues like racism, sexism, or class privilege.

Moreover, as my own life story suggests, we should not entirely surrender to cynicism when assessing university life. Despite its limitations, college does exist, to some degree, as a "life laboratory." This can be (and often is) a place to try out new approaches, learn new skills, discover new worlds. As such it can be tailor-made to fulfill the functions of a "free space" discussed in our last chapter. Our hope is to breed "class traitors," who will use their skills and knowledge against the system that gave them birth.

This is a tricky business to be sure, but necessary nonetheless. Lower-income students will not generally be attending university simply for "life lessons," much less instruction in revolution. They will tend to be there to learn skills and make contacts that can make them less disposable in a world that can throw people away—a possibility most likely for those in tenuous economic circumstances. This pragmatic orientation would hardly be served by alienating gatekeepers who can help sufficiently gifted and deferential individuals to escape their class of origin.

This may be especially true today. As documented in Christian Parenti's *The Soft Cage: Surveillance in America From Slave Passes to the War on Terror* (Basic Books, 2003), a frightening expansion of police and surveillance powers is now underway, aided by new forms of technology. There are thus many reasons to keep a low profile, especially for otherwise marginalized or stigmatized groups. As I was often reminded growing up, one's potential upward mobility might depend on not being labeled a troublemaker.

Fear, then, is a great enemy of activism; we must fight the spread of its grip. Part of the struggle is simply to ensure broader access to this potentially liberating space, through student loan programs, scholarships, affirmative action, and more. However, as I know all too well, student loans are not simple gifts; they require repayment, a reality that itself limits future choices.

The free space offered by college can therefore be significantly less "free" for those hemmed in by practicalities—and may be squandered on partying or other diversions by the less restricted. Of course, whatever our background, we still retain some choices; most of all, our own attitude. The approach we bring to our college experience is also a profoundly important variable.

In my own case, I came to MSU largely to escape the home county. Initially this did not translate into embracing the relatively rich cultural possibilities it could offer. I treated MSU more as a delaying action, giving myself space to plot my next move. I picked a "saleable" major and then coasted along. Not surprisingly, I wasn't feeling it. When school got too boring, I failed a class (in music—simply stopped going) and dropped out. Lacking any better idea, I went back to work on the farm. My experiences during the ultra-rigorous calving season in a harsh winter and spring—combined with the "gotta gettaway" message of punk—were enough to get me back to school in less than a year.

This time I came with a new approach, fueled by desperation and perhaps a bit of courage. I finally broke with the caution and pragmatism of my rural working-class background, embracing the far less bankable promises of punk idealism. Although my financial support was limited, I determined to take only classes that interested me, to not worry about a major or a job after school.

Not surprisingly, shortly thereafter I also took the step into activism. Without this more devil-may-care attitude, I would never have found my way into a class on "Radical Political Ideologies," fronted by a slow-talking but passionate veteran of the '60s upheaval, Ray Pratt. Some of the other students may have been bored, but the revolution that happened for me in this class was undeniable. There I read Karl Marx, Murray Bookchin, and radical feminist Shulamith Firestone for the first time. In the process, I began to concretize some of the thoughts already swirling around my brain courtesy of punk, and started to uncoil their broader possibilities.

Most astonishing of all, the class also led to my first public speaking. By happy accident, Jan Strout, recently arrived Director of Programming Services, heard an hour-long class presentation I gave on "The Ideology of Punk Rock Music"—a talk, by the way, that I could only get through by playing songs every few minutes to overcome my "stage fright." Like Ray, Jan would become a key mentor, friend, and ally. Fascinated by the punk world to which I had opened a window, she asked me to take the talk to various dormitories around campus.

It must have been quite a sight for Bozeman, Montana, circa 1980: a scraggly, bespectacled blonde spitting out a pro-feminist and gay-rights rant, denouncing racism, capitalism, and drinking, all set to an ear-splitting soundtrack of the Slits, Sex Pistols, Gang of Four, Tom Robinson Band, and the Adverts. Now imagine this spectacle played out in front of shy, country-bred co-eds, guffawing, tobacco-chewing cowboys, and puzzled dorm-lobby passersby. It was certainly one of the oddest free spaces I have ever encountered; such is the temporary insanity sometimes induced by genuine passion. Looking back, I was lucky to escape without a beating! Nonetheless, the talks were my first real public speaking, and I came away feeling energized, even empowered.

The presentations also led to my first dive into the graphic arts . . .

if you can call it that. I created the ragged flyer for the series, a DIY monstrosity assembled from pieces cut from Caroline Coon's *1988: The New Wave Punk Rock Explosion*, and clumsily taped to the page. However embarrassing in retrospect, it was a start, just one of many. This step from private dissent to public stand shamed me into stepping onto the picket line with striking janitors a couple weeks later . . . and my life would never be the same.

There also were unexpected side benefits to this personal transformation. My sense of identity grew stronger, broader; soon I was a punk rocker, a political science major with a soaring GPA, and a college radical. If I approached that latter role with more than the average ambivalence (given my background), I also had found meaning and purpose—always precious items in this life.

My activism soon made me something of a public figure on campus. In a certain sense, I even began to (horror of horrors!) "fit in." Even if this largely meant I was consigned to the clichéd role of campus radical, I now at least had more significance in the scheme of things. Put more baldly, I now got noticed. As a result, I began to flourish (in relative terms) socially, becoming courageous enough to go on a couple of dates, even having a girlfriend for a brief period—no small accomplishment for someone as shy and withdrawn as I had been.

In an even stranger twist, progress was also soon apparent in career terms. Work I did during a summer internship with the progressive political action committee MontCEL resulted in victory for Ramona Howe, the first Native American woman elected to a state legislature. This brought me close to the Montana Democratic Party, a link that grew even more intimate when my former MontCEL supervisors, Tony Jewett and Gail Stoltz, joined the party leadership.

I was soon recruited for a job as a researcher with the reelection campaign of Democratic Senator Max Baucus in 1984. Combined with my acceptance to an elite graduate school in D.C. (Johns Hopkins SAIS—described skeptically as "CIA-S" by close friend and mentor Lauren Weinberg), a potentially rewarding and sustainable career in politics and government service now beckoned.

In principle, I thought I might be able to work from within the system for change. On the other hand, was that structure so compromised as to make transformation impossible? And where did my own motivations fit in this puzzle? Did I just want to get ahead in my own way? While I was clearly energized by my college experiences, how could I translate this to empowerment for others?

These are not easy questions to answer. At the time, I wanted desperately to believe that what was good for me was also good for revolution. To do this, I indulged in mental contortions worthy of a yoga master. This is not to say that my college activism around Central America, abortion, the arms race, feminism, and issues of gender violence was not sincere. I am surely proud of my work during the long custodial strike (which was finally won), as well as my persistence in making visible the suffering of Central America, both in Bozeman and back in Sheridan County. Most of all, I still cherish my minor role in the election of Ramona Howe.

There were smaller—yet significant—victories as well. The most touching came when a conservative ROTC cadet (and fellow political science major) approached me shortly before our graduation. Given our divergent views and common academic path, we had been adversaries, often locking horns in class discussions. Over time, a certain wary mutual respect had also developed. I was nevertheless astonished when, in the midst of typical pre-graduation pleasantries, my longtime foe emotionally confided how influential my views had come to be on him. Most moving of all, he shared an unorthodox request he had made to his superiors. In an institution never noted for soliciting opinions from the grassroots, he had asked to not be assigned to the Central American theater due to his personal misgivings over U.S. policy. However quixotic, such moments suggest that my activism was not without its effect—and that we must never give up on others, no matter whom or what they are.

• • •

We now turn to the broader question: Given its inherent limitations, how might student radicalism serve to objectively alter structures, values, and relationships in the society at large, an endeavor which would require connecting to communities far beyond the privileged halls of the academy?

To explore this, let's turn back to where we started this chapter: the disdain held for campus radicals among the relatively marginalized community where I grew up. No doubt part of why the Sheridan County community of my youth didn't like campus activists is that they didn't look like us. As with the punks of a generation yet to come (with their tattoos, piercings, spiky short hair, dyed in outrageous shades), the long hair, bell-bottoms, acid rock music, and recreational drugs of many '60s student radicals were signs of a counterculture. These were meant, explicitly or implicitly, to signify critique of, even disgust for, mainstream society. Is there any surprise that much of that society took the statement as intended, as an attack?

This is no small matter. In *Rules for Radicals*, Saul Alinsky argues, "If the real radical finds that having long hair sets up psychological barriers to communication and organization, he *[sic]* cuts his hair." One doesn't have to entirely agree with Alinsky to recognize this as a problem. Such overt signifiers may be only the most obvious manifestation of an arrogance that can infect and cripple any type of radicalism.

At base, radicals may tend to see ourselves as smarter than the average person. While college students will objectively have more formal education than the mass of people, to think that this necessarily translates to deeper insight is a profound error. For example, as children of the Depression era, my parents understood that the world in no way owed them a living. Perhaps we owed each other a living, but nothing could be taken for granted. To them, it was just common sense: Rights came with responsibilities. However tempting it might seem, to claim one while refusing the other just would not work.

Of course, the '60s-era demand for something close to absolute freedom "to do your own thing" had its value in the face of a repressive society. Still, this was true only to the extent that it restored a balance swung too far in the opposite direction. It is now easy to see how aspects of the '60s rebellion set the stage for the greed and conspicuous consumption of the "Me Generation" 1980s.

Indeed, as historian Patrick Renshaw points out in his introduction to the 1999 edition of *The Wobblies: The Story of the IWW and Syndicalism in the United States* (Ivan R. Dee), the "politics of upheaval" of the 1960s generated an unfortunate recoil. According to Renshaw, the countercultural uprising "badly frightened the 'silent majority,' those God-fearing, taxpaying middle- and working-class Americans who were in many ways the backbone of the country . . . and created a conservative reaction that swept all before it during the Nixon-Reagan years of the 1970s and 1980s." To the extent this is so, no more stinging rebuke to the radicals of those times could be imagined.

This points to what perhaps most rankled those of us in Sheridan County and similar communities: Not only did the students ignore issues that mattered to us—even apparently spoke a different language!—most fundamentally, they didn't seem to care about us. To which I say, fair enough—some of the groups clearly did not care. The Weatherman faction of the Students for a Democratic Society (SDS), for example, straightforwardly dismissed the American working class as irredeemably reactionary and made few efforts to organize within their ranks. Quite simply, the working class was "the enemy."

This critique may be less true of today's student activists, who—neither linked to a larger countercultural movement, nor riding a social upheaval like that wrought by the civil rights movement and the Vietnam War—are perhaps somewhat less likely to flaunt alienating signifiers or indulge in overheated rhetoric.

Nonetheless, there are many ways we can still set ourselves off from the broader population, even on our own campuses. From his frequent campus lecture appearances, *Z* magazine's Michael Albert has observed that "as compared to their classmates, the activists look entirely different, have different tastes and preferences, talk differently, and are largely insulated from rather than immersed in the larger population." Albert continues, "If our core movement [in any given school] of a couple hundred folks spends most of its time relating together and to people very much like themselves, and almost none of its time going into sports bars and fraternities and all the other campus venues where 40,000 other students congregate, how are we going to become a majority project?"

While this failure is hardly unique to the university context, it points to an even more fundamental problem for campus-based activists: connecting to a broader community, including nearby neighborhoods. I have yet to see student radicals convincingly and consistently link to issues that might bridge the divide between them and most of America, much less the world.

In fact, as Naomi Klein recounts, much of campus politics in the late-'80s and early-'90s seemed to focus around what an external observer might well view as arcane issues of identity. "In the outside world, the politics of race, gender, and sexuality remained tied to more concrete pressing issues, like pay equity, same-sex spousal rights, and police violence." Such demands, Klein notes, "were a genuine threat to the economic and social order." However substantive, these struggles "didn't seem terribly glamorous to students on many campuses, for whom identity politics had evolved . . . into something quite different: issues of 'representation'—a loosely defined set of grievances mostly lodged against the media, the curriculum, and the English language."

Incisively, Klein ties this back to the corporate consumer culture most of us have been submerged in: "For a generation that grew up mediated, transforming the world though pop culture was second nature. The problem was that these fixations began to transform us in the processs. Over time, campus politics became so consumed by personal politics that they all but eclipsed the rest of the world. The slogan 'the personal is political' came to replace the economic as political and, in the end, the Political as political as well."

The struggle around "representation," if hardly irrelevant, ultimately became its own trap. As Klein drives home, "In the absence of more tangible goals, any movement fighting about better social mirrors is going to eventually fall victim to its own narcissism." I would argue that self-interested motives have often been present with campus activism. As with other radicalism, student activists may respond as much to their own identity needs as to the practical issues at hand.

Of course, some campus work is less subsumed under this critique than others. In particular, the anti-sweatshop campaigns of the past decade, such as the one I witnessed at Georgetown University, are promising. In part, this hope rises from the fact that, as noted by Liza Featherstone, "Anti-sweatshop activists are the most powerful and visible progressive presence on campus since the South African divestment movement of the 1980s."

The importance of the movement goes beyond this, however. At its best, these efforts have not only tied global issues to local ones, and built bridges to organized labor and church groups, but have also drawn attention to the structural problems of the university-as-corporation. Moreover, the main student group, United Students Against Sweatshops (USAS), is, in the words of Featherstone, "becoming a more broad-based organization, one that spurs students to take on labor abuses on their own campuses as well as in Indonesia."

At the same time, Featherstone, along with some of the college activists who collaborated with her on *Students Against Sweatshops*, frankly admit the shortcomings of their efforts. In particular, they have been far less successful in connecting to local concerns than global ones. Featherstone observes that "to many students of color, anti-sweatshop activism seems like a dodge from injustice at home." This has made building bridges across such lines difficult.

Whatever the racial background of the student activist in question, however, certain fundamental questions about universities and the privilege they convey seem far from addressed. This is suggested by the often tense relations that exist between a campus and its surrounding community, friction that can be especially pronounced along class and/or racial lines.

This seems true across the board, whether it is a left-wing Quaker-inspired college like Earlham in the otherwise working-class town of Richmond, Indiana, or an elite institution like Yale in New Haven. I have even experienced this tense disconnect with an historic African-American beacon, Howard University, on the northern edge of Shaw in inner-city D.C. No matter what their founding philosophy or history, such institutions are often seen as an island of privilege, unconcerned with the plight of an otherwise desperate, hurting community.

One of the keys to building a college experience that can translate to broader horizons of justice is for it to be thus connected in the first place. Some institutions have tried to bridge this gap. Efforts like the Neighbors Project and Project Change (at George Washington and Howard Universities, respectively, here in D.C.), which draw students out of their academic enclaves into community work in nearby low-income neighborhoods, are laudable. At the same time, these outreach projects operate with uncertain resources and a "service" (as opposed to "justice") focus. This should be no surprise, given that they are tiny parts of huge institutions with many competing demands and priorities—monies devoted to sports programs dwarf them.

I have seldom seen campus radicals press demands for such programs, much less pursue their trajectory toward logical conclusions. I certainly didn't while I was at MSU. My very first activism (the janitors' strike) was one of the few times where students seemed to link with the local community across class lines. At the time, Bozeman was beginning to experience what now is clearly recognizable as gentrification. Montanans had long complained about "Californians" moving in, their relative riches bidding up property values and raising the cost of living. The result was the growing displacement of people who had been raised in what were now increasingly desirable, even "hip" communities like Bozeman.

Meanwhile, once-vibrant towns like Butte and Anaconda were being abandoned by the mining companies. The agricultural economy was so troubled that areas like Sheridan County seemed to be dying. Reservations such as the one I grew up on—Fort Peck—were often sad cesspools of poverty, alcoholism, violence, and hopelessness. There was no shortage of local issues to address; still, in my experience, few MSU activists ever did. I certainly did not, despite my own background. If there is one thing I would wish to make right in going back to my school days, it is this. Nearby marginalized working-class communities, when they weren't simply invisible to us, often seemed to be the butt of jokes in my progressive circles, focused (as we often were) on issues far away, in lands across the ocean—our work on the janitors' strike notwithstanding.

How can we play a role in broader transformation if we can't connect to those who could help to make it real? Reaching out to marginalized communities is not simply to invite them to our events. Nor is it sufficient to approach them in sporadic, charity-style activities. Instead, it is to make them central, to allow them to help set our agenda as activists, thus affirming their importance to us with actions, not words. Activists cannot be confined to their own school grounds, although their transient nature will inevitably limit their effectiveness in off-campus community work.

This also connects to a basic organizing principle: The demands most effective in mobilizing a community are those which have emerged from within it. This may seem like common sense, but it rests uncomfortably at odds with the impatient arrogance of would-be revolutionaries, campus or otherwise, who often believe they know what issues are or aren't important to the struggle.

Even more insidious, the approach to politics learned on campus can leave us ill-equipped to translate our ideas into any other non-elite forum. Part of this is the tendency toward "academese," jargonistic gobbledygook that—if we are not careful—communicates effectively only to those already in the know. For example, the concept of an "interlocking axis of oppression" is crucial to my politics. It communicates something essential about the way race, class, and gender are linked, all equally important pieces in a system where some flourish while many others are discarded. However, if I use that expression while speaking to one of the seniors I work with in Shaw (who, I would argue, often exemplify the importance of the idea), the only response is likely to be a perceptible glazing over of the eyes, followed by a polite but swift shift in the topic of conversation.

If we want to break down barriers, to communicate effectively with others, we will seek a common language where everyone involved can comfortably participate in the conversation. Please note that I am not claiming that college is somehow not the "real world" (everywhere that exists, however tiny, transient, or absurd, is "real" in a certain sense—yes, even MTV) or that academic language has no place, for it does. It is simply to say that college, like any subcultural unit, can be so self-referential as to translate only vaguely to the outside world. This only becomes a problem when that community seeks to be more than just one current among many, when it desires to help effect a larger transformation. College activism could play such a role, but often doesn't.

In particular, as already noted, radical tendencies in vogue at many colleges over the past decade have seemed to generate politics that are so theoretical or identity-focused as to thwart any common action, or so out of touch with broader social concerns as to defy translation outside its narrow confines.

Illusions about the actual function of college—or our own mixed motivations—must be exorcised. It would be wonderful if universities were indeed places designed to simply help students discover passion and exercise gifts. With the proper guidance, those two factors might intersect with needs out there in the world, resulting in a job that both pays the bills and helps to transform society, to create justice.

Building institutions to do this would surely be a good idea. College, however, does not exist to build such revolution in any real sense. More often, it serves largely to protect and perpetuate a system based in gross inequity and profit-making. Understanding this is the first step to overcoming the limitations of college activism.

Most observers would probably grant this initial point. The ensuing question, however, is far more unsettling: How does our activism truly serve the causes we claim, rather than our own self-interest? This is the deep query I find myself wrestling with throughout this book, certainly as regards my college activist experience. In retrospect, to the extent we picked up "academic-speak" without simultaneously learning to translate it to everyday English, we were being set up for smug marginality or elite politicking.

It is fair to say that people who are talked down to rarely listen very well. Or, conversely, someone with all the answers may never ask the right people the right question . . . and actually find an answer. The personal challenge is simple yet daunting: Can we affirm ourselves in ways that also leave us teachable, that enable us to truly communicate? If not, we are doomed to talk only to ourselves. The left might be very proud, very smug in our radicalism, but awfully impotent in realizing the ideals we claim to seek.

And we do need answers—be they pleasant or not—lest we surrender the game to the right, seemingly more interested and able to talk in ways that communicate to mainstream America. Is there something here to learn from even that infamous verbal stumblebum, George W. Bush? Although this may sound like blasphemy, I think so.

• • •

For many of us, college activism is an essential start. However, we must then step beyond to the broader, never-ending contest: to continue growing, to keep on course, to stay true even as the backdrop changes, striding through the stages of life toward unknown but beckoning possibilities.

I could easily have been one of those who left their idealism in a time capsule, back in the day, with their other college memorabilia. If I had, my story would have been an object lesson in how the system operates to co-opt dissent. After all, I moved to Washington, D.C. in 1984 to attend Johns Hopkins SAIS, pursuing a career in the Foreign Service or on Capitol Hill.

Fate, it seems, would not have it that way. Instead of a comfortable glide into the lower echelons of the elite, I discovered a tense, gripping cauldron of multiracial, multicultural, class-driven politics. The pain and power of that meeting, combined with my encounter with D.C. punk and Central America, left me transformed once again. After two more years of activism while at SAIS, I would forsake my career path and dive into the challenges of community in my new home, far from Sheridan County.

My experiences in D.C. help to underscore the challenge to which we now turn: how "identity politics" (in particular, those focusing around race, class, and gender) can liberate—or cripple—us.

FOUR:
IDENTITY IS
THE CRISIS

"Without community,
there is no liberation,
only the most vulnerable
and temporary armistice
between an individual
and her oppression."
—Audre Lorde

Gunfire crackled savagely, the short sharp pops cutting through the humid summer air.

I was sitting outside of my Catholic parish, St. Aloysius, watching the door as organizers of a "young adult" social justice event filed in for a meeting. The shots were close—two blocks away at most.

For a moment I stopped breathing, and all was still. Then the sound of screams and shouting echoed in the distance. With that, my stomach clenched into knots, a shudder running through my body, my heart pounding. The insistent shrill of ambulance sirens grew louder. As police cars screeched to a halt near the intersection of North Capitol and M Street, I joined a small community parade walking toward the site of the shooting.

Sadly, the event was not so unusual. St. Al's (as it is more informally known) sits at one of the starkest crossroads in D.C. Several blocks to the south looms Capitol Hill. Going north, half that distance takes you into one of the most troubled public housing projects in the city: Sursum Corda.

The project itself was largely the creation of St. Aloysius. When "urban renewal" turned into "Negro removal" back in the 1960s, a dynamic Jesuit priest named Horace McKenna helped to develop Sursum Corda as affordable housing. Taken from the Latin Mass, the phrase means, "Lift up your hearts."

These encouraging words, so earnestly intended decades ago, now carry a bitter irony. As I know from working with seniors there (and having been jumped twice in the process), Sursum Corda today is a poverty-stricken, gang-ridden complex where desperation festers. There is no more efficient recruiter for the street-corner drug trade than such hopelessness, no better catalyst for violence.

As police unrolled their crime-scene tape, and medical personnel tended to a young African-American man lying in the middle of M Street, onlookers gawked. Some cracked jokes. Little children ran around excitedly, one using his hand to mimic a gun, pretending to shoot at the others.

Standing as a white-skinned dot in the crowd, I said a little prayer for these kids growing up amidst such dehumanizing conditions. Fortunately, it seemed likely that the wounded man would live. He was hustled to a waiting ambulance, in obvious pain but talking freely. After watching the ambulance pull away, I turned around, facing south. There the Capitol dome stood, looming up, white and gleaming, a mere half mile away.

The next morning I checked both the *Washington Post* and its right-wing rival, the *Washington Times*. As far as I could tell, not one word of what had happened was ever reported. Another possibly gang- and/or drug-related shooting in Sursum Corda was, apparently, just not newsworthy.*

What if the person shot had been me, a highly educated white professional, a former Senate employee? This was another matter, of course. That story might well have been on the front page, perhaps even made the national news. The message was bitter but clear: Some people matter, others are disposable. Which is also to say, *identity matters*.

Identity. On one level, it is an entirely random accident that makes somebody white instead of black, born into a rich family in place of a poor one, male instead of female. But such happenstances

---

* In January 2004, Sursum Corda finally found its way to the front page of the *Washington Post*, thanks to three separate shootings in a single week, including the execution of a fourteen-year-old girl to keep her from testifying about one of the previous murders. Gallons of ink were spilled over the affair. Within a couple weeks, the pious talk died down and Sursum Corda began sliding back toward business as usual.

Incredibly, the project returned to the pages of the *Post* just three months later when the U.S. Department of Housing and Urban Development, rather than address safety concerns, moved to revoke the Section 8 status of Sursum Corda and other nearby buildings, potentially displacing thousands of low-income tenants. Fortunately, the tenants—with help from the Alinsky-inspired Washington Interfaith Network—quickly organized to fight HUD's plan. As of July 2004, the fate of Sursum Corda and hundreds of other units of affordable housing still hung in the balance.

determine so much of one's life—even though key determinants of identity like race, for example, have no biological basis, but rise simply from social convention.

At the same time, there is a second, more malleable aspect of identity that is also critical: the issue of personal definition; so tied into personal power. While we will mostly examine the first of these two in this chapter, we must begin with a brief investigation of the latter. Simply put, this version of identity is how we answer basic questions like: Who am I? Why are we here? What is our essential nature? What is possible for me and my world, given these? To answer these queries in hopeful, affirmative ways is not as simple as it might seem to those of us steeped in an activist ethic. Considerable forces are arrayed against an empowered outlook.

Imagine for a moment the world of the unnamed young man shot near Sursum Corda. Although I didn't know him, I have come to know many like him, marginalized kids growing up in the shadow of power and privilege. Despite this proximity to the symbols of democratic idealism, their own lives are profoundly circumscribed. For instance, they are young black men, and thus "untrustworthy," even "fearsome" to many. Is it not possible that such negative social expectations impact self-definition? More practically, they are, statistically speaking, less likely than the average American to get a decent education; more likely to live in poverty, to be unemployed or have a dead-end job.

Beyond even this, our society tells us in so many ways that our possessions are the measure of our human worth. These young men have few avenues to be "somebody" on these terms. In a context like Sursum Corda, drug traffic is perhaps the main economy. In a single busy afternoon, one might make the equivalent of a month's wages at McDonald's or another minimum-wage job.

Is it any surprise, then, that young black men in places like Sursum Corda turn to the "thug life," celebrating hedonism and materialism, living (and dying) by the gun? It is an identity, after all, and one well-suited, in its brutal way, to the environment.

This is not to say that no other way is possible. Of course, there are those who can (and often do) find more altruistic, hopeful identity orientations, even in the most terrible circumstances. Still, while personal responsibility must always remain, and many exceptions to the lure of the thug life exist, we must not be fooled: There is pathology on the loose here. It is the disease of our greedy, materialistic, unequal society as a whole, however, not simply of poor, non-white, inner-city communities.

Even for the more privileged, there are massive, seemingly omnipotent institutions which exist to prevent us from identifying ourselves as anything more than cogs in the consumer machine. In this context, genuine self-reflection, reaching past the pat answers of trashy magazines, television ads, and other social illusions, becomes a potentially revolutionary act. As the X-Ray Spex song that provides this chapter's title pointedly asks, *"Do you see yourself/On the TV screen?/Do you see yourself/In the magazine?/When you see yourself/Does it make you scream?"*

The quest for authentic identity is indispensable. To transform a heartless, cold, commodity-mad world, we must seek the source of those social "facts" that seem so fundamental. Most often, we may discover they are generated by a corporate-dominated consumer society, where—conveniently enough for the seller—meaning comes from a purchase, the hollow act of possession, rather than vital, self-demanding yet life-affirming acts of creation.

Affirming humanity as essentially (if not entirely) good, with an ability to move beyond simple self-interest to seek the common good, is absolutely crucial. Without this, we may see the world's problems but will simply accept them as inevitable, insoluble. Instead of embracing a mission to repair a wounded world, to make it whole and just (what Jewish tradition calls *tikkun olam*), we will turn toward less noble aims and means: looking out for number one, trying to get "ours," while shrugging at the plight of others.

Is this not the essence of the thug life that mainstream America professes to despise? Yet, is this not also what drives so much of our economy, from Wall Street and Madison Avenue on down—the impulse to get ahead at all costs?

Even without the premise I am working with here—that we need each other for revolution—such a world is cold and hopeless. I, for one, can't live in it. Believing instead that I can be part of the solution is vital. The day I realized that I had gifts, however humble, and needed to give them over if I was to be happy (or if the world was to be healed) was a breakthrough; my real *birth*day.

There is a necessary caveat to raise here. While the truth will set us free, it is also extremely demanding. Identifying ourselves as committed to creating change can become a security blanket. This identity can be the shelter to which we retreat for ego support in a chaotic, scary world.

This is not bad in itself, to be sure. However, once we no longer check to see if our sanctuary has become a prison of superiority or complacency, we are lost. Our identity must always strive toward a balance between challenge and comfort, moving us toward deeper understanding, more consistent practice.

This progression is anything but assured. More often ego, self-interest, or laziness intrudes. We see ourselves in one way, but our actions may tell a very different story, may even have the reverse impact than that intended.

Nor is the movement toward each other, toward a combined power that could remake our world in a more compassionate and just manner, inevitable. It depends on our choices. One of the most significant here is how we choose to identify ourselves, especially in relation to each other.

These two aspects of identity meet in how we might join together—coalesce—to transform, to build a multiracial, multi-class, multi-issue movement of the type that is necessary to truly "revolutionize." For me, the latter version of identity compels us to join such a movement, the former helps to determine where we might reside in that entity, what issues might have special urgency.

It is no surprise that the 1960s was a more hope-filled era. At that time there seemed to be a mass exodus of people from one social paradigm toward a more just and compassionate one. Some of this is, no doubt, the rose-tint of sentimentality. It is nevertheless true that dramatic victories were won, not the least of which were the ending of legal segregation and the stopping of the war in Vietnam. Other key steps forward, both large and small, were taken in women's rights, gay liberation, the environment, even animal rights. It is here that the hopeful spirit of the '60s persists, even through the long night of the Reagan/Bush years.

Is there still a movement? It is true that much of the energy of the '60s evolved (devolved?) into single-issue campaigns, struggles that seek improvement on this or that problem, change for this or that group. While these all are generally legitimate places for struggle, the larger sense of community and purpose seems to have been mostly lost. Often these campaigns have only the slightest connection to one another; indeed, some may resist affiliation beyond their narrow bounds for practical reasons.

Even more disheartening, bitter feuds have sometimes broken out between the factions about what is truly important. Former allies have come into conflict, seeming to view change as a zero-sum game where there is only so much to go around. For me to step forward is for you to lose, or vice versa. Any victories won do not necessarily build a movement for more fundamental change.

Indeed, the system often co-opts single issues to preserve its overall power, often aided by the self-interest of those involved. Phenomena like gay Republicans, pro-imperialist "feminists," or the sight of African-American Supreme Court Justice Clarence Thomas misquoting one of America's great revolutionaries (Frederick Douglass) to argue against affirmative action—these are the sadly predictable results of incomplete, disconnected victories.

There are, of course, some compelling historical reasons for this development. In many ways, the "unity" of the movement in the 1960s may have been more apparent than real. This was suspected even at the time. In a work whose influence resounds to this day—1967's *Black Power: The Politics of Liberation in America*—the late Stokely Carmichael (a.k.a., Kwame Ture) and Charles Hamilton argued that African-Americans in this country found themselves in not only a racist, but also a colonial situation. The civil rights movement, they suggested, contained masters and slaves, the colonized and the colonizer, in one mélange that purported to represent "liberation for all." As far as they could see, the movement actually operated largely to the benefit of a certain privileged group: in this case, the whites.

Their response was sure, sharp, and swift. "Before a group can enter an open society, it must first close ranks," Carmichael and Hamilton argued. "Black people must lead and run their own organizations. Only black people can convey the revolutionary idea—and it is a revolutionary idea—that black people are able to do things themselves." For them, the solution was for the black community to organize itself independently. In fact, the Student Nonviolent Coordinating Committee (SNCC)— the group the two were most closely identified with—had already begun to do this, under the banner of "black power." Whites were more or less directly asked to stand aside, to make way for all-black leadership; in the end, to exit SNCC entirely.

There is a certain amount of self-evident truth to this position. Certainly, the emphasis on taking pride in African-American culture and community, while fostering its indigenous leadership, was both winning and widely welcomed. SNCC had long represented the integrationist ideal of "beloved community," of black and white working side by side, however, so the process was also painful. In some ways, it was as wrenching as the disintegration of Students for a Democratic Society (SDS)—then the other major student group, and proponent of participatory democracy—which first descended into fierce factional infighting and, later, outright self-destruction at the height of its power.

SNCC's agonizing march from being a multiracial group to a black power advocate (while dropping its stance supporting nonviolence at the same time) has been documented in many places, so I won't dwell on the specifics. I will note only that by no means was all of African-America aligned behind the black power approach. In fact, there were profound divisions within the African-American community over the question. The term "black power" was itself subject to widely divergent interpretations. Did it mean black separatism? Or simply self-affirmation? Proponents of the idea seemed to have different answers.

Although he never denounced black power, Martin Luther King, Jr. famously noted, "Whenever Pharaoh wanted to keep the slaves in slavery, he got them fighting amongst themselves." Others in the civil rights movement assailed the seemingly suicidal nature of black separatism in a country where African-Americans were less than fifteen percent of the population.

For their part, Carmichael and Hamiton made it clear in *Black Power* that they were not opposed to coalitions per se, deeming them necessary in a pluralistic society. Instead, they asked searching but central questions like, "Coalitions with whom? On what terms? For what objectives?"

From there, Carmichael and Hamilton identified three myths of coalitions. The first was that "in present day America the interests of black people are identical with that of certain liberal, labor, or reform groups." They also denied that "a viable coalition can be affected between the politically and economically secure and the politically and economically insecure." Finally, they disputed the idea that "political coalitions are or can be sustained on the basis of friendly or senti-mental reasons, by appeals to conscience."

These assertions demolished SNCC's own founding declaration. A more direct attack on the existing basis of the civil rights movement—at least as it was popularly understood—was hard to imagine. What were the grounds for successful coalitions, if any? The duo argued that viable coalitions can only stem from four preconditions: a) the recog-nition by the parties involved of their respective self-interest; b) the mutual belief that each party stands to benefit in terms of that self-interest from allying with the other or others; c) the acceptance of the fact that each party has its own independent base of power and does not depend for ultimate decision-making on a force outside itself; and d) the embrace of goals that are specific and identifiable—as opposed to general or vague.

Viewed from today's perspective, some insights contained in this analysis seem undeniable. They surely provide a precious corrective to overly romanticized views of "The Movement." If we are not careful, brushing past hard questions about internal inequities can result in a situation where the privileged still make the decisions, treating less elite parts of a coalition as mere foot soldiers.

The rise of a black power analysis at that time thus makes sense, and was healthy in certain key ways. Such experiences of marginalization within the supposed movement for "liberation"—shared, for example, by many women within civil rights and New Left groups—were painful, and deeply destructive. The reality of such injustice surely accounts for the rise of a separate women's liberation movement, as well as other splits that followed.

These developments, however reasonable, even necessary, have led to a profound dilemma. Carmichael and Hamilton aren't wrong; but by simply noting how we differ, they leave us short of an answer of how to achieve fundamental transformation. By suggesting such major preconditions to making common cause, their approach evokes a pretty bleak scenario. It surely will not be easy to achieve just, effective, and genuine coalitions. But the fact remains that we must, for as splintered groups we will fail to build the power to truly remake our world.

In this way, Martin Luther King, Jr.'s critique rings with a certain essential truth: How can we win this daunting contest for justice if we are not together? While surely a black power organization, the Black Panther Party recognized this fatal flaw and formed coalitions with whites, Latinos, and many other communities, as its former Chairman Elaine Brown has pointed out. This was hardly typical, however. For all the authors' protestations in *Black Power* that advocates of the idea might remain open to coalitions, a real impact of their stance was to profoundly divide—even disable—the civil rights movement.

When Carmichael and Hamilton argue that "group solidarity is necessary before a group can operate effectively from a bargaining position of strength in pluralistic society," it is hard to disagree. Still, it is only a small jump to a far less progressive position, the idea that African-Americans somehow form a "nation," an approach with the implicit goal to organize and build separate from whites or other races, with only the slightest interest in coalition.

Lacking a feminist analysis, *Black Power* can also be seen as opening the way for reactionary, patriarchal black-nationalist politics now most clearly exemplified by Louis Farrakhan and the Nation of Islam. This is not to say that respect isn't due to the Nation of Islam in certain ways, as their discipline and focus have led to some real achievements. Nor is it to somehow say that outsiders can tell an oppressed community how they must organize. But we are useless in our struggle if we do not look honestly at ourselves and share humbly but candidly with our allies.

Beyond this, variants of the black power arguments, now applied to many other "identity" areas, continue to be played out in diverse communities. While growth in sensitivity and justice has sometimes been the result, often there has been a trashing of possible lines of alliance, a shredding of potential power. Each split on its own makes sense, but such division will never lead to larger transformation, especially given how many communities tend to be riven along the lines of gender, sexual orientation, race, class, etc.

It is truly a terrible predicament: We need each other to win the struggle, yet if we don't really share goals or means, or are infected by the ills of the larger society (as we almost inevitably are), how can we be unified? As bell hooks argued in her landmark *Feminist Theory: From Margin to Center* (South End Press, 1984), "Some feminists now seem to feel that unity among women is impossible, given our differences . . . Unless we show that barriers separating women can be eliminated, that solidarity can exist, we cannot hope to transform society as a whole."

How do we get to a politics of common cause from a position that emphasizes difference so profoundly? Can we somehow balance critique with coalition-building? Once we begin to divide, where exactly do we stop?

Take for a moment the movement we have just been speaking of, that of the 1960s. Blacks split from whites; then women from men; then women of color from white women; then gay from straight; then lesbian from bisexual . . . and so on. Given this history, it might seem that the left is far better at the act of splitting apart than that of coalescing.

It is here that the "identity crisis" on the left has become acute over the past three decades, replacing even sectarian ideologies as the factionalizer of first choice. While the right's attack on multiculturalism is in large part a cover for opposing advances for historically marginal-ized communities, there are valid aspects to this critique, even in progressive/revolutionary terms.

Let me be entirely clear here: Affirming all cultures as bearing insights and gifts to share with the world is critical. No less essential is drawing attention to historically overlooked and/or devalued commu-nities. Nevertheless, in the face of seemingly overwhelming difference, efforts like Jesse Jackson's mid-'80s Rainbow Coalition (whose concept was lifted from Fred Hampton of the Illinois Black Panthers) can seem quaint, even wrong-headed. Put simply, given how different we might seem to be, is any unifying bridge between cultures even possible? If not, how can we hope to prevail against the inherently organized corpo-rate powers-that-be and their well-paid puppets?

In 1979, the late visionary African-American lesbian writer and activist Audre Lorde challenged "academic feminists" to examine difference. Apparently they heard, but did not understand. Nearly twenty-five years later, it is in academia that this sort of identity "hair-splitting" has taken root most deeply. Some seem to believe that classroom analysis of difference is the same as transcending our divides, turning them to fuel for communal (as well as personal) power. This is absurd.

To deny our differences is to be blind, if not outright oppressive. Privileged groups must accept primary responsibility in repairing the breaks in community, not somehow blaming more marginalized groups as divisive for simply pointing out the walls that already exist. Yet, to focus on our differences unduly can serve to enlarge them. At its worst, it breaks people down into such tiny clumps as to defy any common ground, stripping us of the power possible in our union.

Even more tragically, we can often lash out at those closest to us, the ones who are our natural allies. As Audre Lorde pointedly noted in her trailblazing work, *Sister Outsider* (Crossing Press, 1984), "Hopefully we can learn from the 1960s that we cannot afford to do our enemies' work by destroying each other." If essential insights, like those contained in *Black Power*, are not balanced by other imperatives, they can begin a slide into self-destruction.

• • •

According to the Random House dictionary, oppression is "the exercise of authority or power in a burdensome, cruel or unjust manner." I would define it a bit more precisely as a systematic, institutionalized mistreatment of any individual or group and/or denial of life's necessities. These include the tangible (health care, food, shelter, employment at a living wage, education) and the less tangible (free speech, expression, spiritual exploration). bell hooks has summarized both of these definitions by saying simply that "being oppressed means the *absence of choices*" (emphasis mine).

Our next step is to affirm what many analysts (including most significantly for me, bell hooks and Audre Lorde) have argued, that there is no one single determinant of oppression. Rather, there are a series of factors, including race, class, and gender, but also sexual orientation, age, nationality, ethnic heritage, religion, physical ability, and beyond, that can be the basis for oppression. Lying beneath these is a "politics of domination" that puts one segment over another, in a never-ending contest for supremacy. Each of these factors can be a significant indicator of the power one will have, the degree of autonomy or self-determination. Some are variable, some are not.

I started out as a member of the working class. Even though some essential aspects of that past persist within me, externally I no longer am part of that class, thanks to my education and experiences. But I cannot so easily change my race or gender. Nor could any attempt at conscious "downward mobility" be real, as I have the tools to step back into the ranks of the privileged at any time.

Oppression, like privilege, can seem invisible, but it is ever-present, including (as we have already noted) within the movements for liberation. This must first be admitted in order that it might be effectively combated or disarmed.

At the same time, however, too much focus on one's oppression can leave one in a victim role, disempowered by definition, terminally divided, or so self-focused that nothing gets done. As feminist historian Paula Petrik, among others, has noted, we need stories of how people have struggled, even won against great odds, not tales that imply unremitting defeat.

I am lucky to have worked for over fifteen years in D.C.'s Shaw neighborhood, home to U Street (a.k.a., "the black Broadway") and what Zora Neale Hurston called the "Harvard" of African-America, Howard University. Amidst the depths of legal segregation in the early twentieth century, Shaw nurtured a community of such power, creativity, and self-reliance as to draw many across racial boundaries to enjoy its fruits.

The whole of Washington society was set up in a way that told African-Americans that they were "less than." Nonetheless, the people of Shaw showed this to be a simple, ugly lie by their achievements. Despite the obstacles, Shaw boasted a cultural vitality unparalleled in white D.C.

There was even a slogan meant to remind those of greater means within the oppressed community to never forget their less fortunate sisters and brothers: *"Lifting as we climb."* It is hardly surprising that much of the groundwork for the modern civil rights movement was laid by Shaw residents like Charles Houston, Mary McLeod Bethune, Mary Church Terrell, and Thurgood Marshall.

Balance here, as elsewhere, is essential. We must neither deny the existence of tensions within our movements (or ourselves) nor allow them to keep us apart, lest we be defeated by our own hand. Key to this is seeing oppression in a broad, inclusive way. We cannot rank any one of the determinants over the others, but must keep all in mind. In particular, we must see race, class, and gender as interlocking elements in an axis of oppression. In short, all are connected; there is no way to truly combat any one without combating all.

This type of definition leads naturally to the building (not burning) of bridges between marginalized communities and their allies; in other words, building toward a real movement. The focus on identity (which, in itself, is healthy and progressive, especially as a corrective to the casual arrogance of many white male radicals) can be taken too far. Self-examination can become self-indulgence, even self-obsession, as if by simply naming our oppression we defeat it. In actuality, if we are not careful, such naming can give it more power, as we identify ourselves with our oppression (not its over-coming) and erect wall after wall, creating an ever smaller pool of potential allies. At its most extreme, this can become the same old American individualism again, denying any ability to ally success-fully across boundaries.

Once devolved to this degree, all that is required to privilege or discount one's opinion is an identity claim, one's assertion that they are part of an oppressed group, or not, as the case may be. This is truly a game that moves as you play. Within feminism, for example, the naïve (even racist) assertions of "sisterhood" have run aground on the shoals of differences in class, race, nationality, religion, culture, sexual orien-tation, and more.

That there is no simple one-size-fits-all version of "sisterhood" is undeniable. But where do we go from there? As bell hooks has asked, how does anything cohesive rise out of this mix of differences? Is sister-hood (or, stated more broadly, solidarity) simply a mirage? Or is the belief that this unbalanced focus on identity is revolutionary the real illusion?

It is here that the ideas of the late Audre Lorde take on a special importance. While they were originally shared mostly in reference to a feminist community, their applicability goes far beyond the bounds of those circles, narrowly understood. In fact, these ideas might be seen as turning the whole issue of difference on its head.

This might seem ironic, as Lorde is often associated with the approach that has fostered some of the most serious splintering. Nonetheless, she exemplified quite a different ethic, one that pushes first past naïve commonality, then past identity, to a deeper solidarity, rising on a more solid foundation: "Mere tolerance of differences is the grossest reformism . . . Difference must not be merely tolerated, but seen as a fund of necessary polarities between which our creativity can spark like a dialectic."

Difference, far from being our downfall, can be our saving strength.

In fact, Lorde argues further that "difference is that raw and powerful connection from which our personal power is forged . . . We must devise ways to use each other's differences to enrich our vision and our joint struggles."

This approach is no simplistic liberal why-can't-we-all-be-friends, power-of-positive-thinking panacea. It rises up from a deep initial challenge: Lorde posits that there is a special necessity for those who are relatively privileged to take the lead in addressing these issues. At the same time, she also notes that those categories are fluid, that we can both be oppressed and oppressor in different ways. Thus, within our communities, we will have to play different roles at different times. Feminist white females may need to challenge their racism; affluent, heterosexual non-white feminists may need to address their classism or homophobia; gay men may need to challenge their sexism; and so on.

The tendency will be to try to focus on one aspect rather than another, if only for simplicity—or in some cases, to evade personal responsibility. Here, the bell hooks/Audre Lorde approach that seeks to not privilege race, class, or gender one over another becomes, once again, key. It challenges us, each in our own context, to see which aspect might be the most important to address in any given moment—but it does not stop there.

Beneath this theory is an overriding aim: the absolute necessity of working together. We must build communities that both support and challenge us, that provide the certain "benefit of the doubt" so essential to turning our difference not into divisiveness, but into a decisive source of transformative power.

This brings us back to our original discussion of the two forms of identity—the subjective search for meaning and purpose, on the one hand; and the objective categories we exist within, such as race, class, and gender, on the other—and how they might intersect to foster revolution. Most basically, to nourish fundamental transformation, we must identify ourselves as turned toward each other, open to alliances, to learning from each other in order to achieve our would-be-revolutionary goals. As Audre Lorde has noted, "Without community, there is no liberation, only the most vulnerable and temporary armistice between an individual and her oppression."

Unless we are to settle for compartmentalized, incomplete personal "revolutions" that don't really affect the larger social structures, values, and relationships of power, *we need each other*. We must be willing to stretch toward one another, to trust and believe that coalition is not only possible, but ultimately necessary.

Jennifer Baumgardner and Amy Richards's *Manifesta: Young Women, Feminism, and the Future* (Farrar, Strauss, and Giroux, 2000) is one such effort to extend and include. Speaking from one feminist generation to both the preceding one and that just arriving, *Manifesta* tries to draw recent cultural phenomena like "Girlie," "Do Me," Riot Grrrl, and the girl's movement into a sort of "big-tent" feminism. The aim is to crack open frozen lines of discourse and create a more inclusive sense of community.

Having affirmed what is progressive in these developments and having drawn their exponents into the discussion, Baumgardner and Richards also throw down a gauntlet. Suggesting limitations and inconsistencies in these often "pop" forms, they gently press toward a more radical application of feminist ideals around race, class, and beyond.

This combination of invitation, affirmation, and challenge seems to be a hopeful direction, broadly applicable to our discussion here. Admittedly, the balance is hard to strike, and sometimes Baumgardner and Richards seem to soft-pedal their critique. Still, creating space for discussion—frank, respectful, sensitive exchange—with the goal of building a more effective movement, is admirable.

Similarly, bell hooks has tried to welcome a broader public into authentic feminist community with works like *Feminism Is for Everybody* (South End Press, 2000). Writing in accessible language and with striking economy and uncompromised politics, hooks clearly aims to rescue feminism from both media misinformation and its own past failures. One very concrete example of the "benefit of the doubt" suggested above is contained in the "Feminist Masculinity" chapter of the book. As articulated in *Feminist Theory* over a decade before, hooks argues that supportive men must be seen as "comrades in struggle," not only a legitimate part of the feminist movement but, in fact, a required one. How else can sexism truly be ended? This is both an invitation and a challenge, for men also have to prove worthy of inclusion. More than just accepting the label, they are expected to engage the feminist "process of becoming" on an ongoing basis.

For me, this is a throwback to my experience in Bozeman, where all manner of leftists, outsiders, and nonconformists mixed, if only because we were so few as to need each other to survive. My "misfits club" of the late-1970s/early-1980s included punks but also engaged feminists, hippies, environmentalists, gays and lesbians, even a vegetarian here and there.

This was in sharp contrast to what I discovered in Washington, D.C., where such groups seemed almost at odds, caught up in internecine politics that were beyond my comprehension at the time. If transgressing boundaries is essential to revolution, it is not always fun. More than once it was made clear that I was not welcome, simply for my gender, sexual orientation, or race. My reaction was understandable, if hardly brave or visionary. For a time, I retreated from the work of bridging communities. Instead, I found my own little subgroup to hang out within, the punk tribe.

I was surely not alone in such choices. The irony is sharp: We, the desperate little clutches of outsiders, grow large enough in size so that we don't need each other for day-to-day survival. This is certainly a sign of some success. The typical result, however, is anything but encouraging. If we are not careful, we can begin to stick only to our little groups. Splintered into different tribes, we can be as likely to critique one another as the larger system we supposedly fight. We make ourselves less powerful in the process.

Again, I don't mean to suggest that being a punk carries the same weight, in identity terms, as race, class, or gender. One can change a funny haircut, remove piercings, hide tattoos; skin color or sex is not nearly so malleable. Nor can you just pretend to be of a certain class. Either you have access to the money (or the advanced degree and/or skills the money bought) or you do not.

This should not blind us to divides within categories, however fixed they may be on their own. For example, the racial and ethnic politics of D.C. are complex, resisting simple categorization of "oppressed" and "oppressor." While the legacy of slavery and segregation remains palpable—enough to fuel mutterings of a "plan" to keep white control of this majority black city—beneath this lurks a chaotic, volatile brew of racial, ethnic, and class divides.

Take D.C.'s Mount Pleasant riots of May 1991. On the face of it, this explosion would seem to fit a neat paradigm: marginalized ethnic community feels the sting of police brutality, anger builds, an outrageous incident ignites an uprising. Sounds familiar, right? Only in this case the victims of police brutality were Latino, the police force largely African-American. The incident that set it off was the shooting of a handcuffed Latino man by a female African-American officer. This illustration only scratches the surface of this city's social complexity.

To say this is not to dispute an ugly, overarching reality that bell hooks rightly describes as "white supremacy." It does add special poignancy to Audre Lorde's anguished recollection that "in the '60s, white america—both racist and liberal—was more than pleased to sit back as spectator while Black militant fought Black Muslim, Black Nationalist badmouthed the nonviolent, and Black women were told that our only useful position in the Black Power movement was prone. The existence of Black lesbian and gay people was not even allowed to cross the public consciousness of Black america."

This is not to suggest that African-Americans were or are any more fractious than any other community. But all of this together should suggest sufficient nuance to deny easy or rigid lines of demarcation. Even Carmichael and Hamilton allow some space for this possibility in *Black Power*. Their concept of how whites might make their contribution was real, if hardly expansive: Whites could aid the black community by educating and organizing their own communities in anti-racist ways. Whites with certain skills (lawyers, for example) could also be directly useful, not in leadership, but in certain limited support functions, assisting black power initiatives.

This prescription, like other aspects of *Black Power*, contains some valuable insight and has been quite influential, applied across other lines of relative privilege and oppression. Certainly, would-be allies of those less fortunate must take care lest they attempt to "help" in ways that still leave their marginalized comrades disrespected, disempowered, and dependent.

But this can also go too far. Two all-too-common reactions to the *Black Power* argument were to become cowed, silenced by the specter of seeming racist or insensitive; or to become uncritical "wannabe" groupies à la White Panther Party and so many other white radicals of the time. Neither approach, however sincerely intended, is of much use, at least in revolutionary terms. How patronizing is it to not speak your truth, humbly and honestly, for fear of offending a comrade-in-struggle? How ridiculous is it to try to mimic another community, to make them into your romanticized vanguard?

While both stances are very human, they don't really advance any revolution of which I would want to be a part. Furthermore, no one can presume to speak for an entire community, much less be a "vanguard," without a serious basis for that assertion. Those who make such a claim deserve to be challenged.

Put simply, no ally in a battle to foster fundamental change—including the relatively privileged—is of much value if they don't share frankly from their own perspective. All opinions can have validity. Truth is of no color, race, class, or creed; it just is. If we are to have revolution, then it must start with humble but real honesty; that self-demanding, often uncomfortable, but precious quality.

"Stretch . . . or die" is a phrase quoted near the beginning of *This Bridge Called My Back: Writings by Radical Women of Color* (Kitchen Table Press, 1983), an influential collection edited by Cherrie Moraga and the late Gloria Anzaldua. As Audre Lorde has made clear elsewhere, to assert that the relatively privileged have the primary responsibility to educate themselves does not mean others have no responsibility. No more patronizing, even racist idea could there be. If those with privilege who wish to be a part of a movement for true liberation must do the most stretching, all, in the end, must extend themselves.

To be in community is to be in conversation, partners in the process of speaking and listening. In the end, we need one another and must learn from each other. This points to the importance of relationships, for we can never encounter one another as equals if we don't also become friends. This can only happen if we create contexts to exchange insight and learn across difference. This doesn't have to be dramatic: connecting college students from diverse backgrounds to befriend, help, and learn from our Emmaus seniors here in Shaw is just one practical example of community-building based in mutual aid.

As William "Upski" Wimsatt notes, cultural forms like hip hop, for example, that enable cross-boundary relationship-building are also important, even if they simultaneously raise issues of expropriation.

Indeed, he suggests the "value of a ghetto education" for whites in *No More Prisons* (Soft Skull Press, 1999). Speaking directly to his original community, Wimsatt asks, "How do you even begin to organize against racism when most of the white and middle-class people who are supposedly against racism are afraid to set foot in the very neighborhoods where the most oppressed people live? And when an entire generation of young people is being classified as criminals?"

It is not simply fear that can stop us. As Wimsatt argues in his earlier work, *Bomb the Suburbs* (Soft Skull Press, 1994), whites may sense a Catch-22 here: "We cannot help blacks without undercutting their self-determination; we cannot be cool without encroaching on their cultural space; we cannot take risks without exercising our privilege to take risks; we cannot integrate without invading." This, Wimsatt admits, can leave us feeling paralyzed—but we must not remain so.

No, the stakes are too high for any of us—whatever our race, class, age, or gender—to stand apart. As Lorde implores, we need to welcome all "who can meet us, face to face, beyond objectification and guilt." Each of us must take part in a lifetime process of extracting the life-negating distortions created by racism, sexism, ageism, and more, from our deepest selves.

This process can mean the strategic creation of separate space for limited amounts of time. Even Martin Luther King, Jr., fearless advocate of cross-racial alliances, recognized near the end of his life that "temporary segregation" might sometimes be necessary, as to accomplish true integration.

As such, the attacks visited on groups like Riot Grrrl, who created "female-only" space in the early-'90s, or more recently, Anarchist People of Color, with "people-of-color-only" space, can be misguided. As long as the ultimate aim is to more effectively link with other communities to build power for transformation, we must affirm such choices as reasonable, even healthy.

The danger, of course, is that instead of moving toward one another, we will drift further apart, crippling movement-building and undermining revolution. Reading Stokely Carmichael's powerful autobiography, *Ready for Revolution* (Scribner, 2003, written with old SNCC comrade Ekwueme Michael Thelwell), it is clear that his opposition to "premature coalitions" persisted until his death by cancer in 1998. One gets the impression that Carmichael didn't believe that sufficient conditions for coalition existed even then, more than three decades after he first articulated this point. And this suggests the fatal flaw in his analysis. We need to build a movement now, not in the next century.

I appreciate Carmichael's challenge nonetheless. As Cathy Wilkerson, formerly of SDS and the Weather Underground, has written, "The question of how white people can truly develop principled relationships with people of color needs exploration. It's not that I think there is one 'right' position but I do think rigorous honesty and thoughtfulness are really important."

The answer—however tentative and incomplete—is not to hate (or fetishize) our roots, nor to turn ourselves into uncritical followers of a leader from a more oppressed community. Rather, we must immerse ourselves in other cultures (especially those of the marginalized), using any privilege in the service of those in need, while simultaneously learning from them.

Identity is indeed the crisis; if Lorde's contention that "we have no patterns for relating across our human differences as equals" is true, then we must challenge ourselves to uncover the ways. It will not be easy to build bridges toward a truly liberating and inclusive movement, rising from a collection of reasonably equal individuals. To believe we can hope to triumph otherwise is to indulge in the most destructive of illusions.

We must discover how to allow our differences to generate a synergy that is far more powerful than the simple sum of its parts. As Lorde has said, "We share a common interest, survival, and it cannot be purchased in isolation from others simply because their differences make us uncomfortable . . . In our world, 'divide and conquer' must become 'define and empower.'"

Until we all learn to do this, there will be no end to the flood of disposable people like the youths of Sursum Corda. Such "outsiders" are necessary in a profit economy that uses surplus people to fuel the machine. We must build a movement of those "outside" so as to make this cycle impossible, unthinkable.

If we truly want transformation, we will be ready to do the hard work, to ask the tough questions, especially of ourselves. We may need to define (or redefine) our personal and group identities, but in ways that leave us open to coalitions. We will be aiming for the standard set by Carmichael and Hamilton—"co-equal partners who identify their goals as politically and economically similar"—but we will start wherever we already are. There is, in the end, no other way.

To say this, though, is to beg the next set of questions. Once empowered, once together, what might be those goals? Who or what do we join together to fight? What is the "system" behind the oppression we have been discussing?

The answers are slippery, and can harbor even more would-be-revolutionary illusions.

United States Senate

OFFICE OF THE SECRETARY

SENATE LIBRARY

norable Jo-Anne L. Coe
ary of the Senate
(Room 221)
Capitol

Secretary of the Senate,

It is with some regret that I must infor
n aide in the Senate Library effective w
riday, June 14th, 1985.

I am deeply appreciative for this oppo
ough the kind patronage of Senator Max
the day-to-day operation of our nation
s than candid if I were not to admit t
t disturbing to me.
mosphere of Capitol
d the rest of the

Nonetheless,
njoyed getting to
with wha

D.O.A.

RIGHT TO BE WILD

ALL PROCEEDS FROM THIS RECORD
GO TO "FREE THE FIVE"

BURN IT DOWN!

HOT TOWN—
PIGS IN THE ST

BUT THE STREETS
BELONG TO THE PEO

DIG

EMMAUS SERVICES

FOR THE AGING

BABYLON BURN

YOU MUST BURN

FIVE: DESTROY BABYLON

"It's the system
Hate the system
What's the system?"
—The Jam

First came the hands, seemingly out of nowhere from behind the wall, grasping its top. Then came the head, the shoulders, the legs. A ripple of disbelief passed through the crowd at WUST Radio Hall, or, at least, through those attentive enough to notice the odd developments.

A compact, well-muscled figure rose confidently. Soon his entire body—topped off by a cluster of lengthy dreads—was perched precariously in the shadows on the ten-foot-high wall behind the stage.

A few yards away, in the harsh glare of the stage lights, a band had finished tuning and now stood glancing at each other, seemingly oblivious to the wallcrawler lurking behind them. As if at some unseen signal, the drummer suddenly lashed out twice, the guitar and bass responding. The song lurched forward, then accelerated like a steam train. The dreadlocked figure on the wall tensed and sprang from his perch. He flew through the air, toward the center of the stage. All sinew and grace, the man landed lightly and grasped the microphone in a single smooth motion. Miraculously, he was precisely on cue, riding what was now a massive sonic juggernaut in full catapult roar behind him.

Throwing his entire body into the song, the singer wailed above the din, *"So you say you're gonna live the truth/Well, have you checked out the future of the youth?/There doesn't seem to be much left for them/But there is an answer for all of Jah children . . ."*

Almost instantaneously, frenzied dancing erupted. Amidst the blur of bodies, a gigantic chorus rose from the crowd. The singing meshed with the intently focused African-American quartet onstage; out of the motion, sweat, and sound, something immense and unified seemed to materialize.

The band, of course, could only be Bad Brains, led by Paul Hudson, a.k.a., HR. If the sign of a truly great performer is the ability to absolutely suspend normal time and reality among his or her audience, HR had this and then some. He was the embodiment of sheer, unadulterated belief. To describe him as riveting, convincing, utterly compelling, is still to fail by half. Never have I seen anyone so deep inside what they are doing, so alive with fire and fury and faith. This was especially true for HR when backed by his brother Earl, Darryl Jenifer, and Gary Miller (a.k.a., Doctor Know), whose own gifts, focus, and power only spurred him on.

I was lucky enough to see the band near the height of its power several times. Songs like "Rock for Light," "F.V.K.," and "Destroy Babylon" were potent enough on vinyl. Live, they exploded into something staggering, even magical. To be in the midst of that explosion was to be pulled into what scholars of the spirit call "liminal" space, the threshold where boundaries dissolve, reality melts, and a cosmos of possibilities crackles. When the music rumbled and roared, with HR at the center of the hurricane shrieking, *"Organize/Centralize/It's time to fight for our lives,"* I was ready to sign up for the battle, no doubt whatsoever.

I was not alone in this. As nearly the entire crowd picked up the *"Destroy Babylon"* chant, it was impossible not to believe that Babylon—the metaphor for all corruption, evil, and oppression—would fall. This, I thought, was not a song about revolution; this *was* revolution.

That's how it felt, anyway. Then the moment passed, the song was over, and the building (in this case, the original 9:30 Club) was still standing, along with the White House and the Capitol. Soon enough, the show itself was history.

That's when it all got terribly complicated again. Illusion brushed against possibility, both whispering soft, alluring words. Sometimes it is so hard to distinguish one from the other. *"The bourgeoisie better watch out for me/All across this so-called nation/We don't want your filthy money/Don't want your innocent bloodshed/We just want to end your world"*: HR's words were stirring—but how to make them real? While I felt the rush of power and insight, and tried to live it, it wasn't easy, not back in "normal time."

It never is, of course. While art can give us fuel for living, the real creativity is in our living itself, each one of us. Moments like those recounted above may give us the belief, the hope to embrace transformation—but they can only go so far in bringing it to reality.

Questions will always be there; for example, who exactly is "the bour-geoisie"? How do we "end their world," at least without shedding (possibly innocent) blood? How much money is too much? If I have some, am I Babylon? In the end, the complexity of the real world can be paralyzing.

It certainly didn't help when rumors of HR's shady business dealings swirled, when he exploded in violence against friends, both male and female. Most shattering was his willingness to justify violence against women as "protecting" them. Equally disturbing was his outspoken antagonism toward gay people who, on religious grounds, he considered "Babylonian." While all people fail to fully live up to their ideals, these last two exam-ples were not such a simple shortcoming. They were something deeper: an essential failure to recognize and affirm a shared humanity.

It felt like the tragic flaw in HR's otherwise galvanizing ideas of love, unity, and revolution. Peeling back the rhetoric, that beautiful vision now lay exposed, seemingly riddled with arrogant, rigid, even hateful elements.

Trust the art, not the artist, I thought. But inside I realized again a deep truth, something no amount of charisma can disguise: *Not everybody talking about revolution is talking about the same thing.*

As we've seen, astute definitions can be crucial, in part because they may lead to asking the right questions. Lacking such, answers may never be possible. If we share a desire to fight oppression as defined in the last chapter, a veritable hydra of queries begins to rear multiple (and some-times ugly) heads. Who exactly is our enemy? The state? Corporations? Technology? The police, the army? The greed within us all? Is power to be sought or fought? Any of us could spend a lifetime trying to answer these questions, and still not succeed. In the face of this enor-mous challenge, our discussion here will have to be relatively shallow, but hopefully useful and provocative nonetheless.

Our first answer is to realize that we will never have *the* answer, just our best approximation at any time. As such, we must always remain humble, ready to learn more, to be taught. This is not an invitation to inaction; anything but. Instead, it is an invitation to engage a certain "revolutionary humility," to realize that while we will always act without certainty, we still must act. If done with some genuine openness to reflec-tion, our next actions might be a bit more informed, a bit more effective.

The late radical Brazilian educator Paulo Freire has argued that reflec-tion and action are essentially interrelated. One should never happen independent of the other; they are part of a healthy, even liberating cycle.

The symbol used by Emmaus Services for the Aging, where I have worked for most of the past two decades—a blue heart on a white circular background, with one arrow going into the heart and another rising out of it—captures this idea with simplicity and beauty. Reflection stirs the heart into action (and vice versa), while the circle suggests a cycle leading one to the other, then back round again, hopefully with increased depth and effectiveness.

Given this approach, you might not be surprised to hear that my idea of whom or what might be our "enemy" has evolved over my years of justice work. While my activism was largely born from a "smash the state" anarcho-punk milieu, I have increasingly found this stance more than a little lacking. Quite simply, it is plain that the destruction of the state is not the same as destroying oppression. Indeed, the state (at least in its modern form) arguably grew precisely to temper the exercise of raw power by the rich, traditionally in league with the military and an officially sanctioned church.

Perhaps this sounds naïve, but I will press the point. The obvious flaw in the classical Marxist analysis is that it could not have predicted how modern capitalism would allow government to temper its own self-destructive excess for the maintenance of the overall order. Traditional Marxist theory surely did not foresee nor can it easily account for the rise of the modern welfare state.

This does not mean that I consider the state entirely benign. Nor am I unaware of more recent ideas of how class war is forestalled here by "exporting the contradictions," by exploiting people overseas for profit to "buy off" our working class and poor with consumer goods and social programs.

This may well be true. Still, all of this suggests that the state, like capitalism as a whole, has its range of motion limited to some degree by popular will. If you don't believe this, just look at the present struggle over neo-liberal economic policies and the related resurgence of so-called "free trade" agreements. If capitalism really is all the same; if it doesn't matter who runs the government or what policies they pursue; then why all the fuss over the WTO, NAFTA, FTAA, and other such agreements?

The answer is that it *does* matter, that the capitalist model is more or less oppressive, unjust, and eco-destructive, depending on how it is applied. This flexibility has been the bane of would-be revolutionaries for more than a century. Some even seem to wish for extreme free market policies and cutbacks in social spending so that the suffering spurs people to rise in revolt.

I understand the theory, but can't wish for such a process, as the death of untold millions seems intrinsic to this approach. For me, at least one thing is pretty simple: Revolutionaries ought to care about people for who they are and what they want, not just as an expendable means to some end called "revolution." More practically, I don't believe the mere existence of mass suffering leads to uprising, much less revolution, at least as I define it. Instead, people have to be organized, have a vision of a better life, and the belief that it can be realized. Otherwise, they will more likely turn on one another than unite to overthrow "the state."

To argue that the state is not necessarily the enemy is not to say that most of its power isn't in the hands of the rich and privileged. Of course this is true; the state often (but not always) operates to achieve their ends. The state is nevertheless an instrument. Underneath its machinery is power, that of the rich and their corporations, as well as popular power. These forces vie for control. The rise of relatively democratic regimes, with a modern social safety net, surely suggests that the grip of the wealthy, however excessive, is not total. The state admittedly does also respond to a certain institutional imperative. No matter what an institution was set up to do in principle, practically, the focus of much of the entity's resources and exertion, however masked, is simply its own continued existence.

This, like the influence of the rich, limits the usefulness of the state in achieving transformation. But while we can agree to disagree on how useful the state can ever be as an instrument for progressive ends, I humbly dissent from any ideology that claims it has no worth in this realm whatsoever.

In Sheridan County, the memory of how the New Deal helped save our communities from utter ruin during the Depression in the 1930s was burned into our collective psyche. For my grandparents and parents, like most in our community, the idea that there was no fundamental difference between the Hoover and Roosevelt administrations was downright laughable.

Smashing the state, therefore, never held a very broad appeal in our county. This was not only due to the dangers of loss of government aid (in a community where many had a small margin for survival) but also to the ever-apparent power of the grain, meat-packing, railroad, and mining companies. Some, like my father, struggled to help organize a farmers' union to improve our community's odds in the face of such forces. Without government on our side, we were largely at the mercy of big money.

This is not to say that there wasn't also a resentment of government taxes and regulation. This was especially true among the more prosperous farmers. While my mother, like others in the county, scorned them as having forgotten their leaner New Deal—era days, many turned increasingly Republican as their economic circumstances improved over the decades.

Disdain toward "bureaucrats in Washington" sometimes rivaled our dislike for the dominant corporations. There was also a strong aversion toward accepting welfare. (This is particularly ironic, given how key government price-support programs were to many in Sheridan County.) At its most extreme, this suspicion fostered movements like the Free Men, who opposed paying taxes and denied the legitimacy of any government, save perhaps the most local and direct version. In the 1980s, farmers abandoned by the Reagan government (and all-too-ignored by the left) began turning increasingly toward such racist right-wing movements in desperation.

That this far-right camp sees the state as its enemy ought to give pause to even the most ardent of anarchists. After all, if the Ku Klux Klan opposes the state, this surely suggests government is doing something right after all!

Beyond some ambivalence, most of my community was quite practical, only rarely lured by the likes of the Free Men. They didn't care much about ideology; they cared about putting food on the table. Sometimes a helping hand from government just made sense. I am not claiming here that my experience in Sheridan County is universally applicable. There is, however, a groundedness in this perspective, a certain common sense that is essential for would-be-revolutionaries to engage with, unless we wish to simply talk to ourselves.

I'd also be a fool if I didn't admit that my own education (including in radical ideologies) came thanks to the state, through loan programs and the like. Some of this, of course, was brainwash into a certain conformist, consumerist ethic—but by no means all of it. Given this, I could never entirely dismiss the potential value of the state.

Are corporations, instead, the enemy? Surely the behavior of many companies justifies the title of Ted Nace's powerful new book: *Gangs of*

America: The Rise of Corporate Power and the Disabling of Democracy (Berrett-Koehler, 2003). Impatient with laws and cultural mores that impede their relentless search for profits, corporations often operate in an aggressive and amoral manner; not unlike gangsters, Nace argues.

The influence of the corporate world comes, in part, from their massive financial resources. Indeed, the gross income of the largest of these institutions dwarfs that of many so-called "Third World" countries. Sadly, the scandal goes beyond this. Due to a string of legal rulings, Nace notes, corporations have ended up not only defined as a "person" in Constitutional terms, but ultimately with arguably more rights than people.

Armed with such privileges, some companies have become enormous enough to challenge the sovereignty of the nation-state itself, and regularly desert their historic homes for greener, lower-wage pastures. States can often do little or nothing to stop this, and instead adjust their policies to retain capital and jobs.

All of this is disturbing enough to merit the wholesale assault provided by Nace, as well as other contemporary critics like Naomi Klein, Noreena Hertz, and Kalle Lasn. Each documents the trend of corporate consolidation and the frightening creep of their influence. As D.C. punk band Fugazi puts it in "Five Corporations," it all *"Grows so smoothly/Moves so slowly/Takes completely/It's as if they belong/And they've been here all along . . . Five corporations/There is a pattern."* Given that five mega-corporations now account for some eighty percent of all U.S. CD sales, this song's depiction appears all too true. While it will take much vision and backbreaking work, we must build counter-institutions like labor unions and regulatory bodies that are equally powerful, and global in nature.

But what exactly are we speaking of in referring to "corporations"? After all, Fugazi itself is technically a corporation. So is the anarchist Brian MacKenzie Infoshop here in the Flemming Center—and Emmaus Services for the Aging, for that matter. Now, the last two are nonprofits, and none are multinational behemoths, but hopefully my point is made. On its own, the word "corporation" can begin to have little or no meaning, lumping Dischord Records, Ben & Jerry's, and *Punk Planet* in with Enron, WorldCom, and Lockheed-Martin.

Let us also remember that companies do provide employment for people. This is a service, in its way: Even if such jobs are not always well-paying, glamorous, or politically progressive, people need work. If we are not careful, we can imply that virtually any job is morally suspect. Critiquing people's employment without offering real alternatives is hardly a winning approach, so plain practicality suggests the need for some nuance here.

Moreover, simply destroying corporations would hardly bring about the "new world." Are not such creatures the result of some deeper dynamic? After all, to be radical is to look to the root of issues; what about a critique that (in the words of pioneer anarcho-punk outfit Crass) calls us to "destroy power"?

This goes past a simple anti-capitalist, anti-corporate, or anti-state critique to question a basic assumption in my analysis, rooted as it is in a calculus of power. In *Post-Scarcity Anarchism* (Ramparts Press, 1971), Murray Bookchin called for the "abolition of power," arguing that "the only act of power that is excusable any longer is that one act—*popular* revolution—that will dissolve power as such by giving each individual power over his or her everyday life."

Is it possible to use power for good? Or is it inherently corrupting, destructive? This ambivalence, common in anarchist circles, finds numerous echoes in the broader contemporary left community. In fact, these mixed emotions run deep even within the mainstream of American history. As the Constitutional doctrines of separation of church and state and separation of powers suggest, the architects of the American Revolution also feared certain aspects of power.

While I agree that questions exist about the dangers of power, I also find this tact lacking in important respects, even disturbing. The problem lies essentially in the *imbalances* of power, not necessarily in its fundamental nature.

To be entirely clear, I don't want to destroy power as such, but have it shared more equally. I want to build power among those who are marginalized, to counterbalance that of the privileged. Only from that place can the human rights of all be respected. "Power concedes nothing without struggle" said Frederick Douglass, and struggle implies counter-power.

There is a basic tension here, one that in some ways mirrors the historic contest between anarchists and communists. I tend to agree with the anarchist critique of power's oppressive tendencies. Bookchin's call for the "dissolution of power" makes sense when juxtaposed with the "seizure of power" associated with the authoritarian left. The resultant so-called "dictatorships of the proletariat" have inevitably been pathetic "dictatorships of the Party."

Power surely can be abused; yet I see its use as necessary. Is there a way that power might not be oppressive, but instead saving, even transformative?

Notes from Nowhere, the editors of *We Are Everywhere*, attempt to offer an answer in one section of their anthology: "Power: Building it Without Taking it." There is much to commend in this essay, especially the poetry of the analysis: "Perhaps the greatest advantage of our movement of movements is that it struggles to avoid taking power, seeking instead to shatter it into little pieces, to share it amongst ourselves, to open spaces where everyone can develop the power to create, and to destroy the power that dominates."

The collective hastens to add, "[Our] power is about claiming dignity, taking back our communities, and not about holding a seat in government . . . When those resisting on the streets are also involved in creative acts of building new ways of living, we reduce the danger that our radical political analysis might become disconnected from the everyday needs of ordinary people."

What does this look like? Notes from Nowhere offer up two examples: the Zapatista Army for National Liberation (EZLN), a guerrilla group rooted in the Mayan population of the Chiapas province of Mexico; and, especially, the *piquetero* movement rising from the unemployed of Argentina. Dismissing popular portrayals of the latter as "masked youths blocking roads with burning tires," Notes instead describe the *piqueteros* as "the living embodiment of building power from below."

It is at this point that I begin to get confused. If the above phrase is meant to suggest independent, grassroots organizations bringing collective weight to bear on existing state structures to make them more responsive and democratic, they have a strong case. Clearly, both of these movements have done just that, with some success, amidst terribly difficult circumstances.

If Notes from Nowhere mean to instead argue that either has done away with the state, or sees it as irrelevant, they are on far more shaky ground. Notes believe that "the desire to conquer the state maintains the illusion that the state is the foundation of sovereignty and autonomy," an assumption no longer valid "in the networked world of global capital." However, the actions of the movements they tout make matters far less clear.

As the Notes' essay admits, the *piqueteros* seek "unemployment subsidies, food, and jobs," obviously expected to flow from the state. While the "constructive aspects of the movement, such as bakeries, communal kitchens, and popular education schemes" are real and inspirational, the "solidarity economy" of the *piqueteros*, "an autonomous, nonprofit system based on need," is the creative response of people in a crisis. It is a necessary supplement, but by no means a replacement for, the broader system.

All of this reveals a more complex scenario than the editors of *We Are Everywhere* would care to admit, as neither example translates smoothly to a simple anti-state critique. Nonetheless, we will examine the ideas used to open Notes' "Power" essay, and echoed throughout it—those of neo-pagan writer and global-justice activist Starhawk—to help explore on the distinction implicit here.

Starhawk addresses questions of power head on in *Webs of Power: Notes from the Global Uprising* (New Society, 2002), and in her earlier book, *Dreaming the Dark: Magic, Sex, and Politics* (Beacon Press, 1988). The latter book, she writes, "is about the calling forth of power, a power based on a principle very different from 'power-over,' from domination."

For Starhawk, "power-over" is "the power of the gun and the bomb, the power of annihilation that backs up all the institutions of domination," a force to be rightly feared. There is another energy that she describes as "'power-from-within,' the power we see in a seed, in the growth of a child, the power we feel writing, weaving, working, creating, making choices." This energy has little to do with threats of annihilation, and much to do with the root meaning of the word *podere*, Latin for "to be able." Starhawk argues that this force is "the power of the low, the dark, the earth, the power that rises from our blood, from our lives and our passionate desire for each others' flesh."

This earthy, life-affirming power, also implicit in Bookchin's analysis, is essential for answering the central questions of this book and of our time: How do we overthrow not just those presently in power, but the principle of power-over? How do we shape a society based on the principle of power-from-within?

As Starhawk makes clear in *Webs of Power*, part of the answer flows from "power-among" and "power-with." The first is the kind of authentic, enlivening leadership that rises organically from the synergy of the group, while the latter is the power of us together, a potentially revolutionary "we."

These concepts help to tie individualist concepts of power to the collective one necessary for transformation, at least in principle. Of course, an ugly reality implicit in my power analysis is glossed over. What if my power-from-within comes into conflict with another person's power-from-within? How do we balance contradictory demands, or protect the weaker from the stronger? Is there a legitimate place for force, can we really expect to make it entirely irrelevant?

Here it becomes clear that neither Starhawk nor Bookchin offer a definitive resolution of the left's ambivalence toward power. But if many unanswered questions remain about precisely where to strike this balance, these ideas help to clarify the sense in which I use the word "power." Like Notes from Nowhere (I think), I believe that we need to build power to ensure that everyone has real choices in their lives, i.e., are freed from oppression.

In this way, power is not our enemy. As Henry Cortes, Southwest Regional Director of the Industrial Area Foundations, a national network of community groups founded by organizer Saul Alinksy, has said, "Power is nothing more than the ability to act in your own behalf . . . Power is such a good thing that everyone should have some." We all must become willing to address our struggle in those terms. Only by wielding counter-balancing power can we expect our rights to be respected, our needs met, our world transformed.

How we might structure this world-to-come is harder to say. With or without the state as such, it will surely involve some form of organization. This begins, of course, with how we organize ourselves now.

This is a central knot with which to wrangle. But, lest we stray too far afield, I now return to one of our original questions: If not precisely "power," "corporations," or "the state," is it "the system" that is our enemy?

This is a very vague term, arguably too diffuse to be of any use. As such, it has been justly ridiculed by many observers as the epitome of empty rhetoric. It does have the advantage of being more inclusive, of suggesting more layers to the structures of domination, if it can be somehow defined more clearly. This need is evoked with stark sarcastic beauty in the Jam quote that begins this chapter. Just what is this "system" that we fight?

This is a very hard but essential question, since I fear there are some fundamentally incompatible answers. For instance, is the system capitalism, or is it modern technological society itself? This is no minor distinction. Some radical environmentalists argue that population growth (itself the result of modern technological advances) is the key cause of ecological problems. David Foreman of Earth First! once suggested that the Earth could healthfully sustain only some fifty million. Given that we now have more than six billion people on Earth, the implication of this stance is cataclysmic. Come the revolution, where exactly are the other 5,950,000,000 people going to go?

In short, to hold to such an ideal is to envision suffering and destruction on a scale never before seen in recorded history.

Brief, dark murmurs from Earth First! that AIDS might be the Earth's approach to solving its population problem was at least honest in its horrifying misanthropy. This dilemma cannot be ignored. While I believe that "deep ecology" holds some key insights, it is fair to say that I cannot conscience such an outlook.

I also don't believe that technology, as such, is the enemy. Whether humans are capable of using the tools of this modern era responsibly remains to be seen. Still, no more ludicrous denial of human possibility could be imagined than to assume that we cannot. I refuse to believe that people are so feeble.

The identification of capitalism as the "enemy" seems more plausible, at least on its face. Again, definitions are key here. For me, capitalism represents an economic and social system where ultimate control is in the hands of the rich, where profit means more than people, where everything (including humans and the Earth itself) is for sale, driven by the never-ending pursuit of consumption and growth. In other words, money is God, and all are expected to bow down.

The destructive side of this approach should be obvious; so is its appeal, at least for those able to buy into the consumer parade. As we have already seen, reforms introduced into capitalism have enabled it to reduce social tensions to at least reasonably sustainable levels, in political if not ecological terms. This seems true even while the gap between rich and poor continues to stretch.

Pure capitalism, like purity of any stripe, is hard to find. Especially in the aftermath of the fall of the so-called Communist Bloc with their centrally planned economies, modified free market capitalism, however flawed, seems to lack a plausible alternative. Where, then, does this leave us?

At the risk of stirring up yet another hornet's nest, I would argue that we must begin by admitting an uncomfortable truth. Despite the current popularity of the term "anti-capitalist," I find it unsatisfactory. How can we define ourselves by what we are against and expect to win? *To defeat capitalism, some credible alternative system for making sure that the needs of all are met is essential.* Without this, we will never be taken seriously by the world's marginalized.

Diehard neo-Situationists, who revere spontaneity as their God (but who fortunately have never had the responsibility for feeding millions of mouths), will no doubt disagree. But, to me, the following is unassailable: Having a system is not bad in itself. Rather, the most salient questions are: What kind of a system, set up by whom, for whom?

The task of envisioning and building a new, more humane and democratic system may be less glamorous than destroying the old one. Yet, no one on the margins should be expected to really listen to us till we can provide some reasonable answers to the most mundane yet critical questions of society. Nor can we ignore production to simply look at distribution of goods and services.

Just as we refuse to let the beguiling rose-tinted rhetoric of neo-liberal economics championed by the World Bank and IMF stand unchallenged, we must not market any illusions of our own. In the end, we will not be judged by our good intentions, but our results. Sincere failure might buy sympathy in some circles, but not generally among those on the margins.

While it is common leftist rhetoric to posit that the poor have nothing to lose, rarely is that actually the case. In fact, they have much more to lose from an idealistic failure than any other group. Such people often have a very narrow margin for survival; they will either have their needs met or they will die.

Given this, one can excuse a certain amount of skepticism on their part. This is why I call for a "practical revolution," one that is rooted in day-to-day struggles. As Jose Ortega y Gasset has written, "Revolution is not the uprising against pre-existing order, but the setting up of a new order contradictory to the traditional one." I believe that the left has to begin to build institutions that can meet basic needs, especially where mainstream ones are failing to do so.

The Black Panthers set a powerful example with their community programs, intended, as Elaine Brown has noted, to assist "survival pending revolution." While this theme will be developed in more depth later, for now I will just note that this is an essential foundation for transformation. Here we could build credibility among "the people" and nurture relationships across boundaries. In short, we could make our rhetoric credible—even compelling—by achieving concrete improvements in people's lives *now*.

Does this often happen? Not in my experience. Many radicals see this as reformist, nurturing dependency, not building "dual power" from which to contest the state. While this can be true, it surely doesn't need to be.

As a result, we are often just as divorced from "the people" as the pop political pundits, who commonly see the mass through the pollster's lens. We have not often succeeded in linking grassroots movements to the power in current institutions or—should that machinery prove unable to carry out true democracy—to creating new ones.

Our failure to make these connections, to build these bridges in any convincing, organic, or sustained way, is why the radical left in this country has withered to virtual irrelevance. In my experience, we rarely even ask ourselves hard but necessary queries like: Where is the working class in this country, how can we connect to them? Will a movement for transformation also need ties to the middle class? What is the motivation to join this endeavor, how can such a coalition be sustained?

We are often disgusted by the apparent bankruptcy of our American electoral system, having become a mockery of democracy, so sold out to big money, so caught up in "society of the spectacle" hype-mongering and illusion. Is it really any wonder that so few people even vote any more?

I am as angry as anyone about this. It is a tragedy, and one that I don't ultimately accept. Instead, I recognize that the right to vote is the result of generations, even centuries, of struggle. How can we be so blind as to simply toss that away? The anarchist in me argues that if voting changed anything, they'd make it illegal. Indeed, that is exactly what they did in the South after Reconstruction ended. Jim Crow laws kept blacks from the polls—until people organized and ended that disgrace with the civil rights movement of the 1960s.

The result has been palpable change. Surely the transformation has not been as extensive as we would like, but that is our challenge now, to see this journey through. To simply discard this mission is to spit on those who came before us, who sometimes gave their very lives so we could have this chance. In the end, I encourage people to vote with no illusions on election day *and* to vote every day with their consumer choices, by organizing in their workplaces and communities, and much, much more.

I know full well how disillusioned many are by the electoral system in this country. This includes, perhaps most of all, millions of the most marginalized and forgotten. I still believe, however, that these millions could be mobilized with a compelling vision, backed by credible actions and organization.

The Democrats are surely not doing this. Indeed, their last serious stretch toward a grassroots democratic vision seems to have been Jesse Jackson's Rainbow Coalition of the mid-'80s. Sadly, that never really blossomed past a vehicle for Jackson's personal ambition.

Like their Republican colleagues, the Democrats are largely under the sway of the rich, while failing to reach out to those in need. Our rhetoric may be different, but our distance from the dispossessed can be just as great. This was made especially clear to me during the A16 protests against the World Bank and International Monetary Fund (IMF) in April 2000. This was the first big global-justice action since the N30 demo in Seattle, where an unlikely alliance including labor and eco-activists helped to shut down a meeting of the World Trade Organization.

Hopeful, optimistic energy was rippling through the often stagnant D.C. air. At last, the plight of the poor seemed to be not only on the radar of the mass media and the international economic institutions, but perhaps even on their agendas. We had helped put it there with tireless organizing and coalition-building as well as creative, disruptive actions. It felt like we were on the verge of a breakthrough.

But in the impoverished Shaw neighborhood, just a mile or two from the World Bank and IMF, the atmosphere was anything but hopeful. As I moved among the low-income residents of that community, doing my ongoing work, the impending protests evoked little excitement, and even some outright hostility.

In Claridge Towers, a major public housing building, some of the seniors had placed a *Washington Post* article on the downstairs bulletin board. It detailed the projected expenses of policing the protest. These costs were measured in hundreds of thousands of dollars, maybe even millions—in a city where painful budget cutbacks had already decimated key social programs.

As I talked with residents about the protests, both before and after, most expressed little understanding of how this battle might connect to their lives. Even fewer exhibited any solidarity with the protesters. As far as they could tell, the demonstrations just made things harder for them. One African-American senior complained, "I saw it on TV and it looked like a bunch of white kids having a party in the street, that's all." Another shook her head, adding, "And all the police are over there, while here we are, left behind with the drug dealers, the dope fiends, and the prostitutes."

I tried to defend the protests, which I had participated in. Facing skeptical faces all around, I explained that the cost couldn't be blamed on the protesters. I noted that the police, eager to avoid a repeat of the embarrassing Seattle scenario, had chosen to use wildly excessive tactics. Not only had they basically shut down much of D.C.'s downtown, they had closed the demonstration's headquarters illegally the day before the protest, and also arrested hundreds without warning.

All of this took money, of course, and lots of it. And that's without even factoring in the potential lawsuits rising from what seemed to be outrageous acts by the cops. How could the demonstrators be blamed for this kind of police misbehavior?

The seniors, most of whom had far more contact with the police than with their would-be advocates, remained unconvinced. And why not? After all, we protesters understood that trying to shut down the World Bank and IMF meetings would surely cost the city a lot of money, but we simply accepted this intentional disruption as necessary to a greater good.

This was a reasonable stand, especially given the gravity of the issue at hand. But why should we get upset if others—most of them less privileged than ourselves—had a different point of view? We could, of course, argue with their priorities, making a case that the A16 actions were taken on behalf of all those in need, perhaps especially here in D.C. After all, D.C. had just suffered through the local equivalent of an IMF structural-adjustment program under an unelected control board. Indeed, the parallels were so close as to be astonishing. Moreover, D.C. still lacked genuine self-determination and faced "taxation without representation" in Congress. Who else should be better able to understand the human costs of such budget-balancing initiatives, to make a global/local connection?

This all made sense as I explained it—but it was news to my friends at Claridge Towers. Why didn't they see the connections? Not for any lack of intelligence, but largely because we, the global-justice movement, had not been there on any consistent, sustained, and credible basis to make the case to them, I fear.

Nor have we been out to listen to their concerns, to learn from them, to let them help to set the agenda. Too often the poor don't know us and don't believe we value their priorities. As a result, they don't particularly trust us, not any more than the police or the IMF.

This gap, I suspect, contributes mightily to the disproportionately white, middle-class composition of the North American global-justice movement. As Elizabeth "Betita" Martinez has noted in her insightful essay, "Where Was the Color in Seattle?" published first by *Color Lines* in early 2000, very significant divides exist between poor, non-white communities and the movement. If we persist in indulging our radical illusions, this chasm will forever remain.

I have come to realize that the biggest value of my many years of grassroots community work may be simply this: Like my Sheridan County upbringing, it helps to keep my radicalism grounded in the mundane practicalities that human lives are built from, especially those of the marginalized.

Clearly, not all radicals agree. In fact, *We Are Everywhere* approvingly quotes this statement from London Reclaim the Streets: "Ultimately, it is in the streets that power must be dissolved—for the streets, where daily life is endured, suffered, and eroded, and where power must be confronted and fought, must be turned into the domain where daily life is enjoyed, created, and nourished."

To me, this reads like romantic tripe. For the poor, the pressing questions are not likely to be whether you are reclaiming the streets, actualizing your full human potential, liberating your desires, or revolutionizing your everyday life. No, the burning questions are more like this: Do you have food, a bed, a job, health care, a safe home, the chance for a decent education? If we don't speak to these concerns in a way that resounds with people who are poor, why should they listen?

To be credible to the marginalized, we have to be present in sensitive, humble, and sustained ways. We can't just show up a few weeks before a protest and try to enlist them in our cause, expecting cooperation or solidarity. No, we have to come together on some reasonably equal basis over an extended period of time. This also means we need to be rooted in such communities, to work together to set a common agenda to some very real degree.

This was brought home to me in a dramatic way in mid-2001 at a monthly meeting of the Fair Budget Coalition (FBC), a group comprised of grassroots justice and service groups like Emmaus. While the FBC is probably the single most active coalition struggling to ensure that human needs are put first in the D.C. budget process, no global-justice groups had ever joined our group or even come to a meeting. Thus, it was exciting when we were visited by a representative of 50 Years Is Enough.

That is, until it became clear that the person simply wanted us to join with actions they had already planned, during another round of World Bank/IMF protests. He didn't seem interested in our history or concerns. When the group expressed some skepticism, he got defensive. Soon he left the meeting, perhaps feeling unappreciated. We never saw him again. In that moment, I had a glimpse into how we in the global-justice movement might appear to those within marginalized communities. It wasn't very pretty, to say the least.

To some degree, the negative image of radicals is no doubt influenced by media distortions. Yet we can't just blame the media. If seniors in Shaw saw A16 as a self-indulgent game of cat-and-mouse between police and protesters, with little connection to their own struggles, they weren't entirely wrong.

Given that many of the activists viewed the police as the enemy, who could blame folks in Shaw for being confused about the protest's objectives? Indeed, who could blame them for having more sympathy, when push came to shove, with the police? The police, if not entirely benign, are at least present in their communities, and thus more known to them. In D.C., many of the cops are from the low-income neighborhoods, seeking a decently-paid, respected career.

I am not so naïve as to argue that police often don't operate to defend the prerogatives of a system that clearly tends to favor the privileged and wealthy. Of course they do; it is the simple reality of power. At base, however, the function of the police contains legitimate, even essential elements. All but the most hidebound anarchist or idealistic innocent will admit to the need to defend the weak from the powerful. In this era filled with genocide, it is surely hard to argue that human beings are entirely benevolent.

There is often a misunderstanding of the role police play in marginalized communities like Shaw. In my experience, police are viewed with great ambivalence. Fear, even rage, exists over police abuses. But there is also a sense that they are playing a necessary role in protecting the community. This is what fueled the anger I saw toward the A16 protesters, the sense that the police were being distracted from their real mission by self-indulgent, privileged white youth.

I realize that this may, again, sound a bit like blasphemy to some of you. If the police aren't our enemy, then who is?

Good question. Believe me, I am no fan of the Fraternal Order of Police; I know the history of COINTELPRO; I was the co-coordinator of the Washington Peace Center which was burglarized by the FBI during the Vietnam War. (The Center won a class-action lawsuit for damages.) I have been arrested numerous times, lied to, threatened, intimidated, even beaten up by officers of the law. For Christ's sake, I was investigated by the FBI in the late 1980s! My phone and e-mail account may well be tapped right now.

At the same time, I have worked side by side with police officers, helping the homeless on our block of 9th Street, giving support and kind words to prostitutes, serving some of the community's most isolated seniors. I know that some brave hearts and good souls are in uniform, people who approach what they do with the same idealism as I, with the same desire to help.

This role was highlighted in the chaos and catastrophe of September 11, 2001. As Starhawk noted not long afterward, "Many police have just given their lives because they stayed in a dangerous situation helping other people get out. A lot of us in the movement talk about being willing to die. They just did . . . As individuals, the police are of a class that doesn't gain from the policies we oppose. Let's not write off the possibility that some of them could be brought to support us."

Even if we may sometimes find ourselves on opposite sides of any given issue, I can't forget that possibility. If I did, I'd be betraying my own revolutionary ethic by ignoring our shared humanity. In the end, I don't believe we can ever give up on each other, not if we really seek transformation. For this revolution, we must see the *person*, and not just the institution. In this way, we can hope to reach them, to bring change. OK, perhaps there are more than a few power-trippers in the police force. However, are we free of those even in our own ranks? I think not.

The police are armed and thus can abuse their power in ways that can—and sometimes do—kill. However, given the very real dangers they often face, what else can we expect? How many of us would be willing to take on that thankless job? The police are part of "the system"—yet so are we. Certainly someone like me, who drives a car, has a computer, pays taxes, has a bank account, is. No one, not even Ted Kaczynski the Unabomber, is truly outside the established structures. Didn't he use the U.S. Mail, after all; didn't he have a Harvard education; didn't he publish his wretched, retrogressive communiqué in the *Washington Post*?

It is true that some folks are less complicit than others, surely a worthy goal. Choosing bikes over cars (whenever possible) is a good idea any day. But is this the big victory we are reaching toward? Not to me, since my definition means my work has to be about the common good, about other people. It can't just be about indulging some dream of purity, retreating to some idyllic lifestyle where I can write off others, drop out, be free of responsibility for the world's evils.

No, my revolution is about dropping in, about "'get up, get into it, get involved,' not 'drop and tune out'" as Henry Rollins once said. The opportunity to "drop out" is a privilege that most people don't have, not if they are going to feed their children, keep a roof over their heads, survive.

• • •

A couple of final points on this subject. First of all, oppressive systems must be transformed, even destroyed—but not people, even those who might seem to be our enemies. To accept the destruction of lives as "revolutionary" is to lose most of what we might have to offer in trying to heal this wounded world.

This brings us back around to perhaps our most fundamental definition, that of "revolution." Given how much I have been tossing this term around, you may be quite surprised to hear that I actually am extremely ambivalent about the word. As I have written elsewhere,

> *The word "revolution"*
> *Burns the tongue*
> *Like "God"*
> *The word says too much*
> *Means too little*
> *(Or is it the other way around?)*
> *Each time spoken*

Its magic ebbs,
Becomes an idol, false
Self-challenge
Shrunk to complacence
Possibility
Withered by illusion.

Some words
Are meant to be lived
Not spoken.

I have been very moved by an idea Fugazi's Ian MacKaye shared in the mid-'80s, the concept of "revolution by example." This is simply about speaking with your actions, about *being* the change you want to see come to pass.

Practically, revolution can simply be a shift in power from one set of elites to another. Most often it can just be what Patti Smith has called, *"One more turn of the wheel"*; or, *"The succession of the seasons,"* as New Model Army has written. Like both of those artists, I am not ultimately interested in that circular process. For me, revolution suggests a fundamental transformation from a death-dealing, profit-obsessed world to a life-affirming, person-focused one. In other words, it is about abolishing unequal, oppressive force through the empowerment of all, a vision shared by both Starhawk and Murray Bookchin.

The revolution I seek is one where the preciousness of life is affirmed for all sentient beings, where boundaries of good and evil are blurred, where enemies still retain their humanity, where allies might be found in the most unexpected places, where everyone—perhaps especially the would-be revolutionaries—are judged not on their rhetoric but on their actions and related consequences.

Sacred cows must always remain open to question. For example, is everyone who opposes abortion our enemy? Is it a contradiction-in-terms to be a "feminist for life"? Likewise, is it wrong to oppose the death penalty and call for a new trial for Mumia Abu-Jamal, while resisting demands that he simply be freed? Is it a betrayal to oppose rhetoric that seems to deny the equal value of the police officer—Daniel Faulkner—who was killed? Not for me.

This may contend uneasily with the realization that having clear enemies can motivate people (the "subjective" aspect once again), but we don't achieve revolution by simply replacing one oppressor with another.

In many ways, revolution begins as an inside job.

This brings us back to where we started this chapter: the glory and tragedy of one of my early inspirations, HR. By the early '90s, when I interviewed him repeatedly for *Dance of Days*, HR was a haunted shell of his former self. Straining through the fog of what I suspected was mental illness, he was either unable or unwilling to address the issues that had so stained his reputation. Even routine questions could elicit odd, rambling, incredible answers. There was as much fantasy as reality involved; to call his meanderings "lies" would be unfair, for it wasn't clear whether he could distinguish any longer.

Fortunately, there were rare moments of clarity, even insight. When I asked him about my old anthem, "Destroy Babylon," and the social upheaval he had once championed, his response was simple and perhaps inarguable: "First you have to destroy the Babylon within your own heart."

His words pointed toward a deep truth. Beyond the betrayal of revolution by his actions (or inaction; his apparent unwillingness to get help), HR seemed to know that he had been—in the words of one of his more recent songs—living a contradiction. Even if he could not find the willingness to embrace it, he knew that there was no greater revolution without the smaller, internal one.

But how do the two connect? Do they, necessarily? Where does self-care, self-exploration, become self-indulgence, self-obsession? As we will see in our next chapter, the pursuit of personal growth as if toward some type of "pure" lifestyle is no less illusory or destructive than the empty rhetoric of "revolution."

SIX: THE GOOD SHIP LIFESTYLE

"It matters not what you believe in
It matters less what you say
But only what you are
It matters what you are."
           —New Model Army

In November 1997, amidst a festive holiday shopping season, the *Wall Street Journal* featured a rather jarring article on its front page.

The eye-catching headline read: *"Shoppers Are 'Pigs': A Holiday Greeting the Networks Won't Air."* *Journal* reporter Robert Bremer opened the piece by evoking an odd, unsettling spectacle for readers of this powerful voice of the American business establishment:

> Picture the scene: Katie Couric and Willard Scott all bundled up and cozy on Thanksgiving morning, watching the Cat in the Hat and Spider-Man float above Macy's department store.
>
> Cut to a commercial: An animated pig superimposed on a map of North America smacks its lips and says, "The average North American consumes five times more than a Mexican, ten times more than a Chinese person, and thirty times more than a person in India. We are the most voracious consumers in the world, a world that could die because of the way we North Americans live. Give it a rest. November 28 is Buy Nothing Day."

This anti-commercial commercial—consistently rejected for airplay by all the major networks, save CNN—exemplifies the subversive approach of Kalle Lasn. The founder of the Media Foundation and *Adbusters* magazine, Lasn attacks corporate consumer society with its own tools. Advertisments become "subvertisments," assisting what Lasn describes as "demarketing."

The aspiring adbuster's best weapons are such acts of creative subversion. Lasn calls them "culture-jamming," a form of direct action with roots that thread through punk, hippie, Situationism, surrealism, Dada, anarchism, and "a host of other social agitators down through the ages whose chief aim was to challenge the prevailing ethos in a way that was so primal and heartfelt it could only be true."

While this "jamming" can take many forms, all aim at *detournement*. This French word translates as "turning around." However, in Situationist hands, as Lasn notes, this involved "re-routing spectacular images, environments, ambiences, and events to subvert their meaning, thus reclaiming them."

Detournement, then, entails creating "a perspective-jarring turnabout in your everyday life." In this way, a subvertisement where a young man and woman appear to pledge allegiance to the McDonald's golden arches becomes both an exposé of the cult-like ideology underlying corporate America and a way to retrieve one's life from the tentacles of the "society of the spectacle."

Such striking, provocative images abound in the pages of *Adbusters* and other Lasn-linked endeavors. As the existence of the above *Wall Street Journal* article suggests, Lasn is a dynamo, even a visionary, terribly hard to ignore. Ideas fly about in his creations with a vigor, verve, and vinegar befitting a former advertising executive turned fervent anti-consumerism activist.

Despite this conversion, Lasn has not forsaken the hyperbole or catch-phrasing of his previous trade. In *Culture Jam: How to Reverse America's Suicidal Consumer Binge—and Why We Must* (HarperCollins, 1999), Lasn declares that "America is no longer a country, but a multi-trillion-dollar brand . . . essentially no different from McDonald's, Marlboro, or General Motors." Corporations no longer sell products so much as their own name and image. We ourselves have been "branded," for in "America™," culture is no longer made by the people, but sold to us by multinational corporations. Our mass media dispense not real news, but a form of "Huxleyan soma," a pleasant mind-control narcotic.

While this means, for Lasn, that "a free, authentic life is no longer possible in America," the threat is far deeper and broader than this simple existential plight. Arguing that "American cool is a global pandemic," Lasn concludes, "The lifestyle of the cool-hunting

American-style consumer is . . . killing the planet." In the face of this looming international ecological disaster, he proclaims that "culture-jamming will become to our era what civil rights was to the '60s, what feminism was to the '70s, what environmentalism was to the '80s."

Pretty strong stuff, no? But Lasn takes it quite a distance further. Picking up the fallen anti-banner of the Situationists, as channeled through ad culture's "can do" optimism, Lasn argues that

> the instinct to be free and unfettered is hard-wired into each of us . . . a drive as strong as sex or hunger. With that irresistible force on our side, *we will strike* . . . We will strike by smashing the postmodern hall of mirrors and redefining what it means to be alive . . . Old political battles that have consumed humankind during most of the twentieth century—black versus white, Left versus Right, male versus female—will fade into the back-ground. The only battle still worth fighting and winning, the only one that can set us free, is The People versus the Corporate Cool Machine . . . We will uncool its fashions and celebrities, its icons, signs, and spectacles. We will jam its image factory until the day it comes to a sudden, shuddering halt. And then on the ruins of the old consumer culture, we will build a new one with a noncommercial heart and soul.

The call to arms is quite stirring, especially to this aging punk who recognizes much of that movement's passion and ideology in it. Indeed, this rallying cry almost seems like a prose rewrite of the L.A. punk anthem, "American Society."

Why, then, do I also have this queasy feeling in my stomach, not so different than what I might feel upon recognizing that I've been sold a bill of goods by the Corporate Cool Machine?

Perhaps because I have been, in a way.

So far, I have been arguing for a rigorous self-examination of our motives and strategies as activists; a destruction of illusions. The aim is to ensure that we are not simply satisfying ego needs, but building power from below, across boundaries of race, class, gender, and beyond. In practical terms, only such a movement could gather the numbers (and, thus, wield the power) necessary to generate fundamental transformation: revolution.

We have also seen how narrow allegiance to subcultures or identity can cripple us, as can uncritical embrace of ideology; all may keep us from the essential task of connecting with each other. Now it is time to turn our gaze toward our own lifestyles and the politics that have grown up around such concerns. In doing this, I hope to reveal how they might help or hinder this quest.

Few could dispute the importance of seeking to ensure that our lives embody our ideals. In *Sister Outsider*, Audre Lorde argues,

> We must root out internalized patterns of oppression within ourselves if we are to move beyond the most superficial aspects of social change. *For we have, built into all of us, old blueprints of expectation and response, old structures of oppression, and these must be altered at the same time as we alter the living conditions that are the result of those structures* . . . As Paulo Freire shows so well in *Pedagogy of the Oppressed*, the true focus of revolutionary change is never merely the oppressive situation we seek to escape, but that piece of the oppressor which is planted deep within each of us, which knows only the oppressors' tactics, the oppressors' relationships [emphasis mine].

I know of no better summation of how personal revolution is connected to a larger transformation. In addition, I heartily endorse Lorde's emphasis that both tracks must be pursued simultaneously. Our unwillingness to truly focus on the internal in this way is one reason why revolution so often becomes the simple exchange of one oppressive power for another; why our own organizations often remain isolated from the people we intend to serve, or descend into factional in-fighting.

This idea also points to the missing link implied in Lorde's famous formulation that "the master's tools will never dismantle the master's house." In short, we can carry the master's brokenness with us, the idea that no community can exist without domination. This manner of operating— often not even recognized for what it is—combined with the seizure and usage of the master's tools (heavily imprinted with this *modus operandi*) will inevitably lead us not to "destroy Babylon," but to unwittingly replicate it.

The necessity of a deeply self-demanding revolution seems obvious. We must not simply engage in economics or politics (narrowly under-stood), but also on the levels of psychology, spirituality, and more. In the end, all of this has to be grounded in our seemingly mundane choices as well, in our lifestyles, our very way of being. In other words, *there is no way to revolution; revolution is the way. We must be the change we seek.*

This may sound like an empty cliché. Still, I see no choice but to admit that our own personal growth must accompany the larger community work—the education, organizing, and actions—if we are to have any real hope of success. We, like our organizations, must struggle to eliminate vestiges of sexism, racism, and other forms of subjugation. Ultimately, we must grow to be truly able to wield power-from-within, not a dominating, exclusive power-over.

In this vision, "leadership" does not go away; indeed, it more often rotates, as we each can play a role as "leader" and "follower" at different times. Indeed, a key measurement of healthy leadership is whether it encourages others to find their own power, their own capacity to step forward and initiate. Most basically, this calls for leadership by example. We cannot ask anyone to do anything we are not willing to do, or that we are not already doing.

The list of challenges in this process could be endless. At the very least, we will have to heal our insecurities, to affirm ourselves while also taming the ego; to seek the common good, not just pursue our own desires. We will need to be centered enough to speak our truth while also being able to hear that of others, past barriers of race, gender, age, sexual orientation, and class. All of this can help us to embrace difference as strength, as Lorde prescribes; to find a synthesis that brings us closer to being able to build real revolution.

This is why revolutionaries as diverse as the communist Che Guevara and Christian apostle Paul have called for a "new humanity." Both, each in their own way, saw personal transformation as possible, as well as necessary, in order to create radically different (and radically more just) communities.

This optimism about humanity can translate to wishful thinking. We might believe not only that people have the potential for such growth, but that they have already entirely grasped that capacity. Such illusions are sometimes hard to identify, much less avoid, but such discernment is absolutely critical. Painful self-examination (with consequent changes in our way of being) is necessary work that will never really end. If revolution is, as Freire has written, "a process of becoming," surely this is true within one's self as well as in the outside world.

Herein lies a main danger of this approach, however: If we seek some sort of "perfect" enlightenment or analysis before acting, we will never act; of this we can be absolutely sure. The only tentative resolution to this tension that I can see rests in the reflection/action model briefly discussed in the previous chapter, leavened with an ethic of "progress, not perfection."

Supportive community can help us to persist in the growth process, to stay true to our course. Others can also help us to strike a just reckoning between consumption and creation. Both are needed. In balance, the pairing is healthy: Each feeds the other, drawing us deeper into the circle of life in all its richness.

Our society, of course, is anything but balanced. We are driven by the never-ending consumer capitalist clamor for "more stuff." Our imperfections and insecurities—preyed upon by the Corporate Cool Machine to sell their goods—regularly sabotage our greater aspirations. There is no way to realize dreams of transformation without also transforming ourselves.

This means a spiritual as well as a political journey. According to pioneer African-American liberation theologian James Cone, "The spiritual and the political are intimately related; the spiritual is the foundation." While this base must be made of rigorous honesty, there are many ways to construct it. I will briefly note just a couple of examples that I have seen work in the lives of people around me.

Twelve Step programs are often disdained in radical circles, mostly for their use of "God" language and a misunderstanding of their desire to remain outside of external controversies. Nonetheless, they can offer a powerful model of this approach, with their use of personal inventories, amends-making, and service.

In our hierarchical, profit-driven health care system, where doctors can almost assume the role of God, such groups represent a radical alternative. Rotating leaders, no fees involved, the "sick" helping one another, with only the loosest of structures—what more profound refutation of our present system could there be? Even the word "God" is left for each person to define for themselves, or to even reject outright, should another word like "greater power" seem preferable.

In their way, these meetings, autonomous except in matters affecting other Twelve Step groups, seem strikingly like anarchy in action. They begin with an admission of powerlessness over some aspect of life, but only in order to harness a deeper, broader power. The aim of the process is a small but very real liberation, one that can help clear the way for larger transformations.

This is not to say that some don't use Twelve Step programs to excuse apathy and disengagement. While real, this failing is hardly inevitable.

However it is done, self-assessment followed by concrete action for personal change is crucial. Vietnamese activist monk Thich Nhat Hanh has written, "Before we make deep changes in our lives, we have to look into our diet, our way of consuming. We have to live in such a way that we stop consuming the things that poison us . . . Then we will have the strength to allow the best in us to arise, and we will no longer be victims of anger or frustration."

If we are to make genuine revolution, such centeredness and clarity can be precious. It is practice, according to Nhat Hanh, not devotion, that matters. Self-knowledge avails us little without some method to realize our insights.

Nhat Hanh's "engaged Buddhism" rises from the practice of meditation to assist in the cultivation of "mindfulness." This is the ability to be in the moment, awake and striving toward reverence for life, generosity, sexual responsibility, deep listening, loving speech, and, finally, mindful consumption. All, Nhat Hanh says, are essential for "self-transformation and for the transformation of society."

This discipline, I would hasten to make clear, is not be confused with asceticism. Such self-denial—abstaining from the normal pleasures of life for its own sake, in pursuit of some illusory purity—is hardly the answer.

"Voluntary simplicity," in which those privileged enough to have excess learn to exercise self-control for the greater good, is closer to the mark. This idea of "living simply so that others may simply live" is no doubt useful for those of us who have grown up enjoying this culture's material riches and spiritual poverty. It has the side-benefit of helping to free us from commodity slavery, as to be able to dive deeply into each other, into life, into struggle.

Some may dismiss this all—especially the brief discussion of spiritual practices—as just so much self-help mumbo-jumbo. Fair enough. I can only say that such healing has been necessary for me, driven as I have been (and often still am) by my human weaknesses. In my experience, many of us would-be "changers of the world" might do better to focus a little more on our own failings, lest we betray, even destroy, that which we claim to want to build. The internal work does not take the place of the external, nor vice versa; both aspects are needed, simultaneously, if we are to move toward realizing transformation.

In certain ways, this is simply what a radical Jewish agitator (ultimately executed by the Roman Empire) named Jesus of Nazareth pointed out some 2000 years ago: *We must practice what we preach.* If we do not, we cannot realize our dreams, and we may actually undermine, even discredit them. One of my assumptions here is that people, whatever our many flaws, are not all that stupid. Even the mainstream folks we might sometimes scorn as "sheep," caught in the Corporate Cool Machine, can be pretty canny, in their way. Most know that talk is cheap; they check to see if you are living what you are talking about. If not, skepticism blooms easily. If our world seems terribly cynical at times, perhaps that is simply because there is just so much bullshit out there.

We owe it to ourselves as well as our cause not to add any more manure to the pile. If we are talking about change, much less revolution, then to be credible, we better be working pretty hard to change ourselves, as well as to build alternative institutions.

For example, if we don't want the police, we must be ready to assume their legitimate functions. If we don't want massive chain stores, then we need to build economic alternatives. If we don't like the overwork, self-destruction, and exploitation of modern life, we must model self-caring, cruelty-free, and simple lifestyles, not the "death-styles" so prevalent in the mainstream.

This is no simple task, but it is terribly important. As New Model Army has sung, *"It matters not what you believe in/It matters less what you say/But only what you are/It matters what you are."* This, if we are to seek revolution in any genuine sense, is the exacting standard we must aspire toward.

I don't mean to suggest that ideas have no power; of course they do. Accepting an ideal can help us move toward it, if only out of embarrassment (this is often my case, it seems) as we seek to not look like a phony. In the end, though, ideas have the power we bring to them with our *living.*

We each must develop a way of being that supports transformation; that gives it a strong, visible (but not arrogant) presence in our own lives. This is essential for our own personal growth as well as for converting others to our cause, by attraction as much as any promotion. This aim toward self-demanding consistency is another hallmark of what I call "practical revolution."

Having said all of this, we must now flip our emphasis, if only for absolute clarity. Alone, steps like "self-recovery" (to use bell hooks's inclusive term for Twelve Step—related processes) or "voluntary simplicity" are weak reeds to lean upon. They hold the greatest relevance for the relatively privileged. More to the point, on their own, such acts can hardly hope to threaten the immense power of the commodity machine.

I agree with holding corporations accountable, as well as with supporting consumer alternatives. There are many examples of companies "doing well by doing good"; enough for the media to have heralded a movement of sorts by the mid-'90s. Ben & Jerry's, The Body Shop, Working Assets, and Tom's of Maine, among others, have combined business and progressive politics in creative (and profitable) ways. Entities like the Calvert Group that promote "socially responsible investing" deserve some praise as well.

This only goes so far, however. Take, for instance, a short but revealing phone conversation I had in late 2003 with Working Assets, my long distance carrier. The company's automated message cheerily proclaimed, *"Thanks for helping us build a better world with every call you make!"* Hearing this left me a bit unsettled, as did an equally high-spirited follow-up blurb that was piped into my ear while I was on hold: *"Want another way to build a better world? How about Working Assets wireless?"*

By the time an actual person—a nice gentleman by the name of Raj— answered my call with a warmly accented, *"Thanks for helping us make a difference! How can I help you?"* I was thoroughly disconcerted. Was this whole "making a difference" riff just sales-schtick to market what, after all, was a profit-making enterprise? Perhaps not, but it had started to feel that way.

I am proud to have a long distance company that posted ads like *"Support Our Troops: Bring Them Home Now"* on D.C. buses during our recent invasion of Iraq. Still, what greater illusion could there be than the notion that we can "buy" our way to a better world?

Moreover, what exactly would our "revolutionary" lifestyle look like? Can you own a car? Drive a car? Can you eat meat? Can you drink alcohol, use other drugs, smoke cigarettes? If so, which ones, when, how often? What about coffee? Can you shop at chains like GAP and Borders? How about Microsoft or AOL, are they off-limits? Or, for that matter, computers themselves? Are plastic "vegan" shoes (which don't directly hurt animals, but won't bio-degrade) better than leather ones (which cause direct suffering to animals, but are arguably more Earth-friendly and may last longer)? Where does this end?

As the above suggests, this "lifestyle" approach may be best at simply dividing us, perhaps even better than the "identity" politics critiqued earlier. No one is going to be able to meet all the possible criteria involved. Where do we draw the lines, on what basis?

I have often seen this dynamic played out within the punk underground, perhaps most egregiously over the question of "straight edge." What was (and is) a simple, smart idea—that we would have an "edge" in fighting the system if we didn't dull our "weapons" with drugs—turned into a cartoon. At a certain point, the entire rich tapestry of resistance that punk could signify seemed to boil down to three things: Do you drink/drug, smoke, or eat meat/other animal products?

I do think that those are important questions for anyone (at least within this privileged society) to engage—as long as they don't become a dividing line between the "righteous" and the "unclean."

In fact, I am straight edge. Or am I? I drink wine as part of Mass. Well, at least I am vegan . . . or maybe not? I do eat grain products. The process of harvesting grains kills many animals, especially (but not exclusively) grasshoppers, as I know from having often been there. If "vegan" means not consuming products that involve animal suffering, how could grain qualify?

I don't say this to discourage people from being straight edge or vegan—far from it. I do, however, wish to discourage, deny, and defeat purism, for it serves nothing except our subjective need to feel righteous, superior to others. However human, this impulse is no friend to revolution.

It is true that our "economic vote" can be very small but significant. We do choose our world, to some degree, by consumer actions; by shopping at a food co-op or unionized grocery store instead of Whole Foods; by choosing to be vegan or vegetarian; by supporting indie stores over chains; even by avoiding plastic bags.

Meanwhile, we must take care not to create an upscale "health food" culture, to instead see that nutritious foods are readily available at affordable prices to all, not just the monied, hip, and well-educated. This could mean that working to make an inner-city Giant or Safeway more responsive to its shoppers might be more important than supporting a co-op in an affluent enclave. Indeed, just making sure that such stores exist in low-income contexts is a worthy challenge, since the chains often bypass such areas as not sufficiently profitable.

Changes in consumption, then, are an important avenue to explore. This is to suggest the value of (self)demanding standards, but worn like a loose shirt, not a straitjacket; with humility, not self-righteousness. Life is very complex, after all, and different people face different circumstances. We need to be flexible, open to other approaches, new ideas.

Such ideas can free us; they can also lead us into some dead ends. For example, in *Visionaries: People and Ideas to Change Your Life* (New Society, 2001), trailblazing Catholic eco-theologian Thomas Berry is quoted saying, "There can be no peace among humans without peace with the planet . . . The underlying assumption is that with a change of worldview will come an appropriately comprehensive ethics of reverence for all life."

While Berry's ideas wisely challenge us to have not just a humanistic, but a bio-centered order of thought, they offer no easy resolution. We don't even seem to be able to keep peace within the movement; how can we also "make peace with the Earth"? What exactly does this even mean? While I understand Berry's statement as metaphor, I find it difficult to translate into a concrete agenda. I don't embrace all that masquerades as "truth" under the bio-centered banner. I have already shared my dissent from the deep ecology attack on population. Perhaps just as ill-conceived is the step past Berry's position—equating the radical ecological cause with that of civil rights.

According to Earth First! activist Christopher Manes, "The protests of radical environmentalists . . . often stress this theme of expanding civil rights." In his eco-manifesto, *Green Rage: Radical Environmentalism and the Unmaking of Civilization* (Little, Brown and Company, 1990), Manes recounts an Earth First! action that involved unfurling a banner that read, *"EQUAL RIGHTS FOR ALL SPECIES,"* at the foot of the Lincoln Memorial, noting that "both the place and the phraseology were chosen for their historical resonance."

Another action at the Montana Department of Fish, Wildlife and Parks made "an even more direct connection between the civil rights movement of the 1960s and the new biocentric civil rights movement," according to Manes. Choosing January 16, the holiday in honor of Martin Luther King, Jr., the Earth First! banners now read, *"We Have A Dream: Equal Rights For All Species."*

Applauding this patently presumptuous equation in an article entitled, "Deep Ecology and the New Civil Rights Movement," Mike Roselle wrote, "We must shift the focus from land management to civil rights for all people . . . the tree people, rock people, deer people, grasshopper people, and beyond." Lest you think that Roselle and Manes walk alone down this incredible path, I offer up another example. In *Animal Liberation and Social Revolution* (Critical Mess Media, 1997), anarchist vegan Brian Dominick describes the "animal kingdom" as "a vast constituency which has yet to receive the right to vote."

What in the world does this eco-babble mean? Animals can't vote, can't assemble in demonstrations, can't have jobs. While we might wish for animals to have the "right to life," even this is a poor conceptual fit. After all, what about predators? Shall we strive to uphold a mouse's right to life over a hungry fox's right to eat? All of this is ludicrous. What is the required lifestyle suggested by this approach; who could ever live up to it?

Beyond being insulting and verging on racist, such half-baked clap-trap is doomed in the marketplace of ideas; in the process, it will tend to discredit the movement. Ecology is already often seen as uncon-nected to the struggles of low-income communities; as more of an esoteric lifestyle concern of the privileged. Yet the poor are generally those most victimized by toxic waste and other pollution. This discon-nect again suggests our failings as activists, not some inevitable blindness on the part of the poorer populations. If the environment is ever to be embraced as a great burning issue in all communities, the movement has to do a better job of addressing its class and racial biases.

Our struggle for a world with reverence for all life, starts, ironically enough, with other human animals. *We have to change minds.* This is no easy task, given that our society has often taught us to view the Earth as simply a grab bag of goodies to be plundered at will. Humans can carry a sense of entitlement that often obscures reverence.

But while the world is surely not ours to do with as we wish, other questions loom. Where does the legitimate right of any creature to survive—often at the expense of another to some degree—come into play? What are its limits?

There is a lot of gray area to be explored here. Strict black-and-white thinking is not really helpful, much less revolutionary. For instance, I don't oppose meat eating in principle, just the inflicting of needless suffering. Having grown up on a beef ranch, I know how much agony meat consumption involves. At the same time, I also recognize that animals feed on each other. Pain is part of life, something that all creatures cause, at least those higher on the food chain.

I witnessed a lot of suffering, but that didn't make me a vegetarian. I stopped eating meat after becoming truly aware (thanks to new friends I met after moving to D.C.) that meat eating wasn't essential, at least not in our current context. Why cause such pain when I could easily eat other foods?

This means that, for example, I don't think the Plains Indians were wrong to eat buffalo. They had little choice, just like the Inuit or other surviving natives may not have, nor any of the less privileged in our world. Indigenous societies are more linked to nature, to the sacredness of all life; among the Plains tribes, there were even ceremonies to ask forgiveness of the animals killed for food.

I surely wish for us to honor the sanctity of life, as we tend to be profoundly "estranged" (to use Starhawk's term) from the Earth. We are so often divorced now from any sense of how our food is produced, the suffering to animals, to people, to the Earth. This pain is not always avoidable, but sometimes can be.

It may seem that I am trying here to convert people to vegetarianism; actually I am not. I am simply suggesting the costs and complexities involved, while modeling a possible process for discernment. My own brother is a beef rancher, struggling to support four kids in a depressed rural economy. I know that my lifestyle, adopted widely enough, would doom his present livelihood. While he might be able to find other means of support, it would probably mean the loss of a farm that has been in our family for generations. It is hard to imagine a more wrenching blow for him or many others who I also love.

There is no pain-free way forward, and no easy answer for what each of us should do. The exact life changes one makes may be far less important than the attitude one brings to it. Why? Simply because any arrogance or self-righteousness is bound to leave division in its wake. This is exactly what we don't need.

Recall my assumption that revolution requires counter-power challenging that of the dominant structures. Can lifestyle changes create this power? In very small ways perhaps they can, by keeping us centered, healthy, and strong . . . but mostly by redirecting money.

Money is power in very concrete ways. Cash rechanneled in a well-planned and visible manner, as in boycotts, can achieve striking results. The shunning of British tea during the American Revolution is one example; the boycott of segregated buses in mid-1950s Montgomery, Alabama, another; the '60s United Farm Workers campaign against lettuce consumption, yet another.

Why did these boycotts work? One reason: *Masses of people supported them.* When enough people are behind a stand like that, in a well-organized fashion, they begin to wield power sufficient to genuinely challenge the status quo.

As Naomi Klein admits, "It may all sound like Alice in Wonderland, but boycotts do affect multinationals." Pointing to a widely supported corporate divestment campaign spawned by abuses in Burma, she explains, "[Corporations] may smile at a tie-dyed college town like Berkeley boycotting everything but hemp paper and Bridgehead coffee, but when rich states like Massachusetts and Vermont get in on the action, the corporate sector is not amused."

This brings us to the crux of my argument here. It has become commonplace for present-day radicals to dismiss phenomena like vegetarianism, straight edge, and eco-friendly shopping as mere "lifestyle politics." Nowhere can the subjective and the objective get more confused than whilst cruising on what UK anarcho-popsters Chumbawamba have wittily described as "the Good Ship Lifestyle." Little different than child-star Shirley Temple's whimsical "Good Ship Lollipop," this ride promises us that revolution means you don't have to get your hands dirty: Just go shopping—or not, as the case may be—and it all magically works out! Ahh, *if only* this were so.

A wonderful point—but now let's expand on it. I would suggest that all radicals are entangled in "lifestyle politics" to the extent that their work is disconnected from concrete improvements in poor people's lives and/or building bridges to realize a broad coalition for transformation. We often embrace activist lifestyles that give us personal meaning but do not objectively alter the structures of domination.

This is why the gradual devolution of a potentially revolutionary idea like anarchism into a form of subcultural "lifestylism" is so disheartening. In a way, it is here that the capitalist system finds its photo-negative, a dark mirroring of its own self-obsession. Somehow the Corporate Cool Machine has managed to trick thousands of would-be revolutionaries into believing that wearing lots of black clothing, decorating themselves with patches, piercings, and tattoos, while talking "militant" somehow threatens the system. How ludicrous!

Venerable anarchist thinker Murray Bookchin—active in radical movements since the 1930s—dismissed this "lifestyle anarchism" as "a juvenile clutter of 'personal insurrections' that consist of offensive behavior, fruitless riots, and outre styles of dress and demeanor as well as in some cases, sociopathic 'actions' and bare-faced criminality, masked with claims that one is an anarchist and therefore is free to do whatever one chooses."

While this rebuke is stinging, it is also uncomfortably on-target. Such a cartoon version of anarchism could never find mass support. Indeed, it seems to draw inspiration from its very disaffection from the mainstream. As such, it has no apparent way to bridge its idealistic aims to a possible reality.

Any politics narrowly based in "anti-corporatism" faces the same dangers. As Naomi Klein argues in *No Logo*, "Anti-corporatism is the brand of politics capturing the imagination of the next generation of troublemakers and shit disturbers . . . Their outrage will fuel the next big political movement." Delivered only a few months before the "Battle of Seattle," this view was surely prescient.

In *Students Against Sweatshops*, Liza Featherstone agrees that the anti-corporate stance has "become the dominant idiom of resistance in the U.S. . . . among middle-class white people." This, she admits, is not all bad: "As the villains everyone loves to hate, corporate power and greed lend coherence to a global youth movement that's too often viewed as diffuse and lacking focus."

In other ways, however, this position can be alienating to some of the very sectors with which we need to ally. Featherstone notes that "many people of color and poor people in the United States say that anti-corporatism fails to describe adequately their experiences of everyday inequality and injustice." As Latina activist Maria Cordera observed to Featherstone, poor people and people of color aren't always so concerned about globalization: "That's not our bread and butter . . . We're worried about how we are going to feed our kids."

Given the relative privilege of many in the anti-corporate movement, this blindness can be self-serving. Featherstone points out, "Talk of 'corporate control' becomes meaningless without some acknowledgement of class power." This bias is made worse when anti-corporate groups make no demands on the state. While such skepticism is understandable, it can be a dead end.

As Featherstone argues, "The lives of poor and working-class people in the United States aren't likely to be radically improved by a movement that eschews state solutions. In the United States, in a time of ebbing government services and worsening economic inequality, to simply repudiate—or, like most anti-corporate activists, to simply ignore—the state is to write the majority of poor and working people out of a movement." Given all of this, it is hardly surprising that Featherstone describes the relationship between anti-racist and anti-corporate groups as "uneasy."

Is anti-corporatism "about social justice or simply an aesthetic objection to bigness"? Featherstone insightfully notes that this is not always clear. To the extent it is the latter, it is lifestyle politics in its most subtle but troubling form.

Even Klein admits that "there is no doubt that anti-corporate activism walks a precarious line between self-satisfied consumer rights and engaged political action." She draws the obvious conclusion herself: "Any movement that is primarily rooted in making people feel guilty about going to the mall is a backlash waiting to happen . . . Genuine political empowerment cannot be reconciled with a belief system that regards the public as a bunch of ad-fed cattle, held captive under commercial culture's hypnotic spell. What's the point of going through the trouble to knock down the fence? Everyone knows that the branded cows will just stand there looking dumb and chewing cud."

This disconnect brings us back around to the potent rhetorical sweep of Kalle Lasn and his ad-busting culture-jammers, whose network-rejected *Buy Nothing Day* ad suggested that North American consumers were "pigs."

On the level of ideas, Lasn has got game. As John Adams once said, "The [North American] Revolution was effected before the war commenced . . . in the hearts and minds of the people." Identifying a problem can contribute mightily to its defeat; of this there can be little doubt. On the level of strategy, however, how precisely to *realize* those ideas . . . Well, that is another matter entirely. As much as any other "lifestylist," Lasn's strategy seems to melt into mysticism. Subjectively, acts of culture-jamming can have great meaning, freeing us in some small yet personally significant way from the commercial brainwash. Still, just how meaningful are they objectively?

Take something like *Buy Nothing Day*. On its own, it is not a terribly effective means to challenge power. It is probably not meant to be, as most recognize that putting a wrench in the machine doesn't destroy it, much less create a new machine. This type of very individualistic rebellion can only achieve transformation as part of a larger, carefully coordinated campaign with many other facets. In a would-be revolutionary sense, the stopping of consumption by a few hundred, even a few thousand people for one day might be nice. But it is hardly sufficient to "bring the walls down," much less pull masses of people together to build power that could then fundamentally revamp the structures.

Consider this scenario, taken from the *Adbusters* website: "Sheer mayhem. That's all we can say. *Buy Nothing Day* was crazy in London where jammers took special medicine so they could puke in unison at the mall. Street theater erupted everywhere, cut-up credit cards littered the streets, and the media covered the action like never before . . . A BND highlight for us was our biggest ever TV jam—a half-minute spot on CNN's Lou Dobbs's *Moneyline*. With the support of hundreds of donors, we scratched millions of money-hungry heads, and played with the media's eye."

I appreciate a good "puke-in" as much as the next (radical) person. But are such tactics likely to change minds? Well, do viruses break us of the "computer habit"? No. In fact, the average person is more often irked than enlightened by such monkey-wrenching.

Of course, this probably doesn't matter to some. It does to me, however, since my assumptions suggest that in order to build power, to make revolution, we need people. If that is the heart of our strategy to nourish a movement—as I believe it must be—then our tactics have to advance that aim.

This is something that Lasn understands enough to pay lip service to, but little more. Indeed, he seems to go out of his way to dissociate the culture-jam movement from not only "cool" and "slackers," but "academics," "lefties," and "feminists." Such gratuitous slams of entire categories of people—mostly obvious allies—are a very strange way to gather strength. Perhaps he means to build a new movement, freed from negative associations that many have with such labels. If so, it is odd that he includes far more stigmatized subsets like "punks" and "anarchists" in his roster of culture-jammers.

In any case, his major tactics to build such a transformative coalition center around the media. Lasn calls for the waging of "meme wars" with subvertisments that undermine existing commonsensical notions. These ideas would be replaced by alternative "memes" that "uncool" consumption and the corporation. In a twist that recalls Saul Alinsky's ideas of "political jujitsu," Lasn wants to "turn the incredible power of the marketing machine against itself," redefining the global economy as a "doomsday machine" to the public.

My own story suggests that such actions can change minds, and thus lives, although they can also alienate as many as they convert. Done skillfully, this *detournement* of consumer capitalism could help to generate a genuine change in ideas, lifestyles, and, thus, power—*but only if that shift in consciousness is followed up by sustained, creative grassroots organizing.*

Lasn brushes past such mundane concerns, claiming that "whoever has the memes has the power." For him, the next revolution will be a "guerrilla information war . . . a dirty no-holds-barred, propaganda war of competing world-views and alternative visions of the future," waged with "cyberjamming," "virtual protests," TV jamming, "leverage points," and "pincer strategies."

Beneath the jargon, some of this makes sense. The use of the Internet has begun to open up fresh channels for information flow and, consequently, new bases of power. Responding to a claim that the Internet is now "the most potent weapon in the toolbox of resistance," Naomi Klein asserts, "That may well be so, but the Net is more than an organizing tool—it has become an organizing model, a blueprint for decentralized and cooperative decision-making." But Elizabeth Martinez has pointed out, "Black and Latino families across the U.S. lack Internet access compared to white communities." Lasn, of course, has already dismissed such concerns as distractions from the real battle.

Even beyond this, Lasn's strategy (if you can call it such) unravels with the most cursory inspection. After all, he cannot get on the major networks. And if he could, where would the money come from to pay for such a campaign? Lasn sees this conundrum, and answers it with a call for a "Media Carta" that would enshrine a human right "to communicate" through the mass media. This, of course, only begs a new question. While this idea of opening the airwaves to populist control is surely appealing, I can't see any hint of how Lasn proposes to accomplish this dramatic reversal.

Is it really true that "the only battle worth fighting is against the Corporate Cool Machine"? Many of the less privileged throughout this world might well disagree, if they understood what Lasn even meant by that florid term. Is the best plan of attack "authentic acts . . . so heartfelt that they must be true," and "small, spontaneous moments of truth"? Not likely. Never mind that any of us might be sincerely, passionately *wrong*; such actions also have to connect to a strategy capable of effecting change.

Such practicalities are where Lasn's vivid vision hits the rocks. His main tips for sparking a "Second American Revolution" are along the line of "Drop Your Facade of Politeness," "Clear a Path for Others," "Reframe

Debates," and "Maintain Your Sovereignty." Such banal abstractions are scarcely more meaningful than run-of-the-mill self-help tripe.

The same crucial ingredient is missing throughout: a direct, organic connection to the people themselves, their needs, wants, and struggles; not in some vague existential way, but in a concrete, bread-and-butter manner. Although Lasn talks about "the People," ordinary folks seem to disappear in his bold scenario. They are lost beneath a "revolution-by-anti-ad" monster riff. However compelling in rhetorical terms, such a revolution is doomed to fail.

Lasn doesn't even seek to hide the elitist nature of his vision. Assuming a certain level of "collective disillusionment" and an inevitable "fumble" of a world crisis by the powers-that-be, he argues, "We just need an influential minority that smells the blood, seizes the moment and pulls off a set of well-coordinated social marketing strategies . . . By waiting for the right moment and then jamming in unison, I think a global network of a few hundred activists can pull off the coup . . . We create a sudden, unexpected moment of truth—a global mindshift—from which corporate consumerist forces never fully recover."

This is an appealing vision—but so is the average commercial.

I'd really like to be more upbeat here, because Lasn's version of lifestyle politics is so artful, so stirring. Indeed, not unlike my beloved punk inspirations, Lasn's vision rings hope in my heart, helps me to believe in a world beyond simple commerce, where value is something deeper than money.

I also know Lasn's dilemma intimately. Indeed, my critique here is much the same as the one I've shared of early Positive Force or NBAU: A very real, very big problem is identified, but the tools at hand are hardly up to the task. I wish we could buy (or, rather, *un*-buy) our way to revolution. Sadly, anything that sounds too good to be true usually is just that—and so this seems to me. Lasn deserves credit for at least trying to connect the dots, something most of us never even attempt.

Naomi Klein similarly seems seduced at times by a potent subjective pull, the intoxication of the anti-capitalist *carnivale*—most obviously when she touts the UK-born Reclaim the Streets (RTS) as "the most vibrant and fastest growing political movement since Paris '68."

As she notes, this is simply Lasn's vision adapted for a new venue: "RTS takes culture-jamming's philosophy of reclaiming public space to another level. Rather than filling the space left by commerce with advertising parodies, the RTSers attempt to fill it with an alternative vision of what society might look like in the absence of commercial control." She approvingly quotes an RTS organizer, John Jordan—now also a member of the Notes from Nowhere collective that created *We Are Everywhere*—describing one of their actions around Claremont Road as creating "a kind of temporary microcosm of a truly liberated, ecological culture."

Jordan elaborates on the grander vision: "The street party is only a beginning, a taster of future possibilities. To date, there have been thirty street parties all over the country. Imagine that growing to 100. Imagine that happening on the same day, imagine each one lasting for days and growing . . . Imagine the street party growing roots . . . *la fête permanente*." In this moment, the echoes of Kalle Lasn's wishful revolutionary scenario are unmistakable.

This idea of RTS and other DIY culture as some harbinger of a new age, linked to a "Great British Ecstasy Revolution"—a view championed in *DiY Culture: Party and Protest in Nineties Britain*, edited by George MacKay, (Verso, 1998)—recalls the most Dionysian pretensions of the '60s counterculture. Like that vanished moment in time, RTS may play a valuable role in the short term, as a response to repressive conditions. It may even create some "free space"; soil in which the seeds of alternative worlds might take root, grow, and blossom.

It will also, no doubt, alienate many working-class and poor people. In the end, such hedonistic hyperbole is ridiculous in its presumption and of little or no use in the transformation I am seeking here. Dancing in this revolution is surely welcome. But if we never get past the party to feeding hungry people, or creating affordable housing, or decent medical care for all, or other mundane practicalities, what use are we to the world's poor? Not much, I'd say.

Klein explains that "spontaneous street parties are an extension of the DiY lifestyle, asserting that people can make their fun without asking the state's permission or relying on any corporation's largesse." All very meaningful, at least for those with privilege. But who is growing food to feed the "permanent party"? Who is taking out the trash? To succeed, this whole enterprise seems to assume some invisible unmentioned class who exist to provide the economic and material basis for our aspiring twenty-four-hour-party-protesters.

Nowhere in Klein's book is it honestly acknowledged what the state can reasonably be expected to do in the face of this permanent, extra-legal street party. Like the average citizen, the police will have little patience for road-blocks and traffic-snarling festivities, so confrontation is nearly inevitable. Thus does the party turn into the "fruitless riot" rightly disdained by Murray Bookchin.

I don't question the emotional pull of the RTS vision, and I appreciate the exuberant creativity and sense of fun they bring to the mix. Still, any belief that simply satisfying our desires, or defying the state and corporations, is some big victory for the oppressed seems far-fetched.

Such is the seductive power of the chimeras embedded within lifestyle politics. While I have argued here for the necessity of personal revolution, I dismiss any notion that simple changes in our consumption patterns—including culture-jamming—will bring real revolution. Any illusion that they could is but one way by which the system operates to help preserve itself.

So where does this all leave us? As the proponent of "anti-manifesto," I have no simple resolution to share here, just a few suggestions. If I am lucky, they may help us to utilize what is best in the "lifestyle" approach, while being realistic about its limitations.

First of all, despite all of its complexity, we must continue to wrestle with the closely linked issues of personal consumption, ideology, and spirituality. We should expect no easy answers, and recognize that well-intentioned people can (and will) come to different conclusions. As such, the process itself may be more important than the outcome. We must give each other the benefit of the doubt, keeping the focus on our own choices while reaching out to one another.

Our aim must be to keep growing, to truly embody the values we hold in our entire way of being. If there is any "revolution by example," we have to represent with our bodies, not just our hearts, much less our words. If we engage thoughtfully, sincerely, in this work, we are bound to find some answers to advance our cause of justice, if only because we are *doing it together*.

Together: This is where we find our transformative power, that of the people.

But what if that righteous power is met by repression; by guns, tanks, bombs? Can we respond in kind? Is violence a realistic tactic or a romantic one? In what way, and when? Can it ever get us to a world free of oppression, coercion? These are the heavily contested questions to which we now turn.

BRING
THE
WAR
HOME!

...TURE AT ABU GHRAIB

...soldiers brutalized Iraqis. How far up does the responsibility go?

BY SEYMOUR M. HERSH

m Hussein, Abu
s west of Bagh-
orld's most no-
torture, weekly
ving conditions.

several thousand, including women and
teen-agers—were civilians, many of
whom had been picked up in random
military sweeps and at highway check-
points. They fell into three levels...

"White Riot" is among the heavies: Clash live tunes, with ...
going. "No more Beatles, Stones, Elvis in...

SEVEN: DON'T MIND THROWING A BRICK

"I've seen the restless children
At the head of a column
Come to purify the future
With the arrogance of youth
Nothing is as cruel
As the righteousness of innocents
With automatic weapons
And a gospel of the truth."
                    —New Model Army

From across the years, the images come; stark, fragmentary, insistent. They are riveting in their primal ugly truth, even glimpsed dimly through the fog of history.

The Saigon Police Chief summarily executing an accused Viet Cong during the Tet Offensive, his gun to the man's head; the soft, sickening jerk of impact, the body's fall to the street, blood spurting.

Napalm canisters cascading end over end from U.S. planes onto grass huts blossoming in fiery red. A young GI torching a home with a Zippo lighter as an elderly Vietnamese woman sobs and shrieks. A tiny, nearly naked girl running down a highway screaming, burning jellied gasoline consuming her skin. A Buddhist monk setting himself on fire outside the U.S. Embassy. An Army officer's words: "We had to destroy the village in order to save it."

There is a monument in Washington, D.C. honoring the 58,000 North Americans who died in this war. However, this grotesque, futile conflict was mostly played out on the lands and bodies of the

Vietnamese people. Probably more than three million died; no one really knows for sure. Part of the war also came home—was *brought home*—to North American streets:

A teenage girl screams over the still body of a student shot by the National Guard at Kent State. Police savagely beat protesters in a haze of tear gas, just outside the '68 Democratic Convention. Frenzied knots of young people in helmets charge down Chicago streets smashing windows, in hand-to-hand combat with cops. Children at a breakfast program, watching uniformed Black Panthers chanting, "Revolution has come/Time to pick up the gun/*Off the pigs!*"

The blood-drenched bed of an assassinated Fred Hampton; the bullet-scarred windows of a Black Panther Party office. JFK, Malcolm X, MLK, RFK all murdered within five years; city streets in flames, creeping within ten blocks of the White House. Torched ROTC offices; the University of Wisconsin's Army Math Research Center stands in bombed-out ruins, a graduate student dead.

Broader historical context is useful in understanding these images. American Indian Movement militants with rifles at Wounded Knee, South Dakota in 1973 ought to recall the sight of 300 Lakota Sioux men, women, and children frozen in grotesque poses after their slaughter there by U.S. Cavalry in December 1890.

In turn, Wounded Knee evokes the bodies heaped up at My Lai, Vietnam, 1968, casualties of another "search and destroy" mission. Or the piles of skulls of Khmer Rouge victims in Cambodia, "collateral damage" of dominoes toppled by the Nixon/Kissinger "secret" bombing and subsequent invasion of that country.

As H. Rap Brown once said, "Violence is as American as apple pie." The United States is a country born of anti-imperial revolution. In some ways, violence is the major constant in our history. Our roots are soaked in blood, including slavery of Africans, genocide of Native Americans.

Yet the question of violence now haunts the North American left, in arguments reverberating from 1960s streets where groups like Weatherman (later renamed the Weather Underground) sought to "bring the war home." Today, these find echoes in the "black bloc" trashing Niketown during the N30 protests; in growing confrontations with police as the global-justice movement strains against the limits of post-9/11 America; in campaigns of sabotage carried out by clandestine groups like the Earth Liberation Front and Animal Liberation Front.

Few topics can so quickly divide a room full of activists. Is property destruction even violence? Perhaps not, but the lines can become very blurred. What about setting fire to a construction site that later turns out to have had sleeping workers there, as happened at one ELF action in mid-2003? Sabotage could easily have turned to loss of life. Meanwhile, groups from the past like Weatherman and the Black Panthers are either romanticized or reviled, seen as righteous prophets who put their lives on the line or adventurist bullyboys (and -girls) pursuing a cartoon version of "revolution" verging on nihilism.

Underneath the sound and fury, a basic question lingers: Is violence acceptable to bring revolution in the North American context? How one answers this tends to determine on which side one falls in the above dispute.

This is deeply ironic, for in many ways the argument is illusory, or at least poorly framed. To me, this question is less a moral one—is violence good or bad?—than a practical one: Will violence work? If so, how and when?

It is worth noting that the two major emphases of my graduate studies were guerrilla movements—especially Guatemala's Guerrilla Army of the Poor (EGP)—and human rights. There were, to put it mildly, occasional tensions between these two areas of concern, tensions that remain hard to reconcile. I still have no clear resolution to offer. While my own tentative answers deny pacifism as an absolute "article of faith," they also point to the shortcomings and dangers—even addictiveness—of violence, especially for those who seek revolution, a world without oppressive force.

As always, we must start with some basic definitions. What exactly is "violence"? One entry in my trusty Random House dictionary describes it as "rough or injurious physical force, action, or treatment"; a second as "an unjust or unwarranted exertion of force or power."

The latter seems the more useful for our discussion. While this definition raises more issues than it settles, it does frame the question in broader terms. If violence comes not from the simple presence of force, but from an illegitimate use of such, what makes force "just" or "warranted"?

There are many ways to answer this. According to modern political-science theory, the democratic state has a monopoly on the legitimate use of force. In principle, this is because the state is duly constituted by the will of the people; in the words of the U.S. *Declaration of Independence*, "drawing [its] just powers from the consent of the governed." Given due process and other safeguards of individual rights, government becomes, thus, the only body that can claim social sanction sufficient for the application of force. This monopoly is not unqualified. For example, self-defense (narrowly understood) is recognized as acceptable.

North American tradition has also given the world another very significant exception. In the *Declaration of Independence*, violent revolution is explicitly justified as "the Right of the People to alter or abolish" a government that has become "destructive" to those "unalienable Rights" that include "Life, Liberty, and the Pursuit of Happiness."

We may scoff at the seemingly quaint rhetoric of this document today. Certainly, the *Declaration*'s assertion of human equality did not make it so within our own boundaries, much less the world. Indeed, at the time, no one but rich white men were even given the right to vote by the American Revolution.

Despite obvious progress toward realizing this ideal, full equality is precisely what we must still struggle to achieve. Lacking this, the legitimacy of the state and, consequently, any use of force by it can and, at times, *must* be challenged.

To simply dismiss the *Declaration*, however, is to fail to recognize a profound shift from legitimacy based on power (might makes right) or heredity (as in royalist traditions) to the people themselves, "the governed."

Ideas have power, and those of the *Declaration* have been far more influential than most. It is no exaggeration to claim that scores of revolutions have risen around the globe from the concepts in this document. The Viet Cong who defeated the U.S. quoted it in their own party's founding documents, as did the Black Panthers at the end of their Ten Point Program.

Moreover, the notion of accountability as a restraint to the immense destructive potential of violence contains a key insight. In this approach, violence, even more than any other form of power, is seen as a dangerous fire. By its very nature, it can definitively abridge the most basic human right: the right to life. As such, violence must be very carefully controlled, lest it rampage roughshod over the fragile rule of law protecting humanity and our rights.

While this analysis is useful as a starting point, and has aspects to which we will return, it doesn't peer deeply enough. In a radical (meaning, again, "going to the root") sense, are we ever free of violence?

I'd say that the answer is no, not in a world where perhaps thirty children die every minute of every day from malnutrition or its side-effects. *No, in such a world, violence is simple, almost banal, day-to-day reality.* It rises out of poverty, prejudice; quieter than gunfire perhaps, but just as lethal. This, in turn, can lead to the more obvious forms of violence: crime, rioting, bombings, beyond.

The origin of this "cycle of violence" must be pinpointed, if the circle is ever to be broken. As Paulo Freire argues in *Pedagogy of the Oppressed*, "With the establishment of a relationship of oppression, violence has *already* begun."

This insight begins to provide a deeper foundation for our investigation of the nature and meaning of violence. Freire goes on to explain, "Never in history has violence been initiated by the oppressed. How could they be the initiators, if they themselves are the result of violence? Violence is initiated by those who oppress, who exploit, who fail to recognize others as persons—not by those who are oppressed, exploited, and unrecognized. It is not the helpless subject to terror, who initiate terror, but the violent who with their power create the concrete situation which begets the 'rejects of life.'"

To accept Freire's analysis is not, of course, to say that any and all actions are acceptable (much less effective or productive) when done by, or in the name of, the oppressed; by no means. This is nonetheless a crucial understanding if violence is to be understood, or if any "war against terror" is ever to be won.

In some ways, the relevant query is no longer, "Is violence good or bad?" Of course violence is not "good." No, *violence is simply real.*

We have to start from this understanding or we are lost. We cannot fairly critique the violence of the oppressed—or their would-be allies—without first admitting that which exists in the operations and outcomes of the global economic and political system. The aim is to use this understanding to move toward a world without violence (i.e., oppressive force) of any sort. But how exactly do we do this? To me, the fundamental question is what will work in practical terms.

Recall our assumptions that we need power to change structures. While I would hardly agree with any narrow interpretation of Mao's famous dictum that "power grows from of the barrel of a gun," it does carry some truth. Weapons are the most primal version of power, the great tyrannizer/equalizer. Beyond this, money buys guns (and more) as well as the people to fire them. Such, of course, is the special province of governments, corporations, the rich.

Given that we are unlikely to be able to compete on the level of brute, naked force, what do we have to offer in response? Perhaps only masses of people, driven by commitment and cunning born not out of money, but from passion for justice, freedom, self-determination.

That this can be an irresistible force has been shown by the overthrow of dictators like Marcos of the Philippines, the Shah of Iran, and Somoza in Nicaragua. It is also exemplified by the defeat of more wealthy, better armed forces by popularly supported guerrilla armies, as with the U.S. in Vietnam, the Soviets in Afghanistan, and the French in Algeria.

I don't think that money or guns are the most profound base of power; I believe that is always *the people*.* While armed struggle will sometimes be necessary, the only way this can ever work against a better trained and funded enemy is to have enough people standing behind the effort.

Make no mistake: I am hardly some wild-eyed "street fighting man." No, I am simply a realist. Power will concede nothing essential without a struggle. Nonviolent confrontation is, of course, preferable. But when push comes to shove, this contest will tend to involve violence, at least in self-defense. This is shown by the history of my own country as well as much of the world.

In saying this, I accept the critique of a naïve pacifism that has most forcefully been made by Ward Churchill with Mike Ryan and Ed Mead in *Pacifism As Pathology: Reflections on the Role of Armed Struggle in North America* (Arbeiter Ring, 1998). A Native American activist of undeniable commitment and a thinker of some depth, Ward Churchill is no coalition-builder. Rather, he is a man on fire with a mission, seemingly cast in the mold of the ancient Hebrew prophets. A good portion of this calling, apparently, is to save the North American left from the "pacifist menace." In the process, Churchill's book has become a bit of a Bible within some contemporary radical circles.

This is oddly appropriate since, having first been published in a radical therapy journal, Churchill's piece—like much of the "Good Book" itself—is anything but an easy read. Heavily larded with psychological jargon, the essay oozes arrogant condescension, with prose almost as leaden and impenetrable at times as the worst academic Marxist.

---

* Against the ambivalence of some radicals, I affirm the value of money-making in meeting human needs and fueling revolution; it is a means, not an end in itself.

As the title suggests, Churchill has declared war on a shallow pacifism which he sees as having become "axiomatic and all but universal among the more progressive elements of contemporary mainstream North America." This approach, according to Churchill, "promises that the harsh realities of state power can be transcended via good feelings and purity of purpose rather than by self-defense and resort to combat."

Much of the book involves highly debatable interpretations of historical events. (For example, his assertion that the black liberation struggle made more gains *after* Martin Luther King's death and the turn away from nonviolence is hard to sustain.) These vignettes offer the least charitable depictions of pacifism, while hyping armed revolutionaries like Weatherman and the Baader-Meinhoff Group.

Pacifism As Pathology was initially written to justify a controversial workshop—"Demystification of the Assault Rifle"—that Churchill hosted at a radical therapy convention. Any relevance to the world of "radical therapy" aside, Churchill's point that guns ought to be "demystified" is lost on me. I grew up with them all around, just like millions of other Americans. As a kid in Montana, I was a National Rifle Association member, went through their "hunter's safety" classes, even slept with a .22 and 30-06 in a gun rack over my head. I once had the opportunity to shoot automatic weapons—at some innocent ducks—thanks to a well-armed neighbor. (I declined the offer; my friend blazed away alone. Duck lovers will be glad to hear that he was not a very good shot and that our feathered friends escaped unscathed!) Another acquaintance died carrying such an assault rifle on a hunting trip, when its trigger snagged on a barbed-wire fence. Perhaps guns could use *more* "mystification"—we all might be safer.

Fortunately, Churchill has more substantial points to offer. He blasts a weak version of pacifism which he characterizes as asking, "What sort of politics might I engage in which will both allow me to posture as progressive and allow me to avoid incurring harm to myself?" He is correct that such protest can collude with the powers-that-be, creating an empty show of dissent that threatens nothing.

Likewise, his analysis of how such symbolic actions can serve to make us feel good or meet other emotional needs is valuable for the self-examination it suggests. The critique is, of course, equally applicable to many far less "nonviolent" but equally symbolic protests.

Churchill also attacks advocates of nonviolence for allegedly suppressing other approaches. In the process, he makes an early pitch for what today is known as "diversity of tactics": "The more diluted the substance embodied in pacifist practice, the louder the insistence of its subscribers that nonviolence is the *only* mode of action 'appropriate and acceptable within the context of North America' and the greater the effort to ostracize, or even stifle divergent types of actions."

The situation is really quite dire, apparently. "Unless there is a marked change in its obstinate insistence that it holds a 'moral right' to absolute tactical monopoly," Churchill argues, "American pacifism will be left to 'feel good about itself' while the revolution goes on without it." Or, alternatively, "The mass suffering that revolution is intended to alleviate will continue as the revolution strangles itself on the altar of 'nonviolence.'"

Churchill's argument gives little quarter. He does admit that, however misguided, some pacifists (Gandhi, MLK, and the radical Catholic Berrigan brothers, among others) were not simply seeking an easy way out, but risking life and limb as much as any urban guerrilla. He also finally announces—in his obtuse radical therapist lexicon—that "the desire for a nonviolent and cooperative world is the healthiest of all psychological formations."

Such brief pleasantries can scarcely disguise the acid dripping from Churchill's pen. In 2001, he would deny to have claimed that "pacifism *is* pathology," only that it *can* assume such a form under certain circumstances, i.e., pacifism *as* pathology. This delicate distinction is hard to sustain when his own words tick off a series of unqualified "pacifism is . . ." phrases: delusional, suicidal, racist.

This litany leads to Churchill's "therapeutic" diagnosis: "Pacifism—far from being a praxis adequate to impel revolutionary change—assumes the configuration of a pathological illness when advanced as a political methodology. Given its deep-seated, superficially self-serving, and socially approved nature, it is likely to be an exceedingly difficult pathology to treat and a long-term barrier to the formation of revolutionary consciousness in North America."

While I hardly admire Churchill's tone (much less his skewed history), his essay can provide a bracing antidote to liberal politics-of-the-comfort-zone. His effort to encourage thinking in strategic terms, to press past a pacifism that is a blind feel-good faith is also valuable. He doesn't take these insights nearly far enough, however, or ground them in any credible assessment of the current North American populace; a significant, but not uncommon error.

We will return to these ideas in a moment. First, to both extend and ground this discussion, I offer up a case study of the aforementioned Weatherman, later known as the Weather Underground Organization (WUO).

The WUO existed from 1969 till about 1977. With at most a few hundred members, the group was dwarfed in size by its parent, Students for a Democratic Society (SDS), who had around 150,000 at its peak. Nonetheless, according to historian Ron Jacobs, the WUO "bombed its way into the headlines of the early 1970s to become one of the most dramatic symbols of the anger felt by young Americans opposed to the U.S. presence in Vietnam."

Over the past five years, there has been a striking revival of interest in the WUO, no doubt fostered by a certain sense of déjà vu in world events. This focus was brought to a peak in late 2003 by the controversy surrounding the release of imprisoned ex-WUO member Kathy Boudin, convicted as an accessory to murder in a botched Brinks truck robbery in 1981. As *Newsweek* columnist Anna Quindlen wrote,

> In the ways that seem to matter to her the world is remarkably unchanged since Kathy Boudin essentially left it in 1970. There still is a chasm between rich and poor, white and black. Environmental concerns have a habit of giving way to the profit motive. The state of California is in thrall to an actor of marginal talents and a Republican administration in Washington is devoted to self-perpetuation. There is even a nasty little quagmire of a war, one that many believe was ill-conceived from the very beginning. Once again the government of the United States is determined to destroy the village in order to save it, whether the villagers want it or not.

As if on cue, the WUO once again seems to be everywhere, courtesy of books rather than bombs. Ron Jacobs's concise, well-written history, *The Way the Wind Blew*, led the way in 1997. (While it gained little notice at the time, a new edition is now headed to bookstores.) Ironically enough, the release of Bill Ayers's Weather-memoir, *Fugitive Days*, coincided with the 9/11 attacks—unfortunate timing that resulted in the cancellation of some of his bookstore appearances. More recently,

Susan Braudy has created a stir with her gossipy, often unreliable *Family Circle: The Boudins and the Aristocracy of the Left*.

Major features in establishment venues like the *New York Times*, the *Washington Post*, and *Newsweek* have offered clear if muted praise (*"Quieter Lives for '60s Militants, but Intensity of Beliefs Hasn't Faded"*) and condemnation (ex-Weather Jonathan Lerner's *"I Was a Terrorist"*), mixed with Quindlen's more nuanced view. Meanwhile, other ex-WUO members like Cathy Wilkerson and David Gilbert are reportedly hard at work on their own chronicles of that time.

This avalanche of print has been supplemented by two recent feature-length documentaries that have brought the WUO into theaters across the country. The first, Helen Garvy's *Rebels with a Cause*, examines Weather in the context of the demise of SDS, while Sam Green and Bill Siegel's *Weather Underground* focuses solely on the group. Both—particularly the second—have drawn rave reviews and lengthy art-house runs. In 2004, Green and Siegel's film even garnered an Academy Award nomination for "Best Documentary."

This is quite a lot of hullabaloo over a group that, after all, was fairly small in size amidst the massive movement of the time. This is largely because the group symbolized an anger felt by many of their peers. Less admirably, Weather also embodied a certain North American romance with violence, while also raising basic—and still relevant—issues about its efficacy for social change.

In some ways, there are really two fairly distinct Weather entities. First, there is Weatherman, the SDS faction who helped destroy its parent; engaged in futile street fighting in the "Days of Rage"; set a new low for macho sectarianism; and romanticized Charles Manson. This version of Weather finally blew itself up in a Greenwich Village town-house in March 1970 while preparing for a terrorist attack that would have targeted soldiers and civilians at a U.S.O. dance.

Then there is the Weather Underground Organization that rose out of these ashes, the group that David Gilbert touts as "trailblazing." While many will dissent from this view, it is true that this version found greater success. As Gilbert notes, "In a society where every single movie and TV program showed that the FBI 'always got their man' the Weather Underground eluded capture and sustained armed actions for six years . . . carrying out more than 20 bombings against government and corporate violence without killing anyone or so much as scratching a civilian."

The WUO must be understood within the context of the long, bloody Vietnam War and its attendant COINTELPRO programs aimed at crushing internal dissent. The actions of the U.S. government during this era, both at home and abroad, surely justified rebellion, perhaps even violent revolution.

The WUO was hardly alone in their embrace of increasingly violent tactics at the time. Gilbert correctly argues, "The WUO was not formed as some narrow conspiracy, but instead was a focal point within a much broader surge of anti-war militancy . . . Thousands of military buildings and Bank of America branches were burned to the ground as hundreds of thousands of people joined demonstrations that broke government windows, disrupted meetings of big wigs and resisted arrest."

Gilbert—former husband of Kathy Boudin and father of their child, Chesa—is not entirely repentant for such actions. Indeed, he carried the Weather ideas into a later group, the Revolutionary Armed Task Force (RATF), which allied itself with the Black Liberation Army. He is now serving a life sentence for his role in the killing of police officers Waverly Brown—an African-American—and Edward O'Grady, Jr. and security guard Peter Paige in the failed 1981 Brinks robbery.

Few could fault Weather for lacking in courage or commitment. Nor is their critique of the criminality of U.S. policy inaccurate. In a just world, Nixon and Kissinger (among others) would have joined Gilbert in a cell, imprisoned for their own murderous actions. Given this, was the WUO effort to bring the war home moral? It could have been. Surely, the destruction wrought by the WUO was dwarfed by that of the U.S. government. Perhaps the "moral" course of action would be what *practically* stops the greater violence.

There is an obvious danger here. This kind of reasoning can be a slippery slope, leading to all manner of terrible lesser-of-two-evils abuse. Setting this sticky question aside for a moment, fundamental issues remain. Did the WUO actions actually help to stop that officially-sanctioned carnage in any significant way? Did they advance a broader movement to fundamentally transform American society? I don't think so.

To make it plain, while the actions of the U.S. government may well have justified revolution, they didn't necessarily make armed struggle a wise approach. Official criminality does not, on its own, make violent overthrow possible, much less inevitable—that depends first on the attitude of the people and then on appropriate strategy and organization.

In other words, simple courage is no substitute for sound strategy based in a clear, level-headed analysis and a genuine connection to a popular base.

Weather had plenty of the first, but not much of the latter two. Gilbert offers up what might serve as the group's autopsy: "Instead of admitting our fear and inexperience and developing a suitable transitional strategy, we psyched ourselves up by glorifying violence and with macho challenges about individual courage. This frenzy was accompanied by basic related errors of sectarianism, a scathing contempt for all who wouldn't assist armed struggle; and militarism, making the military deeds and daring of the group all-important rather than the political principles and the need to build a movement on all levels."

While Gilbert opines that the group learned from these early errors and mostly corrected its course, this is certainly debatable, for some of these miscues would dog the group till its demise. Indeed, putting military approaches in front of painstaking movement-building might be seen as Weather's fatal "birth defect."

According to Che Guevara's famous truism, armed revolutionaries need the "sea" of mass support for the guerrilla "fish" to swim in and survive. As Che found out in his poorly conceived (and ultimately suicidal) guerrilla campaign in Bolivia, such groups also need a realistic, credible strategy with appropriate tactics. Only this, grounded organically in a mass base, can result in victory.

Did the WUO have the above? Not in any way that mattered. Their problem began with a political analysis which seems elitist, even dilettante, in an odd way. The influential Australian anarchist tract, *You Can't Blow Up a Social Relationship*, argues that, like groups such as the Symbionese Liberation Army (SLA), British Angry Brigade, and Japanese Red Army, Weather's ideology was "a syncophantic Third Worldism which saw activity within imperialist nations as supportive of the 'real revolution' in the Third World."

Indeed, the pamphlet singles out the WUO as having elevated this notion to their "whole ideology and strategy." The practical result was that Weather "denied the task of spreading revolutionary ideas to the majority of the people in their own country . . . Instead the U.S. was to be made immobile while victorious Third World revolutionaries brought revolution from outside."

An excavation of the early Weather line lends credence to this critique. "Fight the people!" key WUO militant Bill Ayers famously argued in the most egregious of possible examples. Besides being a rude kiss-off to the Old Left, this revealed the depth of Weather's disdain for the American working class. The same arrogance was aimed at the larger anti-war community. "If you don't do it our way, you're up against the wall," Kathy Boudin told one old comrade. Weather's essential stance seemed to be, *We are right, and if the American public—or even a majority of the movement—doesn't agree, fuck them!* Understandably, such attitudes did little to endear them to other activists.

Some ex-Weathermen like David Gilbert later critiqued the larger left for not supporting them sufficiently. Gilbert credits "the terrible passivity of most of the white left to the early attacks on the Panthers" with giving the state "a signal that it would not face widespread political costs for proceeding with its full-fledged COINTELPRO campaign." This is not entirely fair. Although Gilbert explains that the WUO's stated purpose was to "draw off some of the repressive heat concentrated on Black, Native, and Latino movements," it is just as likely that they helped to intensify it by their actions. Nothing riles the state more than a challenge to its monopoly on force; anyone who steps to this place will face the consequences, both in repression and possible loss of popular support.

Take, for example, the Days of Rage action of October 1969. In *Democracy Is in the Streets: From Port Huron to the Siege of Chicago* (Simon and Schuster, 1987), James Miller recalls Weatherman's assessment of the 1968 Chicago convention face-off: "The skirmishing between protesters and police 'had done more damage to the ruling class . . . than any mass, peaceful gathering the world has ever seen.'" With such a blinkered analysis, no wonder Weatherman saw an outright assault on police and property as an appropriate sequel. Meanwhile, the movement stayed away in droves from this action to "tear pig city up."

Few even on the not-so-pacifist left embraced the Days of Rage. Most famously, Chicago Black Panther leader Fred Hampton denounced Weatherman and their shambolic protest as "Custeristic." This was striking, since the SDS splinter group claimed the Black Panthers as their inspiration.

Despite a subsequent meeting of the two groups, agreement was still not reached. According to SDS historian Todd Gitlin, Hampton became so incensed with Weatherman Mark Rudd over the police wrath the affair had brought on the ghetto (and, by extension, the Panthers) that he denounced him as "motherfucking masochist" and knocked him to the ground. Hampton's warning that increased repression would be the only result of such ill-advised street actions was underlined by his own murder only a few weeks later.

Once the WUO rose out of Weatherman following the townhouse tragedy in 1970, this arrogant line began to soften, but it was too late. Weather had already discarded SDS, the organization that could have been its link to a genuine mass base, and was isolated within the movement from the outset by its rhetoric and actions.

While David Gilbert argues that the group was then at the stage of "armed propaganda . . . with no illusion of contending for military power," it is hard to see how they could have ever gone to the next level. Once underground, the WUO became increasingly cut off from most of its potential youth support, not to mention the broader American public.

Beyond their dodgy politics, there was the isolation created by their clandestine status. As former German urban guerrilla Bonni Baumann has recounted in *How it all Began*, "Because you are illegal, you can't keep contact with the people at the base. You can no longer take part directly in any further development of the whole scene, with the living process that goes on . . . You are a marginal figure because you can't show up anywhere." Ex-WUO member Cathy Wilkerson has said, "One of the main results of our approach was to take a couple hundred of the country's most dedicated and skilled activists out of circulation for two decades."

Early civil rights/women's liberation activist Heather Booth speaks for many in asserting that the WUO was "counterproductive," hurting the movement for fundamental change through their activities. Former SDS president Todd Gitlin goes even further, seeing the group as emblematic of a knee-jerk anti-American "fight the pigs" impulse that led the anti-war movement to "become less popular at the same time as the war did." This tendency, for Gitlin, accounts for much of the resulting shift toward the right in American society in the late '70s and '80s that followed the apparent victory of the left. To the extent that Weather represented the victory of military approaches over political, combined with the abdication of efforts to dialogue with and transform mainstream America, Gitlin is not far off the mark. Surely their rhetoric was not designed for converting middle America.

Check out, for example, these early Weather witticisms. Bernardine Dohrn: "That's what we are about, being crazy mother-fuckers and scaring the shit out of honky America." Mark Rudd: "It's a wonderful feeling to hit a pig. It must be a really wonderful feeling to kill a pig or blow up a building." John Jacobs: "We are against everything that is good and decent in honky America. We will burn and loot and destroy." While supporters of the group might point to their shift toward more sophisticated and humane politics after becoming the WUO, the group also continued to argue that "revolutionary violence is the only way."

In 1974, the group praised the tiny Symbionese Liberation Army (SLA) for its kidnapping of newspaper heiress Patty Hearst. According to a WUO communiqué at the time, the kidnapping "unleashed an astounding practical unity among people's organizations." This meant the two or three tiny groups then committed to armed actions; Weather historian Ron Jacobs says that by this time, the WUO was down to "a committed core of about fifty individuals."

Weather's support for the SLA continued even after the Black Panthers had denounced the group's leader, Donald Defreeze, as a police agent. The SLA's other "victories" included bank and sporting-goods store robberies, and the cold-blooded execution of Marcus Foster, Oakland's progressive African-American superintendent of public schools. Fleeing the Bay Area, they were finally cornered in the Compton neighborhood of L.A. in early May 1974. After a fierce gun battle in which six SLA members died, the rest scattered. More mayhem ensued, and at least one innocent bystander—Myrna Opsahl, shot in an alleged SLA bank robbery in 1975—died before the group finally gave up the ghost.

What was the WUO's reaction to all of this? According to Jacobs, "A Weather statement given to the press hailed the SLA for their revolutionary actions [and once again] criticized the Left's failure . . . to perceive armed groups as allies and support them." In other words, the movement was to blame here, not the SLA for their blind, murderous actions. Apparently, the WUO's version of what today would be called "diversity of tactics" meant that everyone was supposed to follow their lead and support any tactic, no matter how obviously wrong-headed. Little wonder that the WUO was dwindling to utter irrelevance, especially once the U.S. role in Vietnam more or less ground to a halt in 1973.

Aware of this challenge, the WUO tried to create an above-ground mass organization through the Prairie Fire Organizing Committee (PFOC). This was an implicit admission of the premature nature of its military strategy; such a political organization should have long predated the WUO.

Viewed with hindsight—a luxury they did not have, of course—WUO had little support, only sufficient cover in countercultural circles to survive as a tiny group doing symbolic actions on the margins of American society. Leftist historian Dan Georgakas has opined, "The greatest revolutionary skill demonstrated [by the WUO] was the ability to avoid arrest." Their faith in the "God" of Third World revolution failed them, and any conversion to caring about issues closer to home came too late to account for much.

The end of WUO was brought on by internal splits and subsequent misguided adventures like a thwarted bombing of a California state senator's office and the Brinks robbery. To explain their actions now, former Weathermen like Mark Rudd and Brian Flanagan have suggested that the Vietnam War drove them "crazy." Responding more poetically, Ayers has evoked Bertolt Brecht: "You who shall emerge from the flood in which we are sinking, think, when you speak of our weaknesses, also of the dark time that brought them forth."

Fair enough. Of course, other activists just as sensitive and committed went through the same period without a similar descent into self-defeating madness. In retrospect, ex-WUO member Naomi Jaffe admits that "we didn't know until years later how much impact our [nonviolent] Vietnam protests had on the war-makers . . . I think that is more true of all our protests [today] than we realize."

My critique is not meant to discredit the WUO as people, for many of them are gifted, caring folks who have done much good before and since the WUO. Most have come through the fire battle-scarred but wiser. Mark Rudd has gone so far as to say that "violence won't work" in the American context, given the public's typical association of such non-state-sanctioned acts with insanity or criminality. One doesn't have to entirely agree with Rudd to share skepticism about the present efficacy of armed revolution. Again, remember our basic assumption: "They" have most of the guns and money, while "we" (might) have the people and our wits.

"The object is to win," wrote Ed Mead in his thoughtful introduction to *Pacifism As Pathology*. If the time is not right, if a mass of people are not with you, and all other options are not seemingly exhausted, then to wage armed struggle is foolish, premature, counterproductive, self-destructive; even if justified. According to Mead—imprisoned for nearly two decades for actions taken as part of the George Jackson Brigade—the Brigade, and, by extension, other contemporary groups like the WUO, "incorrectly applied the tool of revolutionary violence during a period when its use was not appropriate."

While explicitly *not* disavowing armed struggle, Mead counts off the cost of this profound misjudgment in deaths and imprisonments. He concludes that "there is nothing wrong with sacrificing today for a tomorrow that is significantly freer of oppression, but in our case the sacrifice did not achieve the desired political goals. That, I think, was our principle error."

This is no minor miscalculation—nor is it unusual. Its very source is often our passion, even rage; the energy that generally brings us to activism in the first place. We see the very real and terrible injustice in the world and want it to end, *now* and not later. *We must act*, we think, and in the end, almost any action will do. The momentum of our emotions can carry us to some scary places. In Bill Ayers's memoir, he quotes Weather compatriot Terry Robbins in the summer of 1969 as saying, "I'd rather die and go to hell than stand still!" Ayers has written that the group's watchwords then were, "Action! Action! Action!" adding, a bit mournfully, "We were kids in combat, with little to lose . . . BRING THE WAR HOME. It was a metaphor, of course . . . [but] metaphors matter: for human beings metaphors are causal—we function on the metaphors we ourselves fashion."

I'd rather die and go to hell than stand still. In a few months, Terry Robbins, Diana Oughton, and Ted Gold would be dead, blown to pieces by their own bomb; a device intended for the aforementioned U.S.O. dance.

The year is now 2004, not 1969, but I know these emotions intimately. How could I not? I have come to adulthood as an activist walking amidst U.S.-supported "secret wars" and death squads. I have seen the stinking refugee camps in Gaza Strip where despair turns kids into suicide bombers.

In the "peace" between two separate U.S. wars in Iraq, perhaps a million people have died—half of them children—thanks to our merciless economic sanctions. The second war itself has been waged in spite of massive global opposition, including millions marching in streets across the world on a single day, February 15, 2003.

The results were predictable. Friends of mine now have loved ones at war overseas, writing anguished letters back home. These nightmarish notes detail the fear, the demoralization, and, above all, the carnage they encounter and sometimes inflict. As in Vietnam, they are strangers in an unfriendly, faraway land fighting a pointless war born out of lies, and now sustained by precious, irreplaceable lives; the lives of North Americans and Iraqis alike.

In the war of images, photographs of friendly Iraqi crowds and fallen statues of Saddam Hussein have now been replaced by ugly new scenes broadcast across the world: mutilated bodies of North Americans dragged through Iraqi streets; young and old exulting as destroyed Humvees burn behind them, one waving a sign which reads "Fallujah: a cemetery for Americans"; a hooded Iraqi prisoner, arms stretched Christ-like, perched on a box with wires attached; a female U.S. soldier dragging a naked Iraqi prisoner on a dog leash.

On the home front, military build-up, union-busting, and tax cuts for the rich have trumped human needs. Bush's consequent budget deficit is out of control, to the extent that the IMF itself has warned that it endangers the global economy. Continued slashing of social service programs is inevitable. This is on top of welfare "reform" signed into law by President Clinton in 1996—a base betrayal of the promises of the New Deal that no Republican could have carried off.

As a result, this country faces a growing chasm between the rich and the poor, the largest since statistics began to be kept during the Great Depression of the 1930s. We have seen a presidential election stolen, as well as a new approach to fighting homelessness: Make it a crime! There is no "war on poverty" today—just a war on the poor.

The prison population has quadrupled in the past two decades. If incarceration is now a major form of public housing, gentrification, in turn, seems to have become the central "anti-poverty" program, remaking our inner cities as playpens for the young and affluent, all while the poor go . . . where, exactly? No one seems to know, or to care very much, for that matter. In the last ten years, almost as many people have been killed in D.C. as in three decades in Northern Ireland, an internationally recognized war zone with twice the population. This is no crisis, though; no, this is business as usual.

People just get thrown away. I see it every day, working in inner-city D.C. *"All the power is in the hands/Of people rich enough to buy it/While we walk the street/ Too chicken to even try it,"* sang the Clash in "White Riot," an homage to the Notting Hill uprising led by dark-skinned British often rejected by white society and brutalized by police. This spark ignited my own insurrection, a little revolution that still strains toward a larger but all-too-elusive one.

Walking streets where fires burned after the assassination of Martin Luther King, Jr.—streets that still sometimes crackle with a raw, savage rage— lines from this Clash anthem still make emotional sense to me: *"Black people got a lot of problems/But they don't mind throwing a brick/White people go to school/Where they teach you how to be thick . . . White riot/I wanna riot/A riot of my own."* The song connects the dots between me, the Clash, and the Weathermen who sang, *"I'm dreaming of a white riot,"* to the tune of "White Christmas" in 1969.

Faced with all of this, I have often wanted to blow things up, to smash windows, to pour out my rage at something, anything. Yet I also remember being in the midst of the second night of the Mount Pleasant riots, eager to be in solidarity with a Latino population suffering under police repression. Bricks and bottles flew, and the police retreated. As the tear gas drifted, so did the crowd's focus.

With the cops gone, looting commenced. While some of it had been targeted—Church's Chicken, notorious in the community for mistreating Latinos, was burned—much of it had no aim, save indi- vidual gratification. Often it was done by folks who, like me, didn't seem to be from the neighborhood, who were just using the riot as a chance to plunder. In the morning, the community would be in ruins and we would be gone, leaving others to pick up the pieces; mostly those already groaning under poverty and police brutality.

While observing some particularly ugly and mindless destruction, I was startled to find myself thinking, *You know, maybe I don't really want a riot, after all . . .* While this may sound silly, it was a moment of real insight. This is not to say that riots aren't a desperate form of communication, an unmistakable message to a society that throws people away. But they are also profoundly destructive; especially to the poor communities they rise from within. I have seen that in Shaw, a neighborhood deci- mated by the 1968 riots. I know the rage there, yes; but I also know the ambivalence of the community toward this history.

By their nature, riots are impossible to control. In practical political terms, they are a blunt object—like a club used to attempt heart surgery. This is why the more thoughtful and community-minded exponents of "revolutionary violence" like the Black Panthers opposed them at the time.

I have witnessed much romanticizing of riots within radical circles, particularly after the L.A. uprising in 1992. More recently, a PF compatriot forwarded a startling essay that had been circulating on the Internet after the U.S. invasion of Iraq. At the time, many activists were frustrated by the failure of their lofty rhetoric: *"When the war starts, the city stops!"* The essay's anonymous author began by critiquing what was passing as "direct action" as largely symbolic, noting that virtually none of it truly or directly "wrenched" the war machine.

This suggested, reasonably enough, that the anti-war movement should reconsider its tactics. This represented a clarity and realism that I found hopeful, given the stark challenges in front of us. The Bush war machine was an imposing juggernaut; to waste precious energy on ineffective, even counterproductive actions was to cripple our chances to ultimately prevail.

From this promising beginning, however, the writer leapt to calling for, among other things, "widespread urban rioting." Reading this, I wanted to shout, *Are you joking?* As if somehow the movement—already so disconnected from the marginalized as well as the mainstream in this country—could just conjure that up, as if war in Iraq was going to spark this!

Even in the 1960s, the riots were never instigated by the Vietnam War. They were generally ignited by more domestic matters: an incident of police brutality, the killing of Dr. King. Despite an appreciation of the righteous anger involved, people were painfully aware of the cost of destruction.

What worries me the most about this is the "macho" factor that is so often present. Even my beloved Clash anthem is infected: Are we really *"too chicken to even try it"*? Is this how to best frame the issue of taking back power we have allowed others to monopolize, as if revolution was some pumped-up game of "double dare"?

Action for its own sake, just because "something *has* to be done," is not justified. Tossing a rock because it feels good is understandable in emotional terms, but hardly laudable. Once again, recall the litmus test suggested back in Chapter One: Does a specific action advance the organizing and empowerment of people, the building of a movement that can change things? If so, great. If not, then it needs to be dumped, plain and simple.

We must also take care to guard against guilt-driven politics. According to former Panther leader Elaine Brown, Weatherman was pushed toward its extremist stance by racially charged goading by the likes of Panther exile Eldridge Cleaver. Safe in his Algerian haven, Brown charges, Cleaver was more than happy to sacrifice lives in pursuit of his grandiose vision of armed struggle; a "revolution now" vision that helped to split and cripple the Black Panther Party.

The same sort of guilt-tripping happens today—and can pass unchallenged. In August 2003, former WUO member Cathy Wilkerson—who, with Kathy Boudin, survived the townhouse bombing—told me, "I recently went to [a panel discussion] where a young woman . . . said that the way white people could really prove that they were genuine allies of black people was to do armed struggle. No one on or off the panel took her on—although I know that most people did not agree with her at all—so her impassioned rap sort of stood as the accepted position . . . I felt like it was 1969 again."

I have sensed this growing frustration, especially now that the rise of a powerful global-justice movement has been blunted by what former WUO luminary Bernardine Dohrn has called "a new imperialism" in post-9/11 America. I fear that this anger could spill over into self-defeating actions, especially if the 2004 elections result in four more years for Bush to complete his national security state. (If he loses, of course, we will face another lesser but still very real danger: the illusion that our work is somehow accomplished.)

A Bush victory seems frighteningly possible, given the present atmosphere in the U.S.A. If we don't wish to play into his administration's hands, we must think deeply, clearly, strategically. Our righteous, impatient rage (underlain by guilt) can pull us along, as it did for the WUO and so many others, down the deceptive short-cut-*cum*-dead end, fooling us into believing that the time is ripe for armed revolution.

The only real way to win against the state (as already noted, inherently organized, funded, and mobilized) is to have mass support. Even this is no guarantee of success as such movements also need adequate infrastructure, strategies, resources, allies. No group can move to armed struggle prematurely and expect to win. If we are not careful, we can alienate people and, as with the Tupamaro urban guerrillas in Uruguay, invite general repression that breaks the back of any broader movement, while sacrificing lives needlessly.

In fact, police agencies have made something of a cottage industry out of "agent provocateurs." These days, cops are using the "black bloc" as a cover for such skullduggery. As Starhawk explains in *Webs of Power*, the black bloc "is not an organization, but a tactic adopted in street protests where groups of demonstrators wear black and cover their faces for protection against surveillance and to demonstrate solidarity. The black bloc sometimes, but not always, engages in principled destruction of corporate property."

Starhawk rightly opposes any demonizing of this group. At the same time, her nuanced defense of their actions treads on very thin ice. As she admits, the black bloc has "perfected the art of looking like archetypal Anarchists: dressed in black, hooded, faces concealed, gas masks at their hips, they look dangerous and menacing—mindless violence personified." Needless to say, this image pushes all the wrong buttons in a post-9/11 North America. While I have many friends who have been part of the bloc, this style of protest-tending-toward-mayhem—often carried out under the cover of larger demonstrations, without the consent of those actions' organizers—is tailor-made for police exploitation.

This tactic has to be reconsidered. As even the Notes from Nowhere collective gingerly suggests in the "Clandestinity" section of *We Are Everywhere*, a growing trend toward clandestine and/or masked actions can play into the hands of authorities, while alienating us from the broader populace and undermining movement democracy and accountability.

As in 1969, a scary dynamic is playing out, one that goes far beyond the black bloc as such. Despairing of making converts quickly enough in the face of huge challenges, activists adopt "direct action" as their tool, often stepping behind masks to do so. These actions can be as noble and self-demanding as building a home in a tree targeted for the axe; or as wrong-headed as the burnings and bombings that drift dangerously toward outright terrorism.

As we saw in our earlier discussion of the Martinsville Wal-Mart eco-sabotage, some direct-actionists are honest enough to admit that they act out of rage, with little strategy to change the broader world. In the end, to whom are groups like the Earth Liberation Front and Animal Liberation Front accountable? How can such isolated, clandestine cells help engender a broader democratic revolution any more than the WUO did?

• • •

This brings us to the final turn of our wheel here, round to a powerful and perplexing rejoinder echoing back from the principled pacifist position. Near the end of *Pacifism As Pathology*, Ward Churchill identifies what "seems the highest order of contradiction, that in order to achieve nonviolence, we must first break with it in overcoming its root causes."

In other words, we use violence to end violence. Makes just about as much sense as "fighting for peace," or perhaps "fucking for virginity." If the pacifist faces many difficult practical questions, this is the major one with which any exponent of armed struggle must, in turn, wrestle.

A related issue is how we can get to real democracy, a world without oppressive force, by using military tools that are inherently anti-democratic and coercive. After all, a simple shift in power is hardly "revolutionary." Look at Vietnam today after its hard-won victory. Even correcting for the immense violence done by the U.S. during and since the war, is that the society we are working toward; is it a model of democracy and justice? Certainly not.

The WUO's rigid doctrine and internal discipline did not bode well for what they would have done, had they somehow been magically delivered into power. Once in control, you have to keep it—and there are few uglier or more corrupting processes in this world.

I wouldn't have wanted the WUO as my "revolutionary vanguard" ruler. As *You Can't Blow Up* suggests, their strategy would likely have produced an authoritarian regime, "because the people have not moved into the building of a democratic movement themselves . . . Unless a mass movement with democratic structures for running the country exists, then an elite will take power" after a violent overthrow. As David Gilbert concedes, "there is still no clear-cut successful model for combining the two critical needs of a fully democratic internal process and of tight discipline for fighting a ruthless state."

I don't have any fully satisfying answer either. Revolution is about affirming the humanity of all, the sacredness of life. War works best when denying humanity, demonizing the enemy; thus making them so much easier to kill without qualm or conscience. To me, revolution and war are profoundly at odds.

Any ideology has a tendency to become terribly theoretical, to slide toward the point where it connects to the flesh-and-blood world hardly at all, becoming just an intellectual exercise. It is the slippery slope where the ultimate revolutionary betrayal lurks; the sad, scary destination toward which Weatherman was lurching. This nightmare grows from what Anna Quindlen has called "ideology divorced from humanity."

In "Bloody Revolutions," the trailblazing UK anarcho-punks Crass ask, *"You talk about your revolution/But what are you going to be doing come the time?/Will you be the big man with the tommy gun?/Will you speak of freedom when the blood begins to run?"* This attack on the "authoritarian left" ends with a sarcastic rejoinder: *"The truth of revolution, brother . . . is year zero."*

Year Zero. This Khmer Rouge phrase is repeated over and over at the end of "Bloody Revolutions," slowly, painfully dragging to a halt. It meant nothing more, in essence, than the words of North American revolutionary Thomas Paine: "We have it in our power to begin the world over again." This, the most fervent dream of any would-be revolutionary, can be turned to nightmare by our willingness to value ideas more than human life.

This is the terrible danger of violence, especially paired with ideology. Once initiated, war takes on its own dynamic, pulling all along in a downward spiral of attack and retribution. Violence is a powerful but very limited tool; corrupting, corrosive to the soul. It is the antitheses of our hoped-for "new world."

David Gilbert has denounced early Weather's "sickening and inexcusable glorification of violence, which grievously contradicted the humanist basis for our politics and militancy." Other ex-members like Brian Flanagan have extended this retrospective criticism, noting the line that connects their actions to that of Oklahoma City bomber Timothy McVeigh or al-Qaeda. For Flanagan, the issue is *certainty.* Whenever we have too much of it, our dream of a better world for all can come to justify virtually any act, no matter how heinous.

Thus the freedom fighter becomes the bureaucrat, the executioner, the oppressor. *"Automatic weapons and a gospel of the truth"* turns dictatorial, even genocidal. There could be no more cruel betrayal of the love for humanity, that must be the heart of any true revolution. Don't get me wrong; if need be, I don't mind throwing a brick, as the Clash prescribed. But I don't mistake this for revolution, not by a long shot.

While violence may be legitimate, even necessary in certain circumstances, it cannot take the place of a political strategy that seeks to convert masses of people. Carried out correctly, armed struggle might be the final, inescapable outcome of a political process, not the circumvention of it. As *You Can't Blow Up* argues, "a developing mass movement will produce repression, but it will produce numbers of people with clear aims and the organized means of reaching them. It will be able to build far more lasting means of armed self-defense . . . A democracy can only be produced if a majority movement is built."

The relevant question, then, is less about violence versus nonviolence; it is about how to build a mass movement. Former "prisoner of war" Ed Mead has pointed out that in present-day North America, "Peaceful tactics comprise the only form of political struggle that can be sustained during this particular historic period. Armed actions [except for armed self-defense] would not further the struggle for justice at present, but they could plainly hurt it . . . We are nowhere near [a revolutionary] situation today."

JOIN A POSITIVE FORCE DC DISCUSSION GROUP STUDYING:

THE AMERICAN RADICAL

GREEN

ISSUE #15 - WI

$4 USA, $5 CANADA,
$6 EUROPE, $7 WORLD
FREE TO PRISONERS

ring The War Home!
Actions Against the War Machine

"Tomorrow, we must immediately take the war to the enemy, leave him no rest harassing him, cutting off his breath.

REVOLUTIONARY
ANTI-CAPITALIST
BLOC

EIGHT: THE AMERICAN IN ME

"The world is my country,
All men my brethren,
And to do good is my religion."
—Thomas Paine

The stench is what I remember most vividly now—burning rubber mixed with wood, paper, and human flesh.

Only moments before, all was different. I had heaved a long, exhausted sigh, buckling up my seat belt while sitting on the runway of D.C.'s National Airport. A long night of last-minute preparations and almost no sleep was now behind me. At last I could relax into a final breather before the trek that lay ahead.

Tomorrow—September 12, 2001—I would begin the second of three *Dance of Days* book tours at an arts center in Minneapolis, Minnesota. That meant 8000 miles in three weeks; 5000 of those by car, all by myself.

Still, I was excited. Slipping on some earphones, my thoughts drifted to dear friends I would soon see. I closed my eyes, reclined, and smiled. It would be so nice to get away from my intense work in D.C., reconnect with friends, have time to think, all while seeing the wide expanses of North America again.

My reverie was rudely interrupted by an airport representative who brusquely announced, "Gather up all your personal belongings. We are asking that you leave the plane immediately, as the airport will be closing at this time."

An audible groan passed through the plane. A couple hundred disgruntled air travelers rummaged around their seats, spilling out onto the tarmac to join an impromptu caravan headed to the airport's front doors.

I was probably grumbling more than most. *Just another bomb threat*, I thought. *We'll move outside, stand around for a few minutes, then come back in, go through the whole boarding rigamarole again.* The delay would doom me to miss my connection in Pittsburgh. I was exhausted, bone-tired.

Then I walked out of the front doors, into the smoky chaos. In that microsecond, everything else melted away. The smell was terrible, with clouds rising from a point just beyond our view, about a mile away where the Pentagon stood.

For a minute or so, I stopped thinking about my plans. Having grown up on a farm where we often burned discarded items, I knew my scents. *That's not just rubber or wood,* I thought grimly, *that smell is bodies.*

For a time, the world stopped. Hundreds milled about on the grassy slopes and asphalt streets outside the airport. People with cell phones began to report that planes had hit the World Trade Center and that it was on fire. A huge explosion had rocked the Pentagon, too, although no one knew just what had happened. One thing was soon clear: There wouldn't be any more planes flying today.

Making my way slowly back into D.C. by public transit, I saw the Pentagon on fire in the distance. I shuddered, thinking both of the many protests I had attended there and of Denise Baken, a friend from my Catholic parish, one of thousands employed at the building.

We rode in shocked silence. Finally, one African-American woman spoke up: "Well, at least maybe we will *finally* come together as a country now; get over all this black-versus-white garbage." A white man in business suit and tie across the aisle quickly agreed. As they chattered on, seeming to find hope out of tragedy, I was left feeling uneasy. *Unite around what, exactly?* I thought.

I had little time to process these complex emotions. A couple hours (and many quick decisions) later, I was on my way to Minnesota in the only transport I could find: a blue Camaro borrowed from a generous friend, racing to make the 1300-mile journey in time for my first event.

At every gas station, I found the same scene: a dozen or so people huddled around a TV set, watching the day's horror unfold in stunned silence. Back in the car, I took the (for me) radical step of turning on the radio, hoping for some news. When the talk grew too bloodthirsty and jingoistic, I turned it off.

Another response, increasingly visible as I went, was impossible to ignore. As if by silent command, the stars and stripes were going up everywhere, on highway overpasses, on billboards, even on cars. The phenom-enon left me a bit nervous, coming from a left-wing tradition that associates such display with right-wing views, with blinkered patriotism.

Somehow, though, this was deeper than simple politics. In the face of immense national trauma, people were reaching out for comfort, for connection, for community. Was it also the sign of a country set against the larger world, sliding toward blind revenge? I couldn't tell. Being a man on a mission, I didn't tarry with my thoughts. I hurtled on, heading west across America, past the fading day, through the darkness, searching for hope in a sea of flags.

In a way, that is where I have been ever since, where all of us on the left have been. While the wheel is still in motion, the short-term result of the terrorist attacks on September 11 was to profoundly solidify the position of a dubiously elected president, George W. Bush.

"Dubya" has cleverly used the tragedy to advance his far-right polit-ical agenda. Military build-up, stiff restrictions on civil liberties, and greatly expanded police powers have combined with two separate wars to bring the U.S. to the brink of the nearest thing to fascism since the darkest days of Richard Nixon.

Most frightening of all, this "war on terror" seems intended to be a war without end, not so different from the shadowy clashes that serve to justify the totalitarian state described in George Orwell's *1984*. Words like "empire" now roll off the lips, not of radicals, but of Bush administration–linked strategists. In this new day, they barely seek to disguise the imperial flavor of U.S. policy, but rather try to redefine it as a positive good. This is no small transformation, given that much of American tradition recoils from empire, born, as this nation was, out of an anti-imperial revolution.

The mere fact that some are becoming so bold as to step from behind the smoke and mirrors—albeit still cloaked in talk of spreading "democracy"—reveals the depth of our present danger. In this scary moment, the North American left faces its starkest challenge: Will we find a way to reach masses of North Americans, based out of what is best and true in our own tradition? Or will we surrender to an understand-able (but self-defeating) anti-Americanism, thereby playing into the hands of the Bush administration?

These point toward a deeper question: *Can the United States of America somehow be re-enlisted to the cause of revolution?*

Perhaps it is useful here to remember Antonio Gramsci's call for pessimism of the intellect mixed with optimism of the will. This task will not be easy. Still, I will argue that, given the current realities of power, North Americans must rediscover that which is most compassionate and democratic in our heritage, lest we—and our world—descend into a valley shadowed by countless unnecessary deaths.

Many of my comrades on the left might disagree, in practice as well as in principle. At least since the Vietnam War, our indigenous left has been tinged by a sometimes subtle but often very real anti-Americanism.

Take, for example, this call to action, drawing its images from Herman Melville's classic novel, *Moby Dick*: "I'm monomaniacal like Captain Ahab. He was possessed by one thought: destroying the great white whale. We should be like Captain Ahab and possess one thought—destruction of the mother country." This was how Weatherman Mark Rudd opened what became the final SDS conference, the Flint "war council" of December 1969.

To be fair, this statement placed Rudd on the fringes of the anti-war movement. Yet it was far from unprecedented. Indeed, during Vietnam-era demonstrations, the burning of the American flag—a symbolic representation of Rudd's call—became almost *de rigueur* within some activist circles. If flags are less often torched at domestic protests today, the underlying ambivalence remains.

In my experience, leftists make jokes about the flag; we don't tend to wear it. The concept of "nation" itself can seem suspect. Borders, after all, are just lines humans draw; only as real as we decide they should be. Too often they become walls keeping us apart, setting us against one another.

Radicals are right in resisting such nationalism. In seeking an inclusive global outlook, however, we can forget to meet people where they are. For most, nationality still matters immensely. To think we can transcend this with mere intellectualism, or without engaging in sensitive and sustained dialogue, is to delude ourselves; to indulge in deeply self-destructive illusion.

Nationalism is also not the same as patriotism, the simple love of and support for your country and its ideals; yet few in the contemporary left fully embrace the latter. More typical is the "Report Patriotism" poster done by Bay Area artist John Yates: While parodying Bush calls for citizen participation in thwarting terrorism, the work equates patriotism with jingoism. Another image—this one by Mike Flugennock, taken from D.C.'s Mintwood Media Collective 2004 calendar—has a pig in a U.S.A. hat, driving a bloody SUV (with stars and stripes prominently displayed) over a pile of Iraqi bodies.

D.C.'s own punk visionaries, the Nation of Ulysses, proclaimed (with tongue not entirely in cheek) a *12-Point Program to Destroy America*. One of the album's songs was "Target: U.S.A.," its title a brazen double dare echoing a hysterical book touting the terrorist threat to this country. While such right-wing screeds (also including Daniel Flynn's *Why the Left Hates America* and Ann Coulter's *Treason*) are often laughable, they also carry shreds of truth. Any well-informed person with a reasonably open mind and heart must carry some ambivalence about this country, given its often terrible history.

Beyond this bloody past, there is a garish, commercialized present: the corporate-ruled, consumption-mad America roasted by Kalle Lasn and others. Cigarettes, beer, automobiles, condoms: Everything sells better wrapped in the stars and stripes. "Shop for America," we are told. Far too often we obey, turning our supposed ideals into a tragic, eco-deadly farce.

Is America a dream or a nightmare? As James Cone suggests in his trailblazing book, *Martin & Malcolm & America* (Orbis, 1991), this is the question two of the great African-American leaders of the last century wrestled with throughout their public lives. King and Malcolm were a study in contrasts. Despite their differences, even opposition, the same fate awaited both: assassination. Malcolm X, the champion of black nationalism, fearless scourge of the "white devil," was cut down by his own. Meanwhile, King, equally courageous advocate of white and black working together for justice, was killed by a white man. America seemed without mercy, for "violent" or "nonviolent" alike.

Little or none of this is exactly as it seems, of course. We will soon circle back for a deeper look at how these two were linked, across their differences. In their "yin and yang," we might find a resolution for the uneasy mix of idealism and injustice that the United States of America represents.

In any case, I know this ambivalence intimately, having been raised to love this country. Something of an amateur historian as a youth, I soaked up patriotic tales of the American Revolution: Lexington, Concord, and "The Shot Heard 'Round the World"; Paul Revere's midnight ride; Crispus Attucks and the Boston Massacre; Betsy Ross and the flag; the Boston Tea Party; more.

This awe and wonder had a less savory side: disdain for others. I have a clear memory of standing in a Montana pasture on a gorgeous 4th of July morning; I was eight years old. Looking up at the sky, filled with pride, I felt profound pity for anyone unfortunate enough to be born anywhere else. The United States was number one; nobody else could quite measure up.

This arrogance began to fade to cynicism as the years passed, buffeted by Watergate, Vietnam, and other sordid affairs. Eventually, I began to use my indoctrination into American revolutionary idealism as a yardstick to measure the reality of my country. Not surprisingly, I found it wanting.

In 1976, a favorite teacher lured me into an American Legion speech contest on "How to Celebrate Our Bicentennial" with the promise of prize money. When she assured me that I wouldn't have to give the speech in public, but just before a small committee, I agreed. In a hastily scrawled set of remarks, I took the opportunity to suggest that America might celebrate the Bicentennial by truly living up to its ideals, not pretending to have already done so. Needless to say, I didn't win. Coming in third out of three contestants, I still managed to get five dollars out of it. *Not a bad bargain for a few minutes of work*, I thought.

However cynical I had become, the supposed ideals of my country nonetheless meant something to me, as I knew that they did, at least rhetorically, to many others. I really bought the American story, even made it mine! Looking back, I can now identify this as a key taproot of my present radicalism.

I cried visiting the Lincoln Memorial for the first time in 1984. There, carved in marble, were words that had come to mean so much: *"Government of the people, for the people, by the people."* The same happened at the Statue of Liberty, reading Emma Lazarus's famous inscription: *"Give me your tired, your poor, your huddled masses yearning to breathe free, the wretched refuse of your teeming shore. Send these, the homeless, the tempest-tost to me. I lift my lamp beside the golden door."*

Perhaps these tears were for my own innocence lost. Underneath my teen-punk skepticism, I still believed enough in this country to go to an elite school like SAIS in the mid-1980s, to entertain a career in the Foreign Service, even to work on Capitol Hill for a time. *I will fight from within,* I thought, *I will uphold human rights and democracy against all odds, no matter what.*

It was a seductive thought, and not entirely wrong. No doubt others can take this path wholeheartedly—but not, it turned out, me. As I walked amidst the poverty, violence, and desperation of Shaw, the South Bronx, Guatemala, El Salvador, and Gaza, it became increasingly difficult to see my residual American idealism as anything more than a way to justify my own career ambitions. Eventually I had seen enough to worry that our very position in the world would inevitably keep us from actually living our ideals.

As I wrote in a "goodbye to it all" speech intended for my 1986 SAIS graduation ceremony, "My greatest fear is not that we as a nation have often betrayed our ideals—that I know to be true—but that we now, by our very position in the world, can do little but betray them. How can we stand for equality? We are the elite. How can we stand for justice? We benefit, more than most, from the current unjust world order. How, indeed, can we stand for democracy? Other countries might democratically choose actions against our interests . . . In the end, I fear, we do only what serves our interests and preserves our lifestyles."

(This speech, too, was rejected by an unsympathetic committee; a less-confrontational student address was chosen. Determined to have my say, I asked a close friend to type out the speech, added a drawing of a teary-eyed Statue of Liberty borrowed from a Dead Kennedys record, and made copies. Disdaining cap and gown for a Guatemalan shirt and blue jeans, I handed my speech out at the graduation, much to the consternation of some who attended.)

I still don't have an entirely satisfactory answer to why North Americans would embrace change if it might threaten our privileged lifestyles. In this way, songs like the Nation of Ulysses' "Target: U.S.A." or Fugazi's "Smallpox Champion" (referring to the infamous distribution of smallpox-infected blankets by some white settlers to Native Americans) make sense to me. Maybe the United States couldn't be part of the solution; no, not if *we* were the problem.

"The American in Me," a song by the early Bay Area punk group, the Avengers, expressed this bluntly: *"It's the American in me/That makes me watch the blood/Coming out of the bullet holes in his head/It's the American in me/That makes me watch TV . . . It's the American in me/That says it's an honor to die/In a war that is just some politician's lie/It's the American in me/That never wonders why . . ."*

From this perspective, my once-precious identity as a citizen of the United States of America took on a decidedly less hopeful hue. No longer was I an heir to a legacy of revolution, democracy, and human rights. Instead, "the American in me" became almost a disease, a brokenness that needed to be cut out, conquered, cured—anything but celebrated.

Yet something of my past lingered, together with a nagging practical question: *If we give up on any possible redemption of this country, what is our alternative?*

Some people seem to have an answer—but it is not a pretty one. Listen to Ward Churchill, for example: "On 9/11, nineteen guys equipped with thirty dollars of box cutters did one trillion dollars worth of damage to the structure of the U.S. economy, did more bleeding, in the terms of value that [the system] understands, than every boycott and every march and every campaign that we have undertaken since Vietnam. And they did it in about twenty minutes."

Lest Churchill's apparent cheerleading for the mass destruction of civilian life and property be misunderstood, he adds, "If [the left] had been more effectual in some sense at some point, this might not have been necessary. But as it stands, it was absolutely necessary and it was absolutely empowering."

All of this and more is captured on an AK Press/Alternative Tentacles spoken-word CD entitled, *Pacifism and Pathology in the American Left*. This 2003 sequel to the *Pacifism As Pathology* book—recorded live on November 16, 2001—showcases Churchill's verbal skill and macho swagger to horrifying effect.

Churchill begins his speech wearing a "stars and stripes" hard hat given to him as a gag gift by the event organizers. Sadly, he discards any concern for the loss of North American lives just as quickly as he tossed aside the helmet. For him, it is all very simple: U.S. criminality, combined with the functioning of its economic system, results in millions of "rotting, stinking corpses all over the world."

Churchill zeroes in on the suffering of Iraq, where the people have endured a U.S. war, followed by punishing sanctions, and, since March 2003, U.S. invasion and occupation. In an odd echo of Bush administration rationalizations, Churchill evokes Iraqi pain to justify actions taken by outsiders; in this case, al-Qaeda. Left unsaid is that Osama bin Laden's post-9/11 communiqué focused as much on the irksome presence of U.S. troops near holy sites in Saudi Arabia and the plight of the Palestinians as on Iraq. Also glossed over is the fact that while both bin Laden and Saddam Hussein are former U.S. allies, as Islamic fundamentalist and Leninist secularist, respectively, they are also deadly enemies.

Churchill blithely merges these two very distinct parties into one very murky entity: "Even if they get beat, what matters is that they actually drew blood where it counted. Because it is their blood being shed out there." While the exact identity of this "they" remains a bit shadowy, Churchill's message to U.S. citizens is far less so: "If you want your children to be safe, stop killing other people's babies, or looking the other way while they die."

Dismissing "knuckle-headed Americans," Churchill deems the World Trade Center to have been a legitimate military target by pointing to the presence of one of world's major bond trading companies in the Twin Towers. Lest we get too attached to the humanity of such people, Churchill describes them as "little Eichmanns . . . technicians that make the New World Order function" and thus have blood on their hands. Not-quite-so-Nazi-ish people like janitors and fire fighters are categorized as "collateral damage" in Churchill's best imitation of the North American leaders he despises.

Challenged by some in the crowd, Churchill seems to give ground, only to turn the point back around: "Yes, a single action like 9/11 is insufficient to accomplish anything—it needs to be followed up on." Describing this as the crowd's "homework assignment," Churchill eggs them on, urging them to "get busy." While he never clarifies what that exactly means, the implication is clear: Now is time to strike, while the American Leviathan is staggering, off-balance—and to strike in a way that is somehow analogous to 9/11.

This echoes Weatherman's 1960s belief in Third World revolution "encircling the pitiful, helpless giant," with mother country radicals striking blows at the heart of the beast, helping to bring it crashing down. In this parallel, Churchill plays the role of Eldridge Cleaver, goading others to ill-defined action. What might emerge from the chaos seems of little import; surely it *must* be better.

Incredibly, Churchill is not alone in this. "Bring the War Home," trumpets *Green Anarchy*, an Oregon-based "Anti-civilization Journal of Theory and Action" with a circulation of 9000; "It's time to move from protest to RESISTANCE!!" This evocation of Weatherman is no accident; the group disseminates a publication touting the Weather Underground and Black Liberation Army as "Forgotten Heroes" through its Green Anarchy Distribution Center. (Beyond works by the Unabomber and others about various "urban guerrilla" groups, a talk by Ward Churchill is also available. The wry '80s-era bumper sticker *"U.S. Out of North America"* being no longer sufficient, the video is entitled, *U.S. Off the Planet.*)

The pages of *Green Anarchy* are littered with rage-soaked celebrations of deaths of U.S. soldiers in Iraq, political assassinations, and other attacks on "pigs" (odd language for a publication that celebrates the Animal Liberation Front), with calls for economic sabotage, including not only computer systems but the electrical grid itself. In critiquing the overall failure of battles with police at recent mass demonstrations, the journal's editors note that some advise "that we abandon these activities for more underground and illegal action, while others wish for [protesters] to become more autonomous, elusive, prepared, and destructive at these events." *Green Anarchy* seems to favor "a holistic approach in which we will be able to successfully strike on multiple fronts." In the end, the coming collapse of civilization will make way for a new and better world order.

Forgive us knuckle-headed Americans if we don't share such blood-red-tinted optimism! As *You Can't Blow Up a Social Relationship* asserts, "The total collapse of this society would provide no guarantee about what replaced it. Unless a majority of people had the ideas and organization sufficient for the creation of an alternative society, we would see the old world reassert itself, because it is what people would be used to, what they believed in, what existed unchallenged in their own personalities."

Even *You Can't Blow Up* overlooks a far more mundane but hardly insignificant reality. Given the unavoidable massive disruption in food production brought about by a social collapse, this is one of the few scenarios that might guarantee far more people dying than under the current system. In the case of the United States, one also has to worry about small matters like nuclear weapons being used in desperation or otherwise going astray.

The idea of economic sabotage itself is deeply problematic. Is the economy our enemy? If so, how do we intend to feed, house, clothe, and educate people, to provide jobs and health care? Except in very specific circumstances, such tactics are understandably unpopular, even among the poor, simply because of the suffering they inevitably create.

Recall that war kills not simply by direct wounds, but indirect as well; money spent on the military can't meet more pressing needs. If this is so, an analogous impact is also true: Money lost due to sabotage can't be put toward meeting human needs. Set aside for the moment the massive financial cost of 9/11. According to *USA Today*, "monkey wrenches" such as computer viruses and worms have cost over $209 billion in the past five years. Properly directed—no easy task, I'll admit, but doable, with enough mass support—this sum alone could feed the world's hungry populations.

Even amidst the mania of 1969, this faith in the redemptive power of chaos hardly seemed a successful approach. Today, it faces at least one key additional problem. Ex-WUO militant Cathy Wilkerson correctly notes, "Now the wave of violence sweeping the world is reactionary," committed by the likes of al-Qaeda, Hamas, Islamic Jihad, and other fundamentalists.

The bloom has clearly gone off the global revolutionary rose. In 2004, we are no longer talking about Che Guevara or even Ho Chi Minh. With the exception of Mexico's EZLN, we are left with failed authoritarian left butchers like Saddam Hussein and fundamentalists like Osama bin Laden. Such are hardly true friends to those they claim to represent, much less to anyone on the North American left.

While fundamentalist groups are, in some sense, an understandable response to injustice and dislocation wrought by globalization and modernization, we should not fool ourselves with any romantic depiction of them, their means, or their ends. As Todd Gitlin has pointed out, "The murderers [of 9/11] did not, like the Vietnamese of the '60s and '70s, distinguish between the American people and the American government." Let us not make the same mistake.

Given this, what could reassert itself after a "collapse" might be an "old world" indeed—medieval, in fact. On the domestic front, outright fascism is far more likely than some kinder, gentler, egalitarian outcome.

While I understand (and, to a large degree, share) the rage at American blindness and self-centeredness that drives Churchill and *Green Anarchy*, this raw emotion is not innately constructive. In fact, it is not even remotely helpful, given the legitimate grief and immense trauma experienced.

I also know that it is not easy to strike a balance here. Nonetheless, this is what I tried to do while on my book tour in the days directly after the 9/11 attacks. Each night I began by dedicating the event to Sandra Foster, daughter of Barbara Hill, a key African-American pillar of my Catholic parish, St. Aloysius. Life in the North Capitol community that borders St. Al's can be harsh and unforgiving. Raising her kids amidst this chaos, across from the embattled Sursum Corda, Barbara did the very best that she could. Sandra wanted out of that dead-end world and, with her mother's support, chose a path familiar to many in her community: the U.S. military; in this case, the Department of Defense (DOD).

It was a bit of a devil's bargain, perhaps, but no one else was offering to pay for college. Through the DOD, Sandra found a path to an education and a decent-paying desk job. It was there that she was killed when the plane hit the Pentagon; the third of Barbara's four children to die in the past decade.

By telling this story, I wanted to honor Barbara, Sandra, and all those who died or lost loved ones on 9/11, while also challenging racism—but I didn't stop there. I went on to tell the story of a priest I had known, Fr. Segundo Montes, who taught at the Catholic University in El Salvador. Montes was dragged from his bed and murdered together with five of his fellow priests, their housekeeper, and her daughter, in November 1989. They were killed by U.S.-trained soldiers with U.S.-made weapons bought with U.S. tax money—just a few of the thousands of innocent victims of that government-sponsored terror campaign.

Next I talked about the Jabaliya refugee camp in the Gaza Strip. This dismal place was (and remains) a breeding ground for Hamas, the fundamentalist group now infamous for their suicide bombings. While visiting a hospital there, my North American delegation had been confronted by a distraught Palestinian mother. As her teenage boy lay broken and bleeding on a dirty cot nearby—victim of an Israeli army supported by my taxes—she screamed at us, "What are you doing here? You are the ones who are killing our sons!"

All of these stories were tragedies. None of them were to be dismissed, somehow justified. The point was not to choose who mattered, but rather to mourn the loss, and find a way to stop the bloodletting. While the North American people must surely open their eyes to the broader suffering in the world (and their role in it), this is not likely to happen by insulting them or dismissing their own legitimate pain.

The left is not always sensitive to this. As *You Can't Blow Up* argues, "Leftists are inclined to dismiss people's outrage [at terrorist attacks] as 'reactionary.' But the killing of schoolchildren, placing of bombs in underground stations, or machine-gunning people at an airport cannot be dismissed, no matter what the context. People's response is, on the whole, genuine moral outrage." If we are not careful, this anger can be manipulated "into a law and order hysteria which allows [repressive] legislation to be passed and the left to be crushed."

This process is already well underway in the U.S.A. A left that adopts the wrong-headed approaches of Ward Churchill or *Green Anarchy* might just as well sign over the deed to this whole country—lock, stock, and 10,000+ nuclear-armed barrels—to the most right-wing, militaristic elements of our society.

What, then, does the concept of "the United States of America" mean? Who gets to define it? Is it possible to reach past the ugliness and betrayal to the beauty and possibility? As Martin Luther King, Jr. and Malcolm X knew, these are not academic questions, but matters of life and death.

To be sure, King and Malcolm X were often not in agreement. King embraced the concept of America. According to biographer James Cone, "No one has communicated the idea of the American dream with greater moral and oratorical power, with greater political and religious imagination, than Martin Luther King, Jr. . . . [His] 'I Have a Dream' speech captured the imagination of America." As a result, Cone argues, King "became the symbol, not only of the civil rights movement, but of America itself: symbol of a land of freedom where people of all races, creeds, and nationalities could live together as 'beloved community.'" This America was far from realized, but King believed that it could be.

King was hardly the only African-American to embrace this idealism. Even Frederick Douglass, a former slave who blistered blind patriotism in his famous "Fourth of July" address, carried this torch. According to historian Waldo E. Martin, Jr., against the claims of white racists, Douglass "envisioned a radically different concept of America as a vastly more open and inclusive composite nationality truly belonging to all and transcending divisive categories like race, religion, gender, class, and national origin."

Another example is the poet Langston Hughes, who once called for a "U.S.S.A."—United Socialist States of America—and often evoked the American dream. Hughes's epic poem, "Let America Be America Again"—written in 1938, amidst economic depression and Jim Crow segregation—captures a mix of heart-wrenching failure and immense power in the American idea as few have done, before or since. King acknowledged that lines like, *"Oh, let America be America again/The land that never has been yet/And yet must be/The land where every [one] is free,"* helped form his own vision.

King's seemingly unshakeable faith in America was not shared by Malcolm X. Only months after King's famous address to some 200,000 people at the 1963 March on Washington, Malcolm X responded at a Methodist Church in Cleveland, Ohio: "No, I'm not an American. I'm one of the 22 million black people who are the victims of . . . this American system. And I see America through the eyes of the victim. I don't see any American Dream; I see an American nightmare!"

The nonviolent exhortations of King have been endlessly juxtaposed against the "by any means necessary" approach of Malcolm X; the latter's "ballot versus the bullet" is the most concise rendition of the split. This divergence reflected not only differences in religion but in class origins as well. King came from a more privileged background: the son of a Southern Baptist minister, raised to follow in his father's footsteps. Malcolm, by contrast, was the child of a broken home, and grew up in urban poverty in the North, where millions of blacks had migrated seeking a better life. Embittered by the failure of this "promised land," he turned to a life of crime, was arrested and incarcerated. While in prison, Malcolm joined the Nation of Islam.

As Cone notes, however, "Popular images of Martin and Malcolm seldom acknowledge their movement toward each other and their break with earlier deeply held convictions about America." According to Cone, the two "came to appreciate each other's views about America."

Practically speaking, Malcolm's wrenching split from the Nation of Islam and subsequent pilgrimage to Mecca—where he was surrounded by Muslims of all races—helped him to reassess King's view. In his last year of life, Malcolm X cooled his rhetoric and embraced the civil rights struggle. He even stepped toward what could have been a powerful alliance with King.

Malcolm X's murder, combined with both white resistance to the civil rights struggle as it moved north and the outbreak of urban rioting, helped to open King's eyes to the depth of racism, economic injustice, and desperation in the United States. By the fall of 1965, King was beginning to leave behind his more romantic version of the American Dream for a deeper, more demanding vision.

King now began to see the insidious connections between racism, poverty, and militarism. This insight became dangerous to the establishment when he began to speak out, first against the Vietnam War (over the objections of many more cautious civil rights leaders) and then in a call for a multi-class, multiracial "March on Poverty."

This effort, "The Poor Peoples' Campaign," was intended to move the civil rights struggle into a new arena, pressing questions of economic justice, even economic democracy. King now acknowledged the elephant in the living room of the supposedly "classless" United States of America. How was democracy in the voting booth possible without at least rough equality in the financial realm? King didn't know the answer, but couldn't ignore the problem.

Given King's support within black and white circles, he was uniquely situated to help turn his ideal into reality. It is no surprise that King was soon deemed "the most dangerous man in America" by FBI Director J. Edgar Hoover. In the midst of mounting federal surveillance and harassment, King fell to an assassin's bullet while supporting a janitors' strike in Memphis.

As with the killing of Malcolm X, however, King's death could not defeat his vision. While King surely grew more radical in the last years of his life, never did he surrender his idea of America. If anything, he made it even more insistent, challenging, and universal, no doubt in part as a response to the resistance he encountered.

In his famous "Beyond Vietnam" speech in New York City, a year to the day before his assassination, King charged the U.S. government with being "the greatest purveyor of violence in the world today." After mourning the destruction of the War on Poverty by the war in Vietnam and quoting Langston Hughes, King called for Americans to support "the world revolution." The fiery speech ended with King explicitly endorsing a "radical revolution of values" in the U.S.A. that would take us past narrow loyalty to "one's tribe, race, class, and nation."

This global stance, King made clear, was implicit in the original vision of this country's founders. Such words did little to quiet the FBI's fears, but they do reveal the effective convergence between King and Malcolm X.

As King moved to deeper critique and confrontation in the last year of his life, Malcolm X had begun to entertain the notion that America could be saved in his final months. As he told biographer Alex Haley not long before his death, "Sometimes I have dared to dream . . . that one day history may even say that my voice—which disturbed the white man's smugness, and his arrogance, and his complacency—that my voice helped to save America from a grave, possibly even fatal, catastrophe."

Both leaders agreed that transforming America would not be easy, but was possible and necessary. Sadly, the two met in person only once, in the year before Malcolm's assassination. Nonetheless, the power of their converging visions still resounds. In the end, Cone argues, they were like "two solders fighting their enemies from different angles of vision, each pointing out the other's blind spots and correcting the other's errors. They needed each other."

Just as we need their shared vision today: a vision rising from the experience of the North American people, expressed in our language; speaking truth with the aim of redeeming the soul of a nation that has strayed from its professed path.

In other words, we need a recognizably North American radicalism, one that evokes not simply the nightmare, but also the dream.

It is useful to know that this country is hardly alone in its ugly past. The history of nations, it seems, is written in rivers of blood. It is appropriate that we focus on our own wrong-doings (as we share special responsibility for them), but hardly to the exclusion of others. This would be ahistorical and unbalanced, anything but revolutionary.

It is true that the gap between ideal and reality has been especially pronounced in the United States. Perhaps our atrocities should stand out with greater relief in that arguably few countries have expressed such a lofty idealism as this country. In order to narrow this gap, *we need to know and claim our own revolutionary heritage, our own radical history.*

Take the American Revolution, for example. According to historian Gordon Wood in *The American Revolution* (Random House, 2002), "It has become fashionable to deny that anything substantially progressive came out of the Revolution. Instead, some historians today are more apt to stress [its] failures . . . As one . . . recently put it, the Revolution 'failed to free the slaves, failed to offer full political equality to women . . . failed to grant citizenship to Indians and failed to create an economic world in which all could compete on equal terms.'" As Wood then notes, "Such anachronistic statements suggest a threshold of success that no 18th-century revolution could have possibly attained, and perhaps tell us more about the political attitudes of the historians who make such statements than they do about the American Revolution."

Indeed, as Wood argued in an earlier, Pulitzer Prize—winning book, *The Radicalism of the American Revolution* (Random House, 1991), "If we measure the radicalism by the amount of social change that actually took place—by transformations in the relationships that bound people to each other—then the American Revolution was not conservative at all; on the contrary, it was as radical and social as any revolution in history. Indeed it was a momentous upheaval that not only fundamentally altered the character of American society, but decisively affected the course of subsequent history."

This, Wood points out, helped to bring about massive changes, both here and abroad: "The Revolution made possible the anti-slavery and women's rights movements of the nineteenth century and . . . all our current egalitarian thinking." The scholar sums up by noting, "The Revolution . . . also destroyed aristocracy as it had been understood in the Western world for at least two millennia. The Revolution bought respectability and even dominance to ordinary people long held in contempt and gave dignity to their menial labor in a manner unprecedented in history and to a degree not equaled elsewhere in the world. The Revolution did not only eliminate monarchy and create republics, it actually reconstituted what Americans meant by public or state power and brought about an entirely new kind of popular politics." It is this base we are called to build upon, to challenge the U.S.A.—in the words of Martin Luther King, Jr.—"to rise up and live out the true meaning of its creed" of human equality.

It has helped me immensely to know that, as the editors of *The American Radical* anthology (Routledge, 1994) note, "In every generation men and women of diverse upbringings and identifications have stood to challenge oppression and exploitation and to reassert the fundamental proposition that 'We the people' shall rule. However varied their respective concerns and aspirations, America's radical activists, writers, and artists have conducted a long and continuing struggle to expand both the 'we' in 'We the people' and the democratic process through which 'the people' can genuinely govern."

In 1775, Thomas Paine debated whether to address his concerns about slavery and women's rights in *Common Sense*, the pamphlet that, more than any other single document, helped to ignite the Revolution. Abigail Adams lobbied her husband, John, about women's oppression even as the "Founding Fathers" debated the form of government for the new nation. In the end, this structure borrowed many of its particulars from the Iroquois Confederacy. From the very outset of the United States of America, some were aware of the contradictions and half-victories involved in their Revolution and strained to press past them. What more natural process could there be; is this not the essence of what might be called revolution?

This might seem irrelevant were it not for the unpleasant reality of post-9/11 America. As the flags suggest, there are millions out there who buy into this "American Dream" on some deep level. The story (or "myth," if you will) of this country matters to them; it is the language they know, the ideals they acknowledge, however incompletely and inconsistently. *This story, then, is a powerful, perhaps essential, place from which to struggle for transformation.*

Our political opponents know this. As *The American Radical* states, "A prominent feature of the New Right's attacks and their efforts to mobilize support has been the use and abuse of history." They have been very successful in this; just note how the flag as a symbol seems to have been ceded to them! Fortunately, this is not the whole story. As Mari Jo Buhle and the other editors of *The American Radical* argue, "Given the nation's foundations in revolution and the recurring role of radicalism in its development, the [North American] radical tradition cannot be completely suppressed or denied."

We can obscure this history by our actions, however, as North American socialist firebrand Norman Thomas knew all too well. The man dubbed "the conscience of America" by the *New York Times*, Thomas struggled for fifty years to keep a fading socialist flame alive in the U.S., risking prison, even death. Gary Dorrien has written,

> Near the end of his life, while taking part in demonstrations against America's war in Vietnam, Thomas was distressed by the character of much of the anti-war movement, which struck

him as childishly vulgar and anti-American. His speech to the National Student Association in 1967 summarized his message to a younger generation: "I don't like the sight of young people burning the flag of my country, the country I love," he said. "If they want an appropriate symbol they should be washing the flag, not burning it."

Can the stars and stripes be claimed as a radical symbol? Perhaps so, even if this rubs uncomfortably against the left-wing grain. Even more than the flag, we need to know and honor our prophets, women and men like Ella Jo Baker, Malcolm X, Martin Luther King, Jr., Thomas Paine, Sojourner Truth, John Brown, Michael Harrington, Paul Robeson, Emma Goldman, Woody Guthrie, Ida B. Wells, Norman Thomas, Abbie Hoffman, Audre Lorde, Frederick Douglass, Cesar Chavez, Eugene Debs, Elizabeth Gurley Flynn, and so many others.

If this seems to veer perilously close to North American chauvinism, don't despair. King's "Beyond Vietnam" speech suggests such a radical patriotism can transcend mere nationalism. James Cone explains that King's dream "was not nationalistic, it was universal . . . [It] spilled over the boundaries of the United States. King urged Americans to 'develop a world perspective.' 'We are caught up in an inescapable network of mutuality, tied to a single garment,' he cried out. 'What affects one directly, affects all indirectly.'"

King saw this was no innovation, for a universal call to recognize and respect connectedness was implicit in the declaration that "all men are created equal." Such a claim had not only global relevance, but an inevitably subversive impact as well, corrosive to any form of oppression. Such ideas helped to set the stage for the current international human rights movement. In this way, to be American is not to necessarily deny any other's equal value; indeed, it is to assert a common destiny of freedom and justice.

Not surprisingly, this dream has had global repercussions. Former King ally Andrew Young has noted, "When the Berlin wall came down, they were singing 'We Shall Overcome,' when the Polish shipyard workers went on strike, they were singing 'We Shall Overcome,' when the students went to Tiananmen Square they wrote 'We shall overcome' on their T-shirts." In a world where the blossoming of corporate logos seems the most visible measure of North American influence, such an insight is heartening, to say the least. King is hardly our only such gift to the world; recall that Vietnamese revolutionaries quoted our *Declaration of Independence* nearly two centuries later.

In fact, this vision actually predates the *Declaration of Independence* in the North American tradition. It certainly appears in the writings of Thomas Paine, who historian Harvey Kaye has called "the first international revolutionary." For Paine, every spot of the world was shadowed by oppression, with freedom always on the run. As a result, he argued in *Common Sense* that "the cause of America is in great measure the cause of all mankind." This was not by way of an imperial America imposing its will on all, but as a model and refuge.

Paine later lived out this universal trajectory of the American Revolution by joining the French Revolution and agitating in Great Britain. His motto was simple: "The world is my country, all men my brethren, and to do good is my religion." Once updated with more inclusive language, this seems perhaps the best expression of North American revolutionary idealism.

Radical patriot Paul Robeson—who sacrificed his entertainment career rather than compromise his revolutionary beliefs—celebrated this country's diversity in one of his biggest hits, "Ballad for Americans." Scholar Lamont Yeakey recounts that this song, written by John La Touche and Earl Robinson, with lyrics identifying the various ethnic groups comprising the population of the United States, was so popular that it sold more copies during World War II than Kate Smith's "God Bless America."

Robeson was nevertheless hounded by the government, and his concerts were sometimes met by right-wing mob violence. Under investigation, Robeson was asked by a Congressional critic why he didn't move to Russia. He retorted, "Because my father was a slave, and my people died to build this country . . . I am going to stay here and have a part just like you."

Our contemporary left would do well to reclaim such stubborn determination. It lives on in figures like filmmaker Michael Moore, who spoke out against Bush policy in Iraq at the Academy Awards in 2003. Asked why he had done so, despite pleas beforehand from event organizers to refrain from politicking, as well as boos during his remarks, Moore replied simply, "Because I'm an American."

The United States is more than a collection of its contradictions and failings; it is also the sum of its dreams. From across the world, people have come to this country, leaving their homes, risking their lives. Some fled from war or oppression; others sought economic opportunity; most come here carrying hopes and visions. It is they who have built the U.S.A., in all its glory and folly.

Perhaps, then, "the American in me" can be a seed of hope, even revolution.

The radical legacy of this country is our right to claim; our responsibility to uphold and fulfill. Beyond the bloody betrayals, there is still an America being born, an idea that is worth fighting for, something in which to believe. As Langston Hughes wrote:

O, yes,
I say it plain,
America never was America to me,
And yet I swear this oath—
America will be!
An ever-living seed,
Its dream
Lies deep in the heart of me.

NINE: LOVERS OF THE PEOPLE

*"We represent the kind of patriotism which loves America with open eyes. We
love her beauty, we love her riches, we love her mountains and forests, and
above all, we love the people who have produced her wealth and riches, who
have created all her beauty . . . who are giving America liberty."*
— Emma Goldman

The funeral was crowded, with many of those attending forced
to stand.

A broad cross section of this sparsely populated agricultural
community had gathered on a Saturday afternoon in March. All were
here to pay their respects after the sudden death of a fourteen-year-old
girl, Janis Salisbury.

The father of the deceased, Rodney Salisbury, was a well-known
and respected town resident—twice elected to the office of sheriff and
now a candidate for state governor. Despite her father's relative stature
and influence, the teenager had died of complications following a
ruptured appendix.

Such untimely deaths were hardly unknown. Few in the area were well
off, and medical help was scarce. Indeed, local cemeteries contained
scores of graves of those who had never even made it past infancy.

This, however, was hardly your average small-town funeral.

The ceremony was held not in a church, but in the local "Farm-
Labor Temple." No priest or minister presided. Indeed, no religious
symbolism was apparent anywhere. This shouldn't have been
surprising, given that the elder Salisbury was a leader of the local
Communist Party. Janis herself had been a militant in the Young
Pioneers, a "red" version of the Girl Scouts.

According to a glowing account of the event in a local newspaper,
the *Producers News*, "The windows and stage were covered with red and

black drapings, decorated with hammer-and-sickle emblems. Over the flowers on the coffin [was] draped the Red Flag . . . Led by the Young Pioneers, the audience rose and participated in the singing of [Communist anthem] 'The International.'"

A local farmer, "Comrade" Hans Ramussen, opened the service with a few remarks mourning the community's loss. This was followed by a rendition of the youth group's "valiant fighting song . . . 'Young Pioneers Are Gay.'" The head of the local Party, Erik Bert, gave a rousing eulogy, pointing out the qualities which had made Janis Salisbury "so true and unwavering a young Bolshevik."

Bert then called on the audience to "follow her example of devotion and self-sacrifice for the working class," fondly reprising the young Salisbury's most fervent vow: "I swear it by the Revolution!" After one more song by the Pioneers—"Red Flag"—and a goodbye by Salisbury's Pioneer cohort, Karenina Petersen, the services closed with another rendition of "The International."

The crowd then walked out the doors—and onto the dirt streets of Plentywood, the major hub of Sheridan County, Montana, 1932. This era is not often mentioned back home. Nor does it live on in any obvious political sense. While often suspicious of government and big business, Sheridan County today is no radical hotbed. Probably not since Minnesotan Hubert Humphrey ran in 1968 has a majority of my county even voted for a Democratic presidential candidate.

Nonetheless, according to historian Charles Vindex, in the decade before the Great Depression, Sheridan County "became widely known as the only American community actually governed by practicing 'reds' who, far from concealing their radicalism, proclaimed it through the columns of a uniquely militant newspaper, the *Producers News*."

A product of the People's Publishing Company, and headed up by a charismatic mountain of a man, Charles Taylor, the *Producers News* helped catalyze what was, in its way, a small revolution. "After 1922, when Rodney Salisbury, Taylor's lieutenant, was elected sheriff," Vindex notes, "Sheridan County became a secure haven for laborers who moved with the harvest. Many were 'wobblies'—members of the [Industrial] Workers of the World (IWW)—determined men who carried red cards and took the rights of Labor seriously."

Vindex continues: "In a sense an American underground, 'wobblies' were repeatedly subjected to murderous attack." Indeed, in

1917, IWW organizer Frank Little had been lynched in Butte, a western Montana town.

The Non-Partisan League, an agrarian socialist group that ran nearby North Dakota for most of a decade, set the stage for the *Producers News*. It is worth noting that this upsurge in many ways predated the Russian Revolution, and only later became more narrowly "Communist." This shift actually helped to doom the movement, and can serve as a cautionary tale.

The ideological specifics here are less important, I think, than a more fundamental question. If a militant socialist movement could win a series of elections in Sheridan County—as it did over the 1920s—why not anywhere?

I offer up this snippet from the history of my home county to make a point: *Under the right circumstances, average people will support radical politics.* This may appear unlikely in a nation apparently on a steady march to the political right. The range of acceptable debate these days is largely framed by the Republican Party; it is not always clear that a Democratic Party still exists.

Given that the left claims to be of and for "the people"—as opposed to the corporations or the rich—this is no small matter, especially since we *need* mass support to counterbalance the inherent power and organization of our more monied opponents. Yet our actions too often make our populist rhetoric sound hollow. As a result, the left has shrunk to near irrelevance in the U.S.A.

To remedy this, we might begin by simply admitting that there is an inherent tension in the relation of the would-be revolutionary to "the people." No one becomes an activist, much less a radical, without a critique, however shallow or incomplete. We experience something as unjust, and we seek to change that; it is a simple trajectory, really. Quickly, however, we tend to run into a problem: Other people are not necessarily so eager to embrace our preferred change.

Radical democracy strives for broad, ongoing participation, especially at the grassroots; even a consensus process where possible. True solidarity presupposes actual concern with the wants, needs, and desires of marginalized people. We have to love and honor people as they are, not just for what we think they can become.

John Lennon's "Working Class Hero" was an anthem of mine in my early activist years. This scathing critique of working-class society climaxes with these lines: *"Keep you doped with religion and sex and TV/And you think you're so clever and classless and free/But you're still fucking peasants as far as I can see."*

This dismissal—not so far, in its way, from the view of Weatherman—was how I viewed Sheridan County in 1979. I was saying goodbye and good riddance to my home and all that it represented. I was primed, in other words, to become that which I had been raised to scorn: a campus radical, a bohemian.

I now see this all a bit differently, and even have pride in where I come from. I acknowledge the plain-spoken wisdom of many common folks, surviving, building families, making do with little or nothing. Above all, I recognize the dignity of working with one's hands, of doing the tedious, backbreaking, low-paying (but essential) jobs few others wish to do.

What is it to the world if we shed all but a few of our lobbyists, lawyers, punk rock bands, politicians, or (anti)manifesto writers? Not much, I'd say. But can we spare the people who grow and harvest our food, build our houses and roads, make our clothing, pick up our garbage? Not at all. The lives and views of the working class thus have to be a central plank in the foundation of any revolution.

This, of course, does not mean that we just accept the (often racist, sexist, homophobic, etc.) status quo if most such folks seem fine with it. No, we also need to honor our truth, our own vision; even if this is a minority view—as, for example, opposition to slavery once was. We must, however, seek to strike a balance that leaves us open to being taught, as well as to teaching; an approach that shows real respect.

My Emmaus work has surely helped to anchor my radicalism. The largest group in our senior population is African-American women living at or below the poverty line. Such folks have been the pillars of their communities, even while being marginalized on the basis of race, gender, class, and now age.

While many Emmaus seniors have not had much formal schooling, they often carry a deep wisdom, being (as one senior's T-shirt proclaims) "Graduates of the School of Hard Knocks." In the face of overwhelming odds—such as legal segregation in the "Capital of the Free World"—these folks have not been beaten down. I came to Shaw to serve and teach; mostly I have learned.

One of the key Emmaus ideas is the building of relationships across boundaries like race, class, and age. This kind of sustained, sensitive outreach rarely happens. Instead we tend to stay with our own kind, finding comfort in the relative unanimity of views—the kind that can make our varieties of "consensus" process more workable.

In the anthology *From ACT UP to the WTO: Urban Protest and Community Building in the Era of Globalization* (Verso, 2002), radical historian L.A. Kauffman is quoted saying that "direct action is the driving force behind the new unrest . . . The key is action, not dull rallies where one speaker after another drones on, or meetings that just lead to more meetings, or studies that never end."

This critique of past left-wing activities is a worthy corrective. The book's editors go on to note, "Most of the new organizing—campaigns against police brutality to AIDS drug price wars—emphasize praxis over long debates. 'Action Speaks Louder Than Words' is the slogan of the Ruckus Society, a group that has been training activists in protest techniques since 1995." This emphasis echoes *We Are Everywhere*, and raises important questions. For example, where do people outside activist circles fit into this approach?

"Don't Just Vote, Get Active" is an initiative of a creative anarchist collective called Crimethinc together with some of its allies. The Internet mini-manifesto that I received in early 2004 was clearly conceived as a counterpoint to Punk Voter and other get-out-the-vote-to-beat-Bush-in-2004 efforts. Its initial points are unassailable. Voting and activism shouldn't be seen as an either/or, but as two sides of the same coin. As I have already said, voting on election day and voting every day with our actions go together naturally.

From this reasonable starting point, the "Don't Just Vote" campaign's call-to-action quickly turns into a thinly disguised polemic against voting, seeming to tout direct action as a panacea for all modern ills. Mocking both voting and advertising jingles, the anonymous authors of this call proclaim "direct action is the real thing . . . You make the plan, you create the options, the sky's the limit."

Much of what is shared in the process could be empowering. I especially applaud the line, "Direct action is the foundation of the old-fashioned can-do American ethic, hands-on and no-nonsense . . . without it, hardly anything would get done." Unfortunately, a slide toward an insular subcultural politics is soon impossible to miss, embedded in the issues the call evokes: "the tyranny of the majority," "living without permission," autonomy, consensus.

Could there be any more esoteric, self-referential approach to the burning issues of our moment?

The ghosts of Situationism hover heavily about the call, with the same mystical appeal and intractable illusions as ever: "It's no coincidence that freedom is not on the ballot . . . Freedom is not a condition—it is something closer to a sensation . . . We must begin to cherish and chase these moments . . . Form your own autonomous group, answering to no power but yourself and create an environment in which you chase down freedom and fulfillment for yourselves."

The anonymous authors argue that consensus democracy—the logical and necessary companion to the direct-action approach—"does not demand that any person accept the power of others over her life, though it does require that everybody be willing to consider the needs of everybody else; thus, what it loses in efficiency, it gains ten-fold in freedom and good will. Consensus democracy does not ask that people follow a leader or standardize themselves under some common cause; rather, its aim is to integrate all into a working whole while allowing each to retain her own goals and ways of doing things."

At base, this seems to deny the need for hard choices and work to build power and create coalitions: "In direct action . . . no vast consensus is necessary: different groups can apply different approaches according to what they believe in and feel comfortable doing, which can still interact to form a mutually beneficial whole." While admitting that some might seek "conflicting goals," somehow the invisible hand of the direct-action revolution will apparently guide all our autonomous actions toward the greater good. Like neo-liberal economics, this is not theory; this is religion.*

Even worse, this is a faith that, unless communicated in a very different way, with fundamentally different priorities, is unlikely to interest anyone struggling for survival, not personal expression. Taken to an extreme, this approach can turn us into radical navel-gazers accountable to none but ourselves.

Even courageous efforts, like taking over abandoned buildings to house the homeless, can become racial flash points; this happened with a 1999 Homes Not Jails direct action on Sherman Avenue near the edge of the Shaw community where I work. The aim was honorable, even inspiring. However, the lack of advance community consultation

---

* To be entirely fair, more recent communiqués from the "Don't Just Vote" camp have tempered some of this rhetorical excess and seem more grounded and inclusive.

created a huge rift between the mostly white activists and the area's long-term, low-income African-American residents. It may have been a learning experience, but little, if any, progress was made in ending the scourges of homelessness and racism.

This is where the direct-action model can practically turn into consumer convenience. You can dispense with all of the unpleasant conversations with people who disagree with your ideas, who might challenge your assumptions—*just do it!* Although the creators of Don't Just Vote would have us believe that "with direct action and direct democracy . . . harmony is the only goal that must be sought between participants; unity, on the other hand, is unnecessary and irrelevant," I think they are fundamentally naïve. This can translate not to American can-do, but to American instant gratification.

As Todd Gitlin has noted, direct action can often be directed too widely, not at a specific, appropriate target, and thus risk alienating more than it converts. Take, for example, the so-called "People's Strike" of September 27, 2002. Organized by the D.C. Anti-Capitalist Convergence (ACC), its aim was to shut down the city as an assertion of solidarity with the poor of D.C. and the rest of the world.

Why this was deemed a useful approach to fighting poverty was unclear to me. While considering myself "anti-capitalist," I nonetheless steered clear of most direct involvement with the ACC. This was largely due to my discomfort with their support for a "diversity of tactics." While I wasn't opposed to the idea in principle—diversity being essential to any coalition—practically, this seemed to translate into supporting dangerously wrong-headed, counterproductive acts.

Despite my misgivings, I assisted the ACC in various ways, including finding free meeting space, out of respect for friends in the group. Indeed, the phone number for the ACC was even registered in my name—an open invitation for me to be wire-tapped or otherwise harassed. On the morning of the action, I was there: to participate where I felt appropriate, but mostly to observe, to ensure that the protesters' rights were respected.

In practical terms, the action was a bit of a fiasco. Predictably, given its origins among a very narrow slice of D.C., the turnout was only a few hundred. When the crowd lurched out of Franklin Park into the downtown streets, it was quickly corralled by police. While some affinity groups managed to escape this encirclement and block some streets before their arrest, police quickly re-routed traffic, and little visible disruption resulted.

The demo failed miserably in its aim to shut down the city. Ironically enough, the ACC's major victory of the day was handed to them by the usually savvy Metropolitan Police Department. The illegal encirclement and arrest of some 400 people—including reporters, tourists, and other curious passersby—during a related (but not disruptive) action in Pershing Park led to a chorus of criticism, as well as a class-action lawsuit against the city.

No less august an establishment voice than the *Washington Post* weighed in on the side of the protesters, railing against Mayor Anthony Williams's "dismaying . . . failure to keep the D.C. police department on the right side of the Constitution." In the end, the *Post's* editors wearily concluded that "taxpayers may once again be called upon to pay for the city's wrongdoing."

This embarrassing blow to an arrogant mayor and law-breaking police chief should not obscure the presumption and elitism of the action, however. This "People's Strike" had little or nothing to do with those it claimed to represent. It was not initiated, organized, nor supported by anything but the tiniest subsection of the people of D.C.

While I respect the intent and courage of those involved, we must do better than this. Otherwise, we help to perpetuate arrogant lies, becoming not so different than those who would presume to call their regime "The People's Republic of China" while ruthlessly crushing any spark of genuine democracy.

This reliance on flashy, rhetoric-drenched, disruptive street demos is hardly unique to D.C.'s ACC. It has become the hallmark of what is often mislabeled the "anti-globalization" movement; what I call the global-justice movement. With roots that reach back through Reclaim the Streets, ACT UP, and punk-influenced endeavors like No Business As Usual and Stop the City, this movement has been associated with large, often confrontational street actions, aimed at international institutions like the WTO, IMF, and the World Bank. In the process, it has brought together a diverse array of forces to press burning issues of human needs, accountability, and fairness as measures for our international economic order. At its best, this movement stands not *against* globalization, but *for* democracy.

This compelling message, with broad appeal to the masses on the losing end of corporate globalization, can get muddled by our actions. As pointed out by Andrew Boyd in *From ACT UP to the WTO*, while the

Seattle protest of late 1999 was empowering for thousands who participated, the energy didn't necessarily translate well to millions who
weren't there: "Those watching on television might have thought it was
just a chaotic party."

Boyd writes that "the carnival protest, possibly by nature, often lacks
a clear or unified message . . . One of the great strengths of the new
style of protest—its plural and expressive character—is also one of its
greatest weaknesses . . . As seen through the media, our demands were
a jumbled laundry list; we were against everything without knowing what
we were for." This shortcoming is particularly crucial if, as movement
veteran Starhawk argues, "the more confrontational the tactics, the
more lucid the message needs to be and the more we need to be sure we
have a base of support for the tactics we employ."

The global-justice movement in the West threatens to turn into a
kind of traveling circus. In *The Trajectory of Change: Activist Strategies for Social
Transformation* (South End Press, 2002), Michael Albert warns, "From .
. . Seattle through Prague and Quebec, the left has organized an opposition that is steadfast and strong, and which is raising havoc with the
masters' plans to further enrich and empower the already rich and
powerful. Yet, we have established an activist style that could plateau
well short of what's need to win change . . . Dissent has come to mean
traveling long distances, staying in difficult circumstances, taking to the
streets in militant actions that highlight civil disobedience and street
fighting, even risking arrest and severe mistreatment."

This concern is echoed by Naomi Klein in *Fences and Windows: Dispatches
from the Front Line of the Globalization Debate* (St. Martin's Press, 2002). In her
influential "What's Next?" essay (also reprinted in *From ACT UP to the
WTO*), Klein pauses in her defense of the unorthodox structure of the
movement to observe that "to keep up the [post-Seattle] momentum, a
culture of serial protesting is taking hold . . . Is this what we want, a
movement of meeting stalkers, following the trade bureaucrats as if they
were the Grateful Dead?"

In "Stuck in the Spectacle," written a year later, Klein expands this
critique. Decrying the rise of a "McMovement" of "McProtests," she
states, "It is an article of faith in most activist circles that mass demonstrations are always positive: They build morale, display strength,
attract media attention. But what seems to be getting lost is that
demonstrations themselves aren't a movement. They are only the flashy

displays of everyday movements, grounded in schools, workplaces, and neighborhoods. Or at least they should be."

Klein then touches upon a key point: "The most powerful resistance movements are always deeply rooted in community—and are accountable to those communities." This echoes Starhawk's concept in *Webs of Power* of "developing bonds to place." As she argues, "If we are going to create a new political/economic/social system, one that truly cares for the environment and for human beings, we may need to become indigenous again, to find at least one spot on earth we can know intimately."

These insights beg crucial questions: To what place do we have true bonds; we, the modern-day nomads of the anti-capitalist carnival? In the simple, incisive words of Ella Baker, who are our people? While hopping from action to action, we shouldn't be surprised if local populations don't tend to support us.

Some illuminating discussion ensued when I shared my experience of this disconnect in Shaw during the A16 actions in a workshop at the 2004 National Conference for Organized Resistance (NCOR). One person recounted the local support seen in Miami during the hard-fought Free Trade Agreement of the Americas (FTAA) protests of late 2003. He largely attributed this to the presence of advance teams in affected neighborhoods a few weeks before, sent to educate and reassure the public about the protest's intentions.

Concerned that my emphasis on outreach was being misunderstood, I was gratified when another person spoke up, someone from a punk background who is now active in local union struggles: "Yes, that's partly true, but the only reason that it was effective was because other people have been there organizing and building grassroots support for ten years beforehand."

This, I fear, is what we, the road warriors of the left, don't wish to hear—that change comes slowly, and that we have to be rooted organically in communities, especially those of the poor or otherwise marginalized. It is not sufficient to rush to the scene to confront the global money-lords whenever they have a meeting.

The two approaches are not mutually exclusive, and, like both Starhawk and Klein, I agree that we have to stay in the streets. However, our emphasis must be reversed; we must prioritize organizing people where they are, embracing their struggles, not just trying to enlist them to our own. Otherwise, our movement will fall short of changing structures, and will instead continue to merely piss on them from the outside.

This seems like common sense, and every book I know on the subject at least pays lip service to the importance of community organizing, of tying global issues to local ones. But most often, this all feels a bit grudging, as if the words are inserted as an obligation, simply because we know that it is important, however unglamorous or unappealing.

This will not do. Popular rhetoric aside, democracy cannot just be forged in the streets. When books like *We Are Everywhere* or *From ACT UP to WTO* focus on the dramatic street actions, and fill their pages with photos of street confrontations, we are becoming the mirror image of the media we despise. We don't need our activism to be sexy—we need it to effective, which means connecting to *people*.

Human beings are literally the flesh and blood that make a movement. Without them, we would-be prophets are, at best, voices romantically crying in the wilderness. At worst, we are Chicken Littles running about crying, "The sky is falling, the sky is falling!" Naomi Klein gets it just right when she (after criticizing the past focus in her own writing) worries that "the spectacle of displaying a movement is getting confused with the unglamorous building of one . . . There are times when radicalism means standing up to the police, but there are many more times when it means talking to your neighbors . . . Demonstrations are not the movement, just the public manifestation of all that invisible work."

This understanding is made all the more urgent by an additional factor: the growing level of violence involved in the street demos. Sadly, one of the "diverse tactics" touted by the likes of the ACC has been a move toward calculated confrontation with the police. This dubious approach, practiced by a small minority in the global-justice movement—in particular, by some in the masked "black bloc"—has receded a bit since 9/11.

This is surely wise, given how such images might now connect to "terrorism" in the mind of the average North American. The issue has not gone away, however, and threatens to re-emerge as frustration grows over U.S. foreign policy, especially the bloody occupation of Iraq. Even reasonably coolheaded analysts like Michael Albert argue that "the basic logic of dissent is unchanged since 9/11 . . . We raise social costs until elites agree to implement our demands or end policies we oppose."

This is a dangerous approach if divorced from a savvy assessment of the present moment. I fear that what I wrote in "Global Justice Movement at Crossroads," published about a week and a half before 9/11 in the *Washington Peace Letter*, remains relevant:

> While the specter of Vietnam is often evoked, not all of the parallels are hopeful. Indeed, the tragic death in Genoa of a protester during an attack on a police vehicle has worked as almost a "Kent-State-in-reverse," diverting attention from brutal police repression to the acts of a relatively small—but growing—number of violent protesters.
>
> This increasingly militant response is not ridiculous. As the movement has faced escalating police violence, there has been a tendency to escalate in kind. However understandable, this trend is self-defeating in at least two key ways, as experience during the late '60s and early '70s has shown.
>
> First of all, it draws our movement off the moral high ground onto a terrain where the authorities are infinitely better equipped to fight. I say this not as some starry-eyed acolyte of MLK and Gandhi. Even such prominent dissenters from principled nonviolence as Malcolm X and the Black Panthers recognized the folly of premature confrontation with the state on such direct physical terms.
>
> At the same time, the descent of our blockades and other creative nonviolent actions into cat-and-mouse face-offs with the police—occasionally dipping to near hand-to-hand combat—increases the movement's isolation from both mainstream and, perhaps even more importantly, marginalized communities by facilitating our portrayal in the media as self-centered violent hooligans.
>
> This gap between our movement and an obvious source of potential mass support has long been a critical challenge . . . When the marginalized whose rights we are allegedly trying to defend don't see the relevance of our actions, it is time to rethink our strategy.

It need not be this way. Indeed, our movement is well ahead of the Vietnam one in that it already has deep, organic links to the working poor through organized labor who, by and large, stood against the anti-war movement. We can build on this—if we remain firm in our [tactical] commitment to nonviolence and focus more of our resources on connecting global issues to local struggles in a credible and sustained way.

In D.C., these issues are especially stark and troubling, since street fighting often pits white protesters against black police. This is hardly a winning combination for our side, given that the police department, like the military, is often seen as one of the few opportunities for career advancement among marginalized communities here.

We cannot afford to ignore such concerns. Even the much touted "Teamsters and turtles" alliance seems to have frayed dangerously, partly over such tactical issues. While labor unions can seem terribly bureaucratic and conservative, they are also essential links to the working class. We must take care to build bridges to such entities, not burn them.

Street violence will not be inviting to neophytes or even, generally, the less privileged. As Albert points out, "Activists get caught up in the notion that it is the battle that matters, and even get caught up in a kind of escalating choice of tactics, ignoring the fact that police can always trump militancy . . . A contest of escalating militancy is a contest we are doomed to lose."

The truth of this was suggested by the horrendous violence witnessed during the 2001 protests at the G8 meeting in Genoa, Italy. Most of the mayhem came from the police or their provocateurs, resulting in the death of at least one protester, twenty-three-year old Carlo Guiliani. Reasonably enough, left-wing critics like Naomi Klein took this opportunity to decry a growing police culture of violence aimed at intimidating protesters and reducing turnout.

Sadly, the impact of such critique was blunted by videotape footage of the killing, which plainly showed Guiliani and other protesters attacking the police car in question with bricks, iron bars, and bottles. This is why I have described the tragedy as almost a "Kent-State-in-reverse"; we the protesters come out looking like the thuggish instigators, with the police acting in self-defense. Albert further argues, "To attack the police with the intent to doing bodily harm simply invites further escalation of their violence. It does nothing to hinder elite agendas. Instead it propels and legitimates them."

Albert admits that "anger-fed violence is hard to avoid in some situations. But avoid it we must," for otherwise "we may be creating seeds for an enlarging operational disconnect between the movement and certain types of organizing, and therefore between the movement and the uninvolved but potentially receptive public . . . We have to correct the appearance that opposing capitalist globalization requires traveling to distant cities and demonstrating in the midst of clubs and tear gas, much less hurling paving stones and dodging rubber bullets . . . Few people are in the position to do this." He concludes, "For us to win, and that's what matters, we must attain massive proportions. We must always have the growth of our movement forefront in our minds."

While this, again, does not mean the elimination of "militant" tactics, it does suggest switching our emphasis to sensitive, sustained outreach and organizing at the grassroots level. Albert notes that "a movement does not grow if it creates a culture hostile to the people it is trying to organize." In the end, if our actions have "no larger, visible, supportive dissident community spread out across the land and from which the ranks of those sitting in or battling will be replenished and even grow, this poses no serious threat to elites."

Our rage, then, can divide us from masses of potential supporters. Of course, self-defeating arrogance is hardly monopolized by the more militaristic on the left. Indeed, my Catholic parish has been rocked by the actions of one of our own after the 9/11 attacks. The woman in question—a white radical pacifist of undeniable commitment—roiled our congregation by praying for Osama bin Laden, while repeatedly calling for all Christians to leave the military immediately.

To some, her remarks suggested that those who died in the Pentagon got what they deserved. Given that one of St. Al's key longtime African-American members—Barbara Hill—lost her daughter in the attack, this approach was hardly likely to increase support for peace in our congregation. This was doubly sad, as our parish—one of the few genuinely integrated congregations in the city, and about as radical as is possible without exiting the Church—was already staunchly anti-war. The activist's actions only resulted in raising racial tensions rooted in a sense that whites care more for global issues than the poverty and violence in D.C.'s own mean streets.

A radically democratic approach starts with the marginalized them-selves, as in community organizing. The organizer's role is to uncover the issues and aims of a given community, to support and nourish their leadership. You do not simply enlist them to a pre-determined agenda complete with strategy and tactics.

While such organizing is difficult, often painfully slow work, it is what I believe we need: a more genuinely democratic, "people's" approach. One of the most powerful models for this has been provided by the Midwest Academy, an organizing institute started by Heather Booth, veteran of the '60s struggles.

Midwest focuses on what it calls "direct-action organizing," so named because it enables the people directly affected by the problem to take action to solve it. This approach is based on three principles: winning real, immediate, concrete improvements in people's lives; giving people a sense of their own power; and altering the relations of power. The entire process, by necessity, is rooted in putting the rhetoric of democ-racy into practice. The community itself identifies a problem, and then turns it into an "issue," which is the proposed solution.

Once the issue at hand is framed, the resulting community organi-zation develops a strategy for its campaign. This is the overall plan, which is then to be advanced, step by step, with a certain set of tactics. *The strategy comes first; the tactics flow out of this general scheme designed to achieve your aims, not the other way around.*

With this plan as a guide, the organization seeks to involve large numbers of people in its campaign and then targets the appropriate decision-maker to achieve its goal. Once this aim is achieved, the victory is used to build the organization and move on to the next issue chosen by the community.

One of the strengths of this method can also be seen as a primary weakness. Rooted in pragmatic assessments of power, direct-action organizing does not initially aim to question the legitimacy of the system itself. Rather, it tries to build power that can achieve gains from the system for its marginalized community.

But what if the system itself is fatally flawed; what then? This is a book allegedly about "revolution," after all, however "practical." Is not the process described above suspiciously like "reform"? Perhaps. In a sense, "practical revolution" might seem hard to distinguish from reform, in that it accepts revolution as a process, not a one-time event.

There is still a difference, though. The key question is this: What is the ultimate aim? If it is a fundamentally different set of relationships, values, and structures, then we are talking revolution, not reform.

Seen in another way, the direct-action organizing model does not contradict this aim. While it starts from within the shell of the old society, it begins to build a new one, through its empowerment and organization.

At a certain point, if the process is faithfully pursued, and the system can't be made to respond to legitimate demands, the power built through this process will naturally turn toward questioning the system itself. *It is from this foundation that revolution might be possible, as bases of organized popular support exist with direct experience of participatory democracy.*

Direct-action organizing is surely not the only way to achieve this end. Another was exemplified by the Black Panther Party. Many people today associate the Panthers only with the gun. This is a sad distortion. As former Party chairman Bobby Seale noted in his 1970 history of the Panthers, *Seize the Time*, the group focused on addressing practical community issues from the very beginning.

One of the Panthers' key slogans was "Serve the People," an idea made real with free breakfasts for school children, senior programs, health clinics, and other community services. The result was broad community support. Elaine Brown, Seale's successor as Panther chairman, points out in *A Taste of Power: A Black Woman's Story* (Pantheon, 1992), "These programs as much as Panther guns triggered J. Edgar Hoover's targeting of the party for the most massive and violent FBI assault ever committed."

After the release of party founder Huey Newton from prison in 1970, according to historian Clayborne Carson, the Panthers "began to deemphasize armed struggle in favor of service programs to the black community . . . The Panthers would come to organize more than thirty such programs to serve the 'survival' needs of black and other poor communities."

This process—well-documented in Brown's book—was a radical step. Most revolutionary groups rejected such work as simple charity, failing to recognize their critical role in winning people's trust by making concrete improvements in their lives. After all, seeking revolution involves risks. If benefits aren't also obvious, if a group doesn't seem worthy of trust, why would people join?

The shift was still controversial, even within the Panthers. Carson indicates, "Newton's decision to change the focus of the Party and its mass political line prompted a break with [Minister of Information Eldridge] Cleaver." From exile in Algeria, Cleaver continued to argue "that the black 'lumpenproletariat' had to be readied for armed revolution."

Newton responded, according to Carson, that such "false bravado was causing the Party to become 'a revolutionary cult group' that had lost touch with the black community." Indeed, Newton now saw that the Panthers' past "emphasis on the gun and the police . . . diminished the Party's long-term ability to effectively organize the black community toward concrete political ends, toward liberation."

Furthermore, Newton began to realize that "Cleaver's profane, bombastic rhetoric . . . increased the influence of those more concerned with displays of bravado than community organizing and isolated the Party as to make it more vulnerable to police repression." For Newton, "The Black Panther Party defected from the community long before Eldridge defected from the Party."

Newton's reasoning around these questions seems unassailable. Indeed, this reinvention of the Panthers—done, I will note, amidst intense repression, while other groups like Weatherman were lurching in the opposite direction—made them potentially far more effective than any other '60s radical group. They were bridging the gap between generations, tying service and community organizing to struggle, while remaining open to cross-racial coalition.

Sad to say, the experiment collapsed. Part of the problem was that the gun had already become so primary in the Panthers' theory and iconography. As a result, the Party opened itself up to assault before it had really organized mass support behind it. One truism of armed struggle should be to not pick a fight with the state till your organization and base is ready for the consequences. Some of the Panthers knew this; others clearly did not.

Internal struggles accelerated the disintegration, helped along by the COINTELPRO program and other state repression. Ultimately, the Party split, largely over the question of whether or not to focus on armed struggle. After what became the Black Liberation Army left the fold, the Panthers continued on, turning to electoral politics on one hand, slipping toward gangsterism on the other. Newton's own drug addiction became part of this downward spiral.

Despite this collapse, the example and history of the Black Panther Party should inspire us to see service and struggle as potentially powerful, mutually reinforcing elements of a revolutionary process.

This is why I have focused much of my work over the past few years on two interrelated initiatives, the creation of the Arthur S. Flemming Center and the "From Service to Justice" project.

My experience has been that the more "revolutionary" groups are generally isolated from the very people they champion. While they may have the vision of a transformed world, they have little means to accomplish this mission. Those involved in direct service, on the other hand, are immersed in marginalized communities; only rarely are they able to raise their heads above the trenches to envision or act for a broader transformation.

Both usually lack a credible strategy to bring a longer-term vision together with the meeting of people's shorter-term needs within a grassroots, democratic process that could build the power to truly alter structures, values, and relationships. Indeed, the two camps often view each other with disdain. The revolutionaries perceive the service providers as simple bandages on the cancer of a bankrupt system, nourishing dependency, not empowerment. The community groups, for their part, see the more overtly militant as dealing in blowhard rhetoric, disconnected from people's daily struggles for survival, more interested in appearing "revolutionary" than actually helping people.

In a way, both are right. Either of these approaches—"justice" or "service"—without the other is unlikely to succeed. Together, they are immensely powerful.

The Arthur S. Flemming Center is designed to bring together these disparate visions. The Center is a cooperative project of Emmaus Services for the Aging and Positive Force DC, as well as about ten other groups. Based in direct service to the surrounding Shaw neighborhood, the Center aims to create a "free space" that mixes services, organizing, education, and the arts. My hope is that, over time, it can help to foster a diverse community that can nourish what might be a genuinely revolutionary synergy.

At the same time, I have helped to initiate the "From Service to Justice" project within a larger group, the Fair Budget Coalition, made up of around 100 grassroots justice and service groups, including Emmaus and Positive Force. The goal here is to develop a broader vision within social service providers, encouraging empowerment and organizing, not dependency.

This notion is being pressed forward within Emmaus itself. Part of this shift has already been manifested in my assumption of a new staff role, "community organizer." This innovation should allow Emmaus to deepen our existing involvement with coalitions and individual tenant organizations fighting for affordable housing and job creation in our rapidly gentrifying neighborhood.

The idea of becoming a membership organization has also been raised. If pursued, this would be a clear step in the "justice" direction, based in the community trust and support developed over nearly three decades of delivering services to and defending the rights of seniors in Shaw.

In part, this is simply a practical response to the reality of deep and ongoing cuts in anti-poverty programs and the consequent need to agitate and organize to protect the social safety net. For me, it is also a nod to the wisdom of the Black Panthers mixed with the vision of the Poor People's Campaign.

As Martin Luther King, Jr. said, not long before initiating that latter project,

> On the one hand, we are all called to play the good Samaritan on life's roadside; but that will be only an initial act. One day we must come to see that the whole Jericho road must be transformed so that people will not be constantly beaten and robbed as they make their journey on life's highway. True compassion is more than flinging a coin to a beggar; it is not haphazard or superficial. It comes to see that an edifice that produces beggars must be restructured.

As King made clear later in that same speech, he expected this "restructuring" to be radical, even revolutionary. While this effort was blunted—partly by his murder—King's ideas remain relevant today, as does Newton's vision for the Panthers.

As already noted, this mix requires the creation and nourishing of reasonably equal relationships across boundaries like race, class, and age. It is here that the idea of full-time revolutionaries (or even professional organizers) can become problematic, as they almost inevitably foster inequality within groups. While organizers are useful, just as a computer technician is for certain problems, they cannot lead truly democratic, community-based groups.

Far better is a more mundane rooting in communities, in relationships that don't set "activists" off from the people. The aim, in the end, is to be *of* the community, not just *for* them. It is from this place of mutual trust, respect, even friendship, that our own insights and skills can contribute to a process that might move diverse communities toward effective, lasting alliance. Exercised sensitively, rooted in democratic community, our vision and experience as organizers or activists can encourage a broader understanding of the issues. Ultimately, this increases the chances for fundamental transformation.

If practically challenging, this can also be bracing, even inspirational, as the quote from Emma Goldman at the beginning of this chapter suggests. For me, to be a revolutionary is to be what both Panther Fred Hampton and Bay Area punk band the Quails have called—with appropriate zest and good humor—"lovers of the people."

This has been a consistent thread throughout this book, which I was tempted to call *Revolution As if People Mattered.* By this, I wish to propose a real, and not merely rhetorical, love for human beings.

In his 2003 book, *Letters to a Young Activist,* Todd Gitlin quotes a dialogue from Jean-Paul Sartre's play *Dirty Hands* that powerfully illuminates this theme. In the play, Party veteran Hoederer faces off with young Communist intellectual Hugo, who considers the older man politically compromised. Hoederer, in turn, accuses the other of loving only principles, not people. Hugo responds, "What interests me is not what they are, but what they may become."

Hoederer's answer neatly summarizes my own aspirations:

And I love them as they are. With all their dirty tricks and their vices. I love them with their hot hands and their skin, the most naked of skin, and their troubled looks and their desperate struggle they fight every day against death and anguish. For me, one [person] more or less counts in the world. It's precious. I know you well, *mon petit.* You are a destroyer. You detest [humanity] because you detest yourself; your purity resembles death and the Revolution of which you dream is not ours: You don't want to change the world, you want to blow it up.

Ironically, at that very moment, Hugo is preparing to fulfill the mission entrusted to him by the Party: to kill Hoederer.

More than simply a critique of the authoritarian left, this scenario rails against the "revolution" I detest, that which turns beauty and love into stinking death. This is "Year Zero" in miniature: the love of ideology, of abstractions of "the people," more than the actual entities. This, like purism, is my foe.

My emphasis here may seem to imply a certain idolatry of human beings, making us the measure of all things. Both the animal liberation and radical ecology movements have rightly critiqued just such a stance. This book is surely trying to articulate an idea of revolution "as if people mattered." For me, however, this is to simultaneously call for "a revolution as if all *life* mattered."

It is ironic but true: Given the frightening power humanity holds over all of creation, if we desire to help non-human animals or the Earth, we must first look to changing the minds of people. For better or worse, we humans hold the power of life or death in our hands. Except in the direst situations, this means that we cannot give up on converting other people. Since I am also seeking real democracy, this change must ultimately be persuasive, not simply coercive.

I believe our movement needs more community organizers; fewer street-fighting men and monkey wrenchers. Without the first, the efforts of the last two are doomed to fall short of real victory: democratic, bio-centered revolution. Grassroots organizing is hard, unglamorous, often thankless work. Not insignificantly, this is how we might both turn the tide in this country and set the stage for far more fundamental international transformation.

In many ways our world is perched on a precipice. It seems that humanity has embarked on a grand but risky experiment. As globalization demolishes traditional forms of social organization, while spreading a rapidly expanding personal freedom (mostly experienced, it seems, as the liberty to consume), will humans prove able to choose wisely, humanely? Or will freedom, used irresponsibly, lead to our own self-destruction? In a world that knows the hydrogen bomb and global warming—among other modern horrors—a positive outcome is anything but assured.

In the end, the matter is fairly simple: Do we believe in people, in their power and possibility? If we don't, we aren't revolutionaries, not in my book.

To claim that people have this potential is not to say that it will be realized. Nor is it to argue that humans are somehow all "good." While we have to believe in people, this does not entail being naïve. Not since my study of death squads and torture in Central America of the 1980s have I had any illusions about the profound evil of which people are capable.

Just because the world has long been a certain way, however, does not mean it must remain so forever. Our world, in all its violence, inequality, and injustice, has been molded largely by the actions of human beings. What one set of hands built, another can tear down, renovate, revolutionize. All of this and more is within our power, of that I have no doubt.

This belief in "the world that could be" must, of course, be balanced by rigorous engagement with sometimes harsh reality, with "the world as it is."

As Todd Gitlin has argued, "We cannot invent the world we are trying to change . . . This was the revolutionary delusion—to extrapolate grand results from your acquaintances, to let the wish be the mother of all assessments. Against this intoxication, the practical activist looks at the world as it is, takes account of not-so-pleasant realities."

Part of this revolution is reaching out to "the people" in a broader sense: our own often middle-to-upper-middle-class communities. Consider this anecdote from Bill Ayers about the 1968 meeting between SDS-soon-to-be-Weatherman and the Viet Cong: "Diana [Oughton] would tell me later that the Vietnamese were only mildly interested in our willingness to die for their cause and much more animated about how we planned to reach our Republican parents, something that didn't interest us at all."

We cannot afford to give up on these people, however compromised or bought off they may appear to be. While we should have no illusions about the greed, cruelty, and cowardice of humanity, we can never lose sight of all that is compassionate, courageous, and undefeatable in them—in *us*—as well.

For me, this has meant completing my own revolutionary loop of sorts. This story started with my estrangement from and disdain for my home. Now I recognize my revolutionary outlook as rooted in that upbringing, in the radical values embedded in my religious tradition, in North American patriotism. Even more than this, I can see the influence of my tireless working-class parents: my father's sympathy for the underdog, my mother's belief that any gift we receive requires sharing with the world, especially those in need.

Perhaps they have also been impacted by my wanderings through worlds alien to them. In any case, I have seen their consciousness grow immensely. Racial justice, environmental issues, gay and lesbian rights, even animal liberation—all of these and more my parents have come to accept, even advocate.

To say that some of these issues are fraught with conflict is to put it mildly, indeed—recall that my family is a beef ranching one. Moreover, our immigrant homestead was on the Fort Peck Indian Reservation; this in a county that was named for General Phil Sheridan, infamous for his statement, "The only good Indians I ever saw were dead." It is also where Sitting Bull surrendered to the U.S. Army after long years of resistance, flight, and near-starvation in Canada. We lived through the rise of the American Indian Movement, the occupation of Wounded Knee. We felt its impact on the reservation. Sometimes the changes hurt, but it brought a deeper understanding of history, of what it requires of us.

Which brings us back around to the revolutionary vignette from Sheridan County that began this chapter. The year of Janis Salisbury's funeral—1932—perhaps marked the high tide of the radical experiment there. By then, the populist agrarian socialism that rose some fifteen years earlier had been transformed to a straightforward Communist Party machine.

This force was formidable enough to inspire the Democrats and Republicans to ally, to run a single candidate. At the same time, an ad hoc left-wing party was created—likely with encouragement and aid from the two major parties—designed to siphon off votes from independent radicals unhappy with the ideological drift of the *Producers News*. In the end, this extraordinary attack from right and left staved off an outright Communist victory.

In many ways, however, the Communist defeat was self-inflicted. For starters, the *Producers News* had become the official organ of the United Farmers League, a feisty Communist-linked union. While still based in Plentywood, the paper now aimed for a broader audience. This shift increased circulation—making the *News* one of the nation's more significant radical voices for a time—but it also weakened its ties to Sheridan County.

Many left-leaning locals began to turn away in disillusion with the increasingly Moscow-influenced stance of the *Producers News*. The paper began to run tedious, fawning articles on Soviet agriculture and other supposed Communist advances—hardly must-read material for the average county resident.

Rumors of corruption began to circulate, not the least of which was the supposed culpability of "Red Sheriff" Rodney Salisbury in a bank heist. While all of this was bad enough, Charles Vindex believes that the Janis Salisbury funeral itself was "a catastrophic blunder." By so rigorously scrubbing away any traces of America and Christianity, local sensibilities were deeply offended.

Once upon a time, the *Producers News* seemed to represent the fears, hopes, and dreams of Sheridan County. Somewhere along the line, this had changed. By 1937, the *Producers News* had faded away for good. First the New Deal, then World War II took hold, ushering in a new era. The halcyon days when northeastern Montana had been home to a cutting-edge radical experiment became a dim memory. Once McCarthyite anti-Communist hysteria gripped the country, the period was buried beneath layers of Scandanavian stoicism; dead, denied, officially forgotten.

The dream, however, could not be crushed. The hope for a better way lived on: the vision of a system that valued the worker more than the boss, the producer more than the corporation, people more than profit.

In a way, this dream lives on in me, in this book.

Today, my mother recalls that her father—my grandfather—was a supporter of the *Producers News*, something she did not speak of for many years. In 1982, I met one of Sheridan County's last remaining old-generation radicals, Buster Crohn. This chance encounter happened when, as a college activist, I brought the film *El Salvador: Another Vietnam* to a tiny prairie church near the Danish immigrant community of Dagmar.

Taking me aside after the showing, Buster chattered excitedly about the past. In these few moments, he told tales of "wobblies," of riding on a combine during harvest with a hammer-and-sickle flag proudly displayed, of dreams dashed.

As Buster spoke, I could see the years melt away. Suddenly this bent eighty-year-old man looked young, his eyes flashing, his step lighter. At one point, he paused, glancing around. Suddenly pulling me close, he said, "They think I'm crazy, but I'm not. I just remember how it really was, that's all." As we said goodbye, Buster thanked me for helping him remember this past, for making it come alive again, even if only for a few moments.

It was I who should have thanked him. After all, in those few moments Buster helped me to believe in the people, to know that the incredible can (and often does) happen, even in the most unlikely places.

TEN: LONG DISTANCE RUNNER

"Many will find out in the course of their lives that truth eludes us as soon as our concentration begins to flag, all the while leaving the illusion that we are continuing to pursue it."
—Alexander Solzhenitsyn

"You know, you must try to never express yourself in an arrogant way. Because when you do that, you encourage opposition. If you talk in a gentle, quiet way, people can begin to see your point of view." These wise words were from my late friend Sita Akka Paulickpulle, an Emmaus senior. In writing this book, I have tried to avoid arrogance while being as frank as possible; biting off huge chunks of issues; spitting out my fears, my hopes, my questions, and some tentative answers.

Through it all, I have taken aim at the illusions that often keep us from realizing our radicalism, from turning our ideals into the reality of a better world for all. While not denying the power of subcultures like punk and student activism, I have tried to show their limitations and suggest ways to expand on what is best in both. The insights and the dangers of identity and lifestyle politics have been probed. Traditional radical concepts that trap us in sloppy thinking and feel-good/go-nowhere approaches have been challenged.

Violence as a tool for transformation has been both affirmed in principle and critiqued in practice. We have seen how patriotism and religion have radical elements and can be possible sources of power, helping us to connect with a broader population. Conversely, arrogant dismissals of potential allies suggest an elitism that can doom our vision.

I have argued for the importance of balance as opposed to purity; of seeking out alliances across boundaries; of rigorously, honestly examining our motives as to ensure that our activism objectively improves our world rather than simply our self-esteem. Above all, I have advocated that we take our populist rhetoric to heart, by meeting people where they are, not where we wish them to be; by setting aside judgment and inviting them into the work. In the process, we may discover ourselves—and our revolution—transformed for the better.

I have tried to identify what seem to me, after more than two decades of activism, to be the illusions that cripple us. All are destructive. Still, there is one particularly persistent and pernicious falsehood, the reef upon which many a once-idealistic, energized activist has run aground. *This is the notion that change comes quickly, or that revolution happens once and then is over.*

Time can seem the archenemy of the would-be revolutionary. *People, animals, the Earth are dying*, we cry, *this evil must change* now.

The world, however, rarely proves so easily malleable. *"All things human take time/Something the damned never have,"* wrote Carolyn Forche in her epic poem "Ourselves or Nothing," quoting Holocaust scholar Terrence Des Pres:

> *Time for life*
> *to repair at least the worst of its wounds;*
> *it took time to wake, time for horror*
> *to incite revolt, time for the recovery*
> *of lucidity and will.*

Long-term change offers little to those millions who live and die in the short-term. It is not wrong to push against such terrible realities, especially in the face of apparent lack of concern with ongoing carnage. But impatience can hurt our cause as much as apathy; balance is the key.

I have felt a desperate urgency at times, most memorably in 1979 after reading Robert Heilbroner's plain-spoken yet doom-struck *Inquiry into the Human Prospect*. The recent cracking of a polar ice shelf—the surest sign yet of global warming—hardly reassures me that modern civilization is sustainable. Still, the practical revolutionary in me notes that the world has yet to end, despite doomsayers down the ages. Meanwhile, the debris of countless apocalyptic sects of every stripe litters the halls of history. Most have faded away into obscurity; others have left their mark in death and destruction.

The politics of apocalypse are rarely humane, much less democratic. Nor are they revolutionary, at least in the sense I have delineated in this book. But if most often associated with millennial religious groups, apocalyptic pleas are far from unknown on the secular left. "There's no time to be nice," read a 1985 No Business As Usual flier, warning of imminent nuclear destruction and advocating an angry, aggressive politics. I have seen similar pleas for action around ecology, animal liberation, and U.S. policy in Iraq, to name just a few.

Such raw urgency may prove successful for recruitment from narrow segments of society. It is hardly likely to result in the broad multi-class, multicultural coalition necessary to stop World War III, reverse global warming, fight corporate globalization, or foster fundamental transformation.

We face truly immense challenges. If not careful, however, we may continue embracing illusions that inflate the enemy beyond any rational recourse. For some, the struggle is no longer against economic inequality, prejudice, or violence. Our foe now appears to be civilization, perhaps even humanity itself.

In the shadow of such a monster, politics fade, analysis seems futile, strategy shudders to a halt. As *we* are the enemy, the battle is unwinnable save through something approaching suicide. We bow down before the insatiable, eternal demands of apocalypse. If everything can't be achieved *right now*, nothing is worthy. All that is left is ultimate catastrophe.

While working for a sustainable system, we must reject such dead-end visions. In their place, we must seek a lasting activism, based in the politics of the long distance runner. Rather than spend ourselves in a frantic sprint to some imagined finish line, we must pace ourselves, stay the course, as to triumph. *To be most meaningful and effective, building revolution must be a life-long process.* This means knowing and cultivating the single passion that can sustain us. Despite my punk experience that *"anger is a gift,"* rage is not the energy of which I speak. No, love, and love alone, will suffice.

This may seem a cliché, borrowed equally from Che Guevara, St. Paul, and the Beatles. Still, as more recent advocates like bell hooks have argued, love is no sentimental platitude or romantic mirage. Love is a radically demanding commitment to life, to humanity, including even our apparent enemies. Real love always comes with a cost, up to and including our own lives.

"There are no others, there is only us." These are the words of my fellow St. Al's parishioner Shabaka. A falsely accused African-American death row prisoner saved only hours before execution, he had every reason to be vengeful, bitter. Instead, once freed, he took a stand with those even more marginalized than himself, working with the homeless at our parish's Father McKenna Center. Shabaka truly appreciates how profoundly we are all connected, how we can't do violence to one another without doing it to ourselves, too.

Such living, breathing examples of the power of love can help us to use our anger more skillfully. Starhawk has pointed out that we must find such ways to "transmute our rage" into energy for change, lest it kill us and our dreams. For me, the gentle strength and insight of an engaged Buddhist path has been healing in more ways than one. Love tells us that confrontation is often necessary. However, we more closely model our desired "new world" by tempering our struggle with patience and compassion.

This love must begin and remain rooted in a deep sense of our own value. We are not here simply as sacrifices on the altar of some revolution made for others; we are precious parts of the world we seek to wrap our arms around, to protect, to nourish, to build. Self-care is not to be confused with selfishness. All the banal yet essential elements of life— enough sleep, healthy food, exercise, reasonable comfort, recreation—these, too, are the building blocks of transformation.

We have seen how some notions of revolution can turn us away from uncomfortable ideas or inconvenient, disagreeable people. In his magnum opus, *The Sixties: Years of Hope, Days of Rage* (Bantam Books, 1987), Todd Gitlin writes, "The movement had been self-enclosed for a long time, progressively more so in the late '60s, for turning toward revolution usually meant turning away from family and the wrong friends, dropping contact with disquieting ideas, confounding books, critical magazines. Of course, the more insulated we were from counter arguments and complicated reality, the easier it was to hold onto abstract revolutionary schemes."

Writer David Edwards has noted in *Burning All Illusions* (South End Press, 1996) that "we build our lives on certain beliefs, then spend much of our time protecting ourselves from conflicting facts, experiences, and ideas." He goes on to criticize "the cult of specialization" that steals our humanity and stunts our sense of social responsibility, turning us into cogs in a machine. While he is surely correct in this, his insight also applies to those of us who rage against that machine. Are not our own radical circles often held together by that same "glue of self-deception"?

The revolution that I am suggesting is a turn toward people, toward disquieting complexity, toward life in all of its challenge and possibility. It is grounded in the love we show each other, in the meeting of needs at once physical, emotional, and spiritual, in seeing all life as sacred.

Perhaps this sounds distressingly "faith-based" to some of you. If so, I first plead guilty as charged, and then rebound with a challenge: Is any activism not faith-based in the deepest sense? After all, we act with incomplete knowledge and imperfect vision, with motives we realize may be clouded by self-seeking. Yet we believe, without proof, that our actions will aid some larger transformation that began long before our births and that will continue well after our deaths.

Can we ever know, for sure, that our acts make any difference whatsoever? I suspect not. Instead, we *believe* that they will. In this sense, all of our actions—however agnostic or atheistic—are an expression of faith. Is there any greater leap than to believe in something as lofty as "revolution"?

Reflecting on the black freedom struggle, liberation theologian James Cone argues that "faith is the most powerful force in the world." While swift to note that "there are many expressions of that faith," Cone states simply that "without that belief that we are more than what the world says we are, [black people] would not have survived."

We, of course, will want our faith grounded as firmly as possible in rigorous use of reason, in the facts before our eyes, in our own experiences. Moreover, the faith I espouse must be lived out, not preached. Without works, such belief is truly dead.

It should go without saying that fundamentalisms of every persuasion ought to be rejected. (This is not the same as rejecting people who embrace these.) By contrast, a mystical approach that emphasizes questions more than answers, the present moment rather than any afterlife, can be a friend to humane, democratic, bio-centered revolution.

Such a transformation will never come if we aren't in this for the long haul—which is no easy task. In *The Trajectory of Change*, Michael Albert asks a key question: "Why do people stay in this business of trying to change the world year after year after year, including in difficult times?" Albert notes that reasons could include "to improve your personal life" and "to have fun." Appropriately, he dismisses neither out of hand—as both are crucial to keeping people in the movement—but does point to how narrow such motivations can become, sometimes standing in the way of actually winning a transformed world.

There are at least two reasons that go beyond simple pursuit of what feels good, according to Albert:

> One is religious, in a sense, and the other is strategic. If you look back in the early part of this century at the people who were revolutionary out of a religious motivation, they were still in the thick of it thirty or forty years later. Somehow their beliefs provide the sustenance that lets them stay in the struggle whether they think they are going to win or not . . . The other group of people who stay in the struggle for the long haul understand the process. They see the victories, and they see the gains, they see the losses too, but they can comprehend them rather than being motivationally destroyed by them. They can deal with the feelings of depression and difficulty, not out of faith but out of understanding . . . At some level they understand something about the world that gives them the ability to get past these frustrations and to feel hope.

In practice, these two motivations are often hard to distinguish. I've sometimes found a greater acceptance of life's difficult mysteries and, thus, a greater persistence within religious activists; yet, it really depends on one's approach. At their best, these two blend into one another; faiths different in shape, not in substance.

Another related and largely unspoken element has hovered around our discussion. This element is music, art, theater, cinema, poetry, beyond; in a word, culture. I have not lingered on this theme, given that it is the main focus of my earlier book, *Dance of Days*, written with my friend Mark Jenkins. It nevertheless must not be dismissed.

In a recent panel at the 2004 National Conference on Organized Resistance (NCOR), Heather Booth decried the apparent collapse of community in North America as documented in Robert Putnam's *Bowling Alone* (Simon & Schuster, 2000). Marshalling a dizzying pile of data, Putnam argues that "television, two-career families, suburban sprawl . . . and other changes in American society have meant that fewer and fewer of us find that the League of Women Voters, or the United Way, or the Shriners, or the monthly bridge club, or even a Sunday picnic with friends fits the way we have come to live."

While this list of lapsed commitments might seem amusing to many radicals, Booth insightfully noted that anything that keeps us isolated from one another—thus reducing what Putnam calls "social capital"—is also likely to injure hopes for movement-building. Putnam warns, "Our growing social-capital deficit threatens educational performance, safe neighborhoods, equitable tax collection, democratic responsiveness, everyday honesty, and even our health and happiness."

During another NCOR panel on the following day, Fugazi singer/guitarist Ian MacKaye pointed out the immense contribution of music communities like punk in bringing people together. Such grassroots scenes, if scarcely as formal as the groups Putnam enumerates, nonetheless create free space where people can discover their own strength as well as that which rises from one another, together; where music and politics can help to spark and sustain transformation.

If powerful, this mix is also volatile; politics may trump art, or vice versa. The balance is hard to strike, harder to maintain. In our modern consumer era, commerce can also disarm culture's power, turning art into simple product. Historian Ron Jacobs has nevertheless argued, "If I were to have one criticism of today's left organizations in the United States, it would be their seeming failure to understand the importance of culture in building resistance."

In the 1960s, the counterculture helped to nourish struggle, as did music during the civil rights movement. Bernice Johnson Reagon of the SNCC Freedom Singers recalls, "As a singer in the . . . movement, I sang and heard the freedom songs, and saw them pull together sections of the Black community when other means of communication were ineffective. It was the first time that I knew the power of song to be an instrument for the articulation of community concerns."

Reagon makes it clear just how powerful this instrument could be with the following anecdote: "In Dawson, Georgia, county seat of 'Terrible Terrell,' where Blacks were seventy-five percent of the population, but only five percent of the registered voters, due to Jim Crow intimidation, I sat in church and felt the chill that ran through a small gathering of Blacks when the sheriff and his deputies walked in. They stood at the door making sure that everyone knew they were there. Then a song began. And the song made sure that the sheriff and his deputies knew that we were there. We became visible; our image was enlarged as the sounds of the freedom songs filled all the space in that church."

Such events, for Reagon, revealed "culture to be not luxury, not leisure, not entertainment, but the lifeblood of a community." I have experienced the same, most often through punk, and know that folk artists like Woody Guthrie, Pete Seeger, Hazel Dickens, and Holly Near have played a similar role. As IWW troubadour Joe Hill once wrote, "A pamphlet, no matter how good, is never read more than once, but a song is learned by heart and repeated over and over again."

Beyond an organizing tool, a glue helping to connect people, culture can be a more secular link to the spirit, the unifying, sustaining force noted above; the channel to something beyond this moment, beyond ourselves. It can be a way to bring us to each other, but it can also be a way to keep us apart. Since we the people are the ones who build culture, we get to choose. Certainly any split between "the politicos" and "the artists" is destructive for our dreams of transformation. People can find hope through art, perhaps even enough to believe in—and realize—revolution without illusion.

• • •

In 1986, I found myself being straight-facedly lied to by an official of the Nicaraguan revolutionary government, the Sandinistas, in a public forum. The deceit witnessed that day was, I later discovered, just one of many; the icing on a cake of corruption that came to rot the core of a once-proud "people's" organization. My blistering rebuttal expressed more than simply a concern for the persecuted Miskito Indians, the issue at hand; it carried an unmistakable tinge of heartbreak, a sense of almost personal betrayal.

Reflecting later on my odd reaction, I understood how deeply I had invested myself in this distant uprising. It is no exaggeration to say that I had given my heart to the Sandinista Front for National Liberation (FSLN), *"The Revolution That Just Might Work,"* according to an article I read at the time. Coming to fruition, as it did, simultaneous with my own activist awakening, the Sandinista experiment represented something larger than life for me. When my beloved Clash named their most ambitious (and flawed) album after them, it not only made sense, but cemented the love affair.

Of course, we are all just people, with the same strengths and weaknesses, including the Sandinistas. They were under immense pressure, not the least from the United States and our own deceitful leaders. Yet, if you claim to be "revolutionary," you must answer to a higher standard. As Starhawk writes in *Webs of Power*, "To even dare to use the word 'revolution' is like someone who has been badly hurt in an affair daring to risk love again."

Partly due to my experience with the Sandinistas, I have avoided commenting here on what seems to be this generation's "revolutionary heroes," the EZLN or Zapatista movement, largely based in Chiapas, Mexico. As friends have trooped back and forth from the region, bringing tales of achievement and courage, I have been reminded of my own journeys to Nicaragua in the mid-'80s. I have sometimes wanted to warn them not to trust too deeply, not to give themselves too freely, for fear that they, too, will feel betrayed and broken one day.

Some of what I see and hear from them is truly inspiring. Other bits sound like warmed-over romanticism, the never-ending parade of glamorous, faraway icons that embody the revolutionary fire: Lenin, Mao, Fidel and Che, Ho Chi Minh, Daniel Ortega, and now, Subcomandante Marcos.

Without passing any judgment on the Zapatistas as such, this focus on revolutions elsewhere can begin to feel like a distraction from the hard work we need to do here, among our own communities. As Starhawk has written, "Revolutionaries are fond of ideals and often work from some internal model of a realized society located in some distant future"—or distant place, I would say—"when the state will wither away or when we will all live cooperatively with no need for control or violence."

The danger in this understandable, even positive process is that rather than using our vision to focus energy on present practical steps to realize our revolution, we make it our idol. Starhawk argues, "A vision can also be an illusion . . . If we are too focused on an ideal future without grappling with the real present problems of moving toward it, then 'revolution' becomes another word for 'Heaven': the distant promise that makes up for a grim reality here on earth."

What if, instead, the future is now, being born out of each action we take, each choice we make? Maybe, as Starhawk suggests, "Revolution is what we are, not what we will become; what we do, not what we will do someday. An unfolding, evolving, enlivening experiment, something we continually reinvent as we go along, a living process happening right now."

We also need to find revolution in people, in each other; perhaps particularly in the people we don't agree with or don't know. If we aren't challenged, we don't grow, and revolution becomes just another mirage along the bloody Jericho road; something we hold to our heart at night, our security blanket. Riot Grrrl cocreator Molly Neuman told me in 1991 that her spirituality is based in "the revolution"; if so, then let it be fuel for growth beyond all bounds, all words, all barriers.

Names for the energy which animates this process exist, but none are without controversy. Starhawk has called this spirit "Goddess." In "Moses and the Revolutionary Community," Jewish thinker Michael Lerner terms it "God . . . the principle of transcendence toward all that the world and human beings can and ought to be . . . that force which makes possible and necessary the transformation of the world."

Such G-words are hardly essential, however, and can be profoundly divisive. I can almost see some of you grimacing out there even as I write this! Having grown up in (and rebelled against) a pretty rigid religious context, I understand such reactions. The spiritual does not have to be about pretentious concepts, oppressive rules, or pie-in-the-sky mirages. Instead, we can simply recognize that which is inside us, and around us, in every mysterious moment.

Such approaches can also be useful in practical terms. James Cone argues that being rooted in the Christian tradition enables him to be "prophetic" (i.e., revolutionary) from "within the mainstream." This is no small matter, given that this country was largely settled by religious radicals fleeing persecution; hence the development of the doctrine of separation of church and state. Much of this country—and the world—remains visibly, viscerally tied to religious traditions.

This, of course, is not all good. But within all of these faiths are revolutionary elements that can be reclaimed to press a progressive agenda. We aid no one but right-wing demagogues like George W. Bush by betraying our populist rhetoric with left-wing disdain for religion. This need not mean embracing any particular faith, but simply showing genuine respect for other humans.

Beyond such practicalities, spiritual approaches can also help inoculate us against the ultimate challenge to any would-be revolutionary: our own mortality.

Most mornings I begin the day with a meditation exercise suggested by Buddhist Thich Nhat Hanh. The practice reminds me that I am growing old, can expect to face ill health and ultimately die. Moreover, everything I hold dear, everyone I love, is likely to be separated from me. All that I can truly possess are my actions, from whose consequences I cannot escape. Beyond this, little is certain. Death is a natural part of life. To know this is essential if we wish to truly live fully. All any of us really have, for sure, is this moment, *right now*. As such, now is the time to live, to learn, to love. By burning away all illusions, we become freer, more powerful, centered ever more deeply in truth, the only possible foundation for real transformation.

This is the essence of this book. It has no easy answers to dispense. It is intended to be part of what Freire scholar Denis Collins has called "a constant co-investigation carried out by students who recognize that knowing is a process of never-ending perception, and educators who recognize that they are themselves students." The point of this endeavor is not to be right, but to advance the progress of discovery.

One of my Emmaus coworkers, Pat Itohan, often says that "we stand on the shoulders of those who came before us." We must always remember and honor the fact that, as sung by New Model Army, *"No rights were ever given to us by the grace of God/No rights were ever given by some United Nations clause/No rights were ever given by some nice guy at the top/Our rights were bought with all the blood and all the tears of our grandmothers, grandfathers before."*

This has been, of necessity, a discussion across generations, both present and past, aiming to build a better future. As Audre Lorde has said, "The generation gap is an important social tool for any repressive society . . . We have to fight against an ageism that gives rise to a historical amnesia that keeps us working to re-invent the wheel every time we have to go to the store for bread."

This is especially important for those of us, like me, who grew into activism amidst youth subcultures. Author Zalman Schachter-Shalomi has written, "We need a new image of elderhood, not as a period of slow, sad decline, but as a time of unparalleled inner growth having evolutionary power, a pioneering journey into our untapped potential." This is to say that what is best in youth is a state of mind, a proclivity for growth. This orientation is forever relevant; there is always more to learn, to become.

Revolution is hardly some naïve dream just for the young and single; no, it is the ultimate "all ages show." Raising a family with love and respect is no distraction. Birthing a new generation who can carry on the work past our own human limits is also a natural part of life and, thus, of transformation.

"We are prophets of a time that is not our own," Oscar Romero, martyred Archbishop of El Salvador, once said. We struggle not just for ourselves, but to pay a debt to our ancestors. As we push past the benchmarks left by those who came before, we also leave our own legacy for our descendents to build upon. SNCC catalyst and life-long freedom fighter Ella Baker (channeled by Sweet Honey in the Rock) wrote, *"That which touches me most is that I had the chance to work with people/Passing onto others that which was passed on to me."*

Which brings us to a final *(is anything final?)* consideration: How do we build lives that can carry these seeds courageously, consistently, accessible to all? No greater father of illusions is there than the idea that simply saying the word makes it so. Paulo Freire is famous for having said that he is "not yet a Christian," that both he and his thought remained "incomplete." I wish to be a revolutionary in the best sense of the word. Similarly, I would like to be a feminist, a communist, a Christian, an anarchist, a pagan, a socialist, a punk, a Buddhist, a democrat, a Muslim, and many other ideals. Am I? No, not really.

But I *wish* to be, which is a start. It helps to recall once again Paulo Freire's idea of revolution as "a process of becoming." *In other words, revolution is the destination and the journey.* It is a path of growth, empowerment, and organization, seeking the healing within us that we also seek for the world. Even after the Revolution, the revolution will go on. We will still be required to take the next step, to keep challenging ourselves, to keep growing.

How do we build the kind of community which honors the individual, which manifests radical (participatory) democracy and still puts food on the table? I would advocate both a long-term vision in theory, education, and organizing, and the short-term meeting of basic needs: food, clothing, shelter, heath care, jobs. Creativity is required to sustain struggle and growth, often as expressed through arts and culture, including religious/spiritual channels. We surely need organizations that can act on all these levels.

Most of all, however, we will need each other. Divided and alone, we are beaten, and our history remains dominated by violence and injustice in all its interrelated forms. This is where humility, persistence, and love for each other rise to our side. Again, the words of Audre Lorde:

"Survival is not an academic skill . . . it is learning how to stand alone, unpopular and sometimes reviled, and learning how to make common cause with those others defined as outside the structures in order to define and seek a world in which we all can flourish. It is learning how to take our differences and make them strengths" *[emphasis in original]*.

Given the immense, unprecedented challenges before us today, revolution (narrowly understood) is not the only matter at stake. As Lorde notes, "The future of our earth may depend on the ability . . . to identify and develop new definitions of power and new patterns of relating across difference."

In a way, this new definition and pattern was manifested in the life of Ella Baker, and beautifully articulated by biographer Barbara Ransby in her book *Ella Baker and the Black Freedom Movement: A Radical Democratic Vision* (University of North Carolina Press, 2003):

> Looking back on Baker's life . . . I am reminded of the eclectic crazy quilt that has hung on my wall since I began this project . . . It reminds me of how she patched together her worldview from the ideological fragments in her repertoire, binding together seemingly mismatched theories and traditions, stitching it all together into something both functional and utterly amazing. The patchwork quilt reminds me of how Baker served the movement: identifying the value in people who were raggedy, worn, and a little tattered—people who were seen by some as the scraps, the remnants, the discarded ones. In each one, as in each strip of fabric, Ella Baker saw enormous beauty and potential. And, like the quilting tradition itself, her life's work was a collective process.

As Ransby notes, Baker did not write a book, "perhaps quite deliberately so. Manifestos make us lazy. Rather she has left us a warm and complex work of art, a reminder of a process, a way of working and living, a way of looking at that which may seem of little value and finding in it enormous transformative power."

Perhaps a similar sprawling, patchwork punk spirit also animates this reluctant (anti)manifesto. I hope that these words do not encourage laziness; that in their simultaneous conviction and doubt, they simply inoculate with disillusion. I have not wished to knock down, but to build, albeit only from the strongest possible foundation. I don't want to make anyone feel small. In the manner of true leaders such as Ella Baker, I wish to call forth the biggest and best from you, my reader. Like her, I really do believe in you. The real reason I have spent countless hours writing these words is to help awaken the immense possibilities we all carry within; to encourage you to also believe, to stretch yourself toward all you were born to be.

At its best, I pray that this book may help to bring together, in some small way, the emotional and the practical, the subjective and the objective. In so doing, we can draw closer to one another, becoming more able to reclaim all the power—all *our* power—from the hands of those rich enough to buy it.

• • •

This is where we must end (and begin again)—with the imagination.

Let us imagine another kind of radical, one who doesn't use four-dollar (or four-letter) words nearly so much, who isn't so intent on setting him- or herself off from the rest of society, who is teachable, who genuinely cares about crossing boundaries, engaging with the insights and problems of the common person.

This is an activist, in other words, who might take the skills and knowledge learned in an elite context and put them to work in a grassroots one, organically linked to and learning from and building with the marginalized, with their leadership, their organizations. We neither overly rely upon, nor flee from alliances with those on the "inside." We don't need to, for from our strong, diverse foundation, undeniable, undefeatable power rises.

First we imagine this revolution—then we grow toward becoming it.

This is not impossible. It does require us to survey the world from the perspective of the other and build our movement accordingly. For those privileged like myself, this means from the point of view of the underdog, the oppressed; *"los olvidados,"* the forgotten ones, the throwaway people.

Allies may come in odd shapes and sizes. Whether you seek electoral advances or transformation by direct action, even armed struggle, to be successful all must be grounded in an organized, mobilized people, in a movement that strives to embody democracy.

In the end, the personal does meet the political; the subjective and objective can and must reinforce one another. As eco-visionary Thomas Berry has written, "People in the 11th, 12th, 13th centuries felt that they were engaged in what they called 'a Great Work'—the establishment of a finer civilization after the chaos of the Dark Ages. There is a Great Work for us to do too, and as we do it, it will not only give us a better world—it will give us a reason to live."

Revolution without illusion means that we will never know just how far toward real justice and respect for life individuals or society can grow. Given that humans are, by definition, imperfect, perfection in outcome seems unlikely. Why not let go the reins entirely, just live for now, for our own desires? For the privileged, this will always be an option. While we can all debate just how far toward the "perfect world" humans are capable of growing, it is undoubtedly true that we can do better than our current mess.

Fundamental transformation—revolution—will not come quickly. But the fight is worth it, this much I know. In fact, amidst maximum confusion and uncertainty, nothing has ever been so clear to me. *"I believe I'll run on/See what the end will be"* goes a Sweet Honey in the Rock song, filled with the deep wisdom of the black spiritual tradition.

What better way could there be to live? Why not reach toward the best in me, in you, in WE; in being here now, being brave now, letting time tell the tale?

During the dark winter at Valley Forge, while a ragged, dejected revolutionary army froze and suffered near starvation, Thomas Paine wrote a simple, stirring call to action that began, *"These are the times that try men's souls."* This call was not wrong, only incomplete. All eras call for integrity, compassion, vision, and self-sacrifice in the midst of conformity, self-interest, and apathy. *We can choose to shirk this challenge—but for our own sake and that of our world, we must not.*

In the end, there is a single crossroads for anyone with enough privilege to have a choice, a place in our soul of ultimate meaning. As poet Carolyn Forche said so perfectly, so poignantly:

There is a cyclone fence between
ourselves and the slaughter and behind it
we hover in a calm protected world like
netted fish, exactly like netted fish.

It is either the beginning or the end
of the world, and the choice is ourselves
or nothing.

We will come again and again throughout our lives to this daunting crossroads. As Gulag survivor Alexander Solzhenitsyn states in the epigraph that begins this chapter, our concentration, perhaps even our courage, can begin to flag.

May we never cease taking the harder, truer path; may we walk there together.

"Step by step
The longest march
Can be won, can be won
And by union what we will
Can be accomplished still
Drops of water turn a mill
Singly none . . ."
—Pete Seeger

"Don't be a hero
Because we don't need them
Be a panther or a poet
Someone to light a beacon."
—The Adverts

"If the house is not yet finished, don't be discouraged, builder!
Keep your hand on the plow! Hold on!"
—Langston Hughes

ART CREDITS AND COMMENTARY

By its very nature, collage art sends multiple, often conflicting messages which depend on the viewer to decipher and interpret. While I am quite uncomfortable with a few of these images, they all represent some part of my story and that of this book. The collages also suggest a process: voices in passionate conversation with one another. I sometimes critique the images in the chapters themselves; the images argue right back, just as they should.

Credits and commentary, clockwise from top left-hand corner:

FRONT COVER: 1) Black Panther button, circa 1969; 2) flyer for Positive Force *American Radical* study group, 2003; 3) photo of Sita Paulickpulle in her apartment on 7th Street NW, Washington, D.C., 2002, with my hands also visible (photo by Sarah Tooley); 4) black bloc protesters run down street with police barricade, A16 protest of World Bank and IMF, April 2000; 5) U.S. flag/peace sign button, circa late 1960s, often worn by me, especially over months in 2002–2003 in lead-up to U.S. invasion of Iraq; 6) photo of Ian MacKaye on stage at PF/Fugazi Gulf War protest in front of White House, January 1991 (photo by John Falls); 7) Dead Kennedys' *In God We Trust, Inc.* Christ-on-a-cross-of-money record cover by Winston Smith, 1981; 8) "Radical Montana" keychain, picked up by me at gas station on road trip through eastern Montana in mid-1990s; 9) "From Service to Justice" poster for Fair Budget Coalition conference in March 2003, designed by me, with MLK photo borrowed from newspaper long ago by Tomas Squip and pasted on wall at Kearny Street group house, rescued and re-used by me; 10) PF/Emmaus book study-group flyer, 2004, with photo from cover of *Ella Baker: Freedom Bound* that PF members and Emmaus seniors studied together; 11) page with first photos of the Clash I ever saw, first mention of "White Riot"—images and words just blew my mind!—from *Rock Scene,* circa spring 1977 (photos by Michael Esteban/Lyzzi Mercier); 12) Positive Force logo, designed by Jim Miller and me from art by Seth Tobocman, 1990; 13) photo of masked ALF member with "liberated" beagle, from "Who is the ALF?" flyer I ran across in 2003.

HERE COMES THE ARGUMENT (Chapter One): 1) cover of *How People Get Power*, first book I read on community organizing, Lauren Weinberg MSU class, approx. 1982–'83; 2) ELF publication I encountered in 2003; 3) photo of man standing in front of anonymous graves in Antigua, Guatemala that I visited in 1985; 4) "The Revolution Starts Here and Now" list from *Riot Grrrl* issue #3, assembled by Kathleen Hanna, summer 1991; 5) photo of masked ALF member with "liberated" beagles, from "Who is the ALF?" flyer I ran across in 2003; 6) and 7) two photos I took of kids in "La Barranca" shanty town in Guatemala City, summer 1985.

OUR LITTLE TRIBE HAS ALWAYS BEEN (Chapter Two): first flyer for event I ever made, April 1980, complete with tape and handwritten time-and-place information—I forgot to put it on the poster! Johnny Rotten photo and words taken from *1988: The New Wave Punk Rock Explosion* by Caroline Coon, 1977; 2) Dead Kennedys button, circa 1984, when I moved to DC; 3) the very first article ever written on Riot Grrrl, for September 1991 issue of short-lived indie paper, *Crack DC*, from great interview in July 1991 with Kathleen Hanna, Molly Neuman, and Allison Wolfe—they were (are) some inspiring folks!; 4) cassette cover for early Chumbawamba material from mid-'80s, the rest of the title is, "The music's not a threat (but the action it inspires can be)"; 5) Positive Force flyer created by Patrick Cranston in background, 2002; 6) "There Will be Two Wars" banner refers to one in Gulf, one here at home in protest . . . John Falls shot of Fugazi members Guy Picciotto, Brendan Canty (behind drums), and Joe Lally from the January 1991 Gulf War protest in front of White House.

BACK TO SCHOOL DAYS (Chapter Three): 1) flyer designed by Charles Primm of MSU Students for Peace, for talk I gave on El Salvador in 1982 or '83—too bad you can't see the rest of the graphic showing a genial Ronald Reagan trying to shake hands with a man being used as human shield by Salvadoran military. Reagan seemed to be willfully ignorant of the carnage his policies created; 2) flyer for series on Central America designed by Sean Knight, then of MSU Students for Peace, later of PF DC, with victims of U.S.-supported death squad . . . title of series taken from a Rolling Stones song!; 3)

Students for Peace cofounder Danny Choriki flyer for 1980 Dutch film *Revolution or Death*; this was the first time I really became aware of the slaughter in El Salvador; my friend Ray Pratt also spoke at the event; 4) SAIS Progressive Student Network flyer I made for brunch gathering before March for Women's Lives, 1986; 5) one of a series of flyers I created to hand out at a protest of a U.S. Representative Ron Marlenee campaign fundraiser in Bozeman, MT—I gave him one when he emerged from his limo, smiling and waving at the crowd . . . Without missing a beat (or cracking his fake politician's smile), he refused to take it, and told me, "Why don't you go back to Russia?" I told him, "Well, because I'm actually from Sheridan County"; 6) smart-alecky flyer from showing of powerful anti–Vietnam War documentary that I brought to SAIS—by this time I had obviously abandoned my career path; 7) flyer from the first concert I ever put on, a Take Back the Night benefit with feminist men's movement folk singer Geof Morgan, for Students Against Sexual Assault, spring 1984—the concert led into the first TBTN march in Bozeman; 8) Justice For Janitors benefit flyer I designed—actually from PF tenth anniversary show in June 1995 for the Service Employees International Union organizing campaign of janitors in big downtown office buildings in D.C., but included here to evoke the MSU Students in Support of the Strikers group; 9) a much-abused folder from good ol' "Moo U." with its classic school motto.

IDENTITY IS THE CRISIS (Chapter Four): 1) program from the funeral of the son of a friend of mine, murdered in parking lot of RFK stadium—w/ love to Ruby and Claire; 2) map of North Capitol/Shaw/LeDroit Park areas of D.C. showing how close Sursum Corda (McKenna Walk is in the project) is to Capitol; note also Howard University on northern edge; 3) cover of amazing Audre Lorde book, with thanks to Kathleen H. for recommending it to me; 4) *Post* article from June 1991 shortly after Mt. Pleasant riots documenting the tension between black police officers and Latinos in community; 5) picture from multiracial March on Washington, 1963; 6) photo of Fr. Horace McKenna with model of Sursum Corda at press conference announcing its construction; 7) booklet detailing history of slavery auctions and more in Washington, D.C.

DESTROY BABYLON (Chapter Five): 1) my rather tart resignation letter from my job at the Senate library, a posh patronage gig I worked during part of my tenure at SAIS—when I gave the letter to my supervisor, she read it and said, "You realize that you'll never work here again, don't you?"; 2) 1984 DOA 45 to raise funds for the "Vancouver 5" arrested for a series of bombings in early 1980s in Canada, including Gerry Hannah of (Canadian) Subhumans; 3) sixties poster with the rhetoric of the time; 4) since I have been here in D.C. I have seen barrier after barrier erected between the White House and the rest of the world . . . Here is a Dan Sinker shot from 2000; 5) before the fall... borrowed from *Dance of Days*, my favorite shot of HR ever, from late 1981, done by Glen Friedman, a serious artist, activist, and true-heart guy; 6) graffiti I photographed just off North Capitol Street in D.C. back in the late 1980s; 7) button with the logo of Emmaus Services for the Aging—all of these are fragments of a commentary on rhetorical vs. real revolution, with no simple answer but lots of concerns and questions.

THE GOOD SHIP LIFESTYLE (Chapter Six): 1) essay I wrote for booklet of PF/Dischord *State of the Union* benefit LP in 1988, with controversial boycott chart done mostly by Tomas Squip, with help from Kelly of PF—note how we tried to qualify the chart as containing "suggestions, not rules to divide us." The boycott of Morton Salt is now outdated since they divested their arms program, I believe; 2) goofy sticker from late 1980s Seven Seconds record—I'd bet money they didn't know the record company was going to put it on!; 3) photo of Cesar Chavez of United Farm Workers from great book on their organizing struggle; 4) PETA fridge magnet bringing that noble little pig Babe into the struggle; 5) Dan Sinker photo of GAP store with anti-sweatshop graffiti sprayed on wall, D.C., 2000; 6) *Adbusters* magazine cover; 7) button given to me by friend at Giant Foods across the street from Flemming Center in April 2004 after their union won the struggle for a new contract with their health benefits largely intact.

DON'T MIND THROWING A BRICK (Chapter 7): 1) nonviolent blockade at A16 protests, April 2000 (by Dan Sinker); 2) poster of Viet Cong soldier for "Days of Rage" as SDS morphs into Weatherman; 3) destruction from 1968 riots in D.C.—photo from 7th and P Streets NW, D.C., two blocks from where Flemming Center now stands. Borrowed from *The Changing Face of Shaw: Stories From the Front Line* report by Manna Community Development Corporation (www.mannadc.org) and D.C. Public Library Washingtonia Division; 4) page with the first photos of the Clash I ever saw, first mention of "White Riot"—images and words just blew my mind!—from *Rock Scene* magazine circa early 1977 (photos by Michael Esteban/Lyzzi Mercier). Note "Red Guard" arm band on Mick Jones, reference to China's bloody "Cultural Revolution," designed to purify their regime of "bourgeois reformist elements." This highlights some of the concerns shared in the chapter; 5) Sad to say, this photo needs no introduction, as it has been broadcast across the world . . . I saw an enlarged version of it in Istanbul, Turkey in May 2004 and have never felt so ashamed to be from the United States of America. I went up to the folks at the information booth displaying the Abu Ghraib photos, told them how much I opposed George W. Bush as an American citizen, signed their petition denouncing the U.S. policies, and wrote two post-cards to be sent to Bush and John Kerry, respectively. Then I walked away with tears in my eyes.

THE AMERICAN IN ME (Chapter Eight): 1) famous "By Any Means Necessary" poster of Malcolm X; just out of sight is the gun he is holding while looking out the window. He was facing many death threats at the time; 2) flyer for 2003 PF *American Radical* book study group, using a famous Robert Mapplethorpe photo borrowed from Patti Smith *Complete* book, 2000. I love the raggedness of the flag with the light still shining through, a good metaphor for the ideals of this country, I'd say; 3) and 4) the next two bits are the cover of the Winter 2004 issue of *Green Anarchy* and an inside page echoing the Weather Underground slogan with a fierce Franz Fanon quote; 5) MLK photo borrowed from newspaper long ago by Tomas Squip and pasted on wall at Kearny Street group house in D.C., rescued and re-used by me on "From Service to Justice" poster for Fair Budget Coalition conference in March 2003, with quote from his 1967 "Beyond Vietnam" speech; 6) members of the Revolutionary Anti-Capitalist Bloc (a.k.a., "the black bloc") in A16 protest, April 2000; 7) U.S. flag/peace sign button, circa late 1960s, that I often wore over the months in 2002-2003 leading up to U.S. invasion of Iraq.

LOVERS OF THE PEOPLE (Chapter Nine): 1) rather dramatic headline from *Producers News*, November 1932, Plentywood, Montana; 2) Black Panther button, circa 1969; 3) front page of official publication of the "People's Strike" demo, September 27, 2002; 4) flyer for PF/Fugazi "Downed City Rise" protest concert in August 1995 at Washington Monument, protesting cuts in social programs by unelected control board—the gas can is a Ryan Nelson drawing suggesting the explosiveness of the situation in parts of D.C.; 5) "Radical Montana" key chain I picked up at gas station on road trip through eastern Montana in mid-1990s; 6) monument just outside of Plentywood, Montana commemorating Sitting Bull, great Native American leader who surrendered to the U.S. Army nearby after long, difficult, and courageous years of resistance; 7) and 8) two photos taken by Emmaus senior Timothy Hillie at the dedication of the Flemming Center community-room mural. The first shows dynamic D.C. poet E. Ethelbert Miller during his reading. The second features the audience, a mix of Emmaus seniors, Positive Force members, and Emmaus staff. This beautiful mural was painted by Amy Farina and Ian MacKaye, based on materials I provided to Amy. It features some inspirational figures (both famous and not-so) in the history of Shaw, with lines from a Langston Hughes poem, "Freedom's Plow": "If the house is not yet finished/don't be discouraged, builder!" These words came to mean an immense amount to me while wrestling with the exhausting and heartbreaking dramas that surrounded the project.

LONG DISTANCE RUNNER (Chapter Ten): 1) labor march during A16 protests, April 2000—note in particular the sign saying, "You are the leader you are looking for"—sense a message to you here? (photo by Scott Sommers); 2) PF/Emmaus book study-group flyer, 2004, with photo from cover of *Ella Baker: Freedom Bound* that PF members and Emmaus seniors studied together; 3) photo of ninety-three-year-old Sita Paulickpulle in her apartment, 2002, with my hands also visible—if you look below Sita's face, you will see her on a War Resisters League calendar in a photo from perhaps the single largest protest in U.S. history; a million people in N.Y.C. against the Reagan nuclear-arms build-up in summer 1982 . . . And yes, aspiring punk historians, that *is* Wendy O. Williams next to her with torn "Ban the Bomb" shirt (photo by Sarah Tooley); 4) graphic from Green Anarchy Distribution catalog with a "primitives versus civilization" motif; 5) and 6) photos by Dan Sinker from A16—we liked the energy of joy and hope in the faces; 7) hammer'n'sickle Christ by Troy Scum—hope Sweden is treating you and yours well! "If you like Jesus, then you'll love communism": if you don't believe us, then do read Acts

2:44 and 4:32, while recalling Karl Marx's famous communist dictum: "From each according to their abilities; to each according to their needs."

BACK COVER: 1) The U.S. Capitol, from D.C. map; 2) the mighty Poly Styrene, circa 1977, in photo borrowed from *The Boy Looked at Johnny: The Obituary of Rock'n'Roll* by Julie Burchill and Tony Parsons, 1978; 3) "Stop the Burning" Earth graphic from a Body Shop campaign against the destruction of rain forests; 4) poster for mid-'90s "Global Party" RTS-type demo from *We Are Everywhere*; 5) Sitting Bull, great Native American leader who surrendered to the U.S. Army nearby after long, difficult, and courageous years of resistance; white protesters clash with African-American police officer; 6) monkey-wrencher from "What Is Security Culture?" flyer I encountered in 2003; 7) "The Earth Is a Common Treasury for All" banner from late-'90s demo, echoing Gerrard Winstanley and the Diggers, borrowed from *We Are Everywhere*; 8) Mark Rudd of Weatherman/SDS mug shot from FBI "Ten Most Wanted" poster, 1970; 9) Huey Freeman comic by Aaron McGruder, borrowed from PF *Anti-Capitalist Reader* book study-group flyer designed by Scott Sommers, 2002; 10) Robert Mapplethorpe photo of Patti Smith from *People Have the Power* single, 1988; 11) elderly woman wearing a Black Panther button while sitting with Panther-provided grocery bag, 1971, borrowed from *Portraits of the Panthers* book.

Thanks to all the artists and activists whose work was used in these pages; your passion and vision helped to fuel my many years of activism as well as this book. If I missed anyone, or got something wrong, please let me know at emmausdc@aol.com.

—w/ love, Mark Andersen, July 2004

INDEX

Let us rededicate ourselves to the long and
bitter – but beautiful – struggle for a new world.
-Martin Luther King, Jr.

EMMAUS SERVICES FOR THE AGING
The Arthur S. Flemming Center
1426 9th St, NW
(at 9th and P, across from Giant Foodstore)

The Flemming Center was initiated by Emmaus Services for
the Aging, a senior advocacy group, with youth activists
Positive Force DC. We are joined by ten other diverse nonprofits sharing a spirit of service, creativity and justice.

Emmaus and its partners seek to build just, caring, and
inclusive community. As the neighborhood changes, we
need to ensure that Shaw's long term, low-income residents
are not displaced. Help us stand for affordable housing and
healthcare, jobs, and other basic human rights!

PLEASE COME JOIN US!

To get more information or to get involved with the Arthur S.
Flemming Center, please contact Mark Andersen at
emmausdc@aol.com or c/o Positive Force DC, 1426 9th Street
NW, Washington DC, 20001, 202-745-1200x15.
www.flemmingcenter.org, www.emmausservices.org, www.positiveforcedc.org

Donations are welcomed, as finances are extremely tight.
Checks for the Center should be made out to Emmaus Services
for the Aging and sent care of Positive Force.

Please feel free to come and visit... and thanks for your support.

ALSO AVAILABLE FROM AKASHIC BOOKS

Dance of Days:
Two Decades of Punk in the Nation's Capital
By Mark Andersen and Mark Jenkins
$19.95, Paperback, ISBN 1-888451-44-0, 437 pages, 300 photographs

Washington, DC's creative, politically insurgent punk scene is studied for the first time by local activist Mark Andersen and arts writer Mark Jenkins. The nation's capital gave birth to the most influential punk underground of the '80s and '90s. *Dance of Days* recounts the rise of trailblazing artists such as Bad Brains, Henry Rollins, Minor Threat, Rites of Spring, Fugazi, and Bikini Kill, while examining the roots of PMA, straight edge, Dischord Records, Revolution Summer, Positive Force, and Riot Grrrl.

We Owe You Nothing:
Punk Planet, The Collected Interviews
Edited by Daniel Sinker
$16.95, Paperback, ISBN 1-888451-14-9, 346 pages

Featuring interviews with Steve Albini, Noam Chomsky, Ian MacKaye, Kathleen Hanna, Jello Biafra, Sleater-Kinney, and many more.

"Not just for fans of punk rock—*Punk Planet* is a fine source of articles about politics, current events, and do-it-yourself culture." —*Utne Reader*

The Five Biggest Lies Bush Told Us About Iraq
By Christopher Scheer, Robert Scheer,
and Lakshmi Chaudhry
(a co-publication with Seven Stories Press, in cooperation with AlterNet.org)
$9.95, a Trade Paperback Original, ISBN 1-58322-644-3, 175 pages

"Highly readable and tightly argued, *The Five Biggest Lies* does more than devastatingly refute the mendacity of the Bush administration's Iraq policy. Christopher Scheer and his cohorts present a chilling portrait of the cabal of neocons who have commandeered American foreign policy, revealing the arrogance, assumptions, and contradictions that have had such disastrous consequences for our nation—and the world."
—Arianna Huffington, author of *Pigs at the Trough: How Corporate Greed and Political Corruption are Undermining America*

These books are available at local bookstores.
They can also be purchased online through www.akashicbooks.com.
To order by mail send a check or money order to:

AKASHIC BOOKS
PO BOX 1456, New York, NY 10009
www.akashicbooks.com, akashic7@aol.com

(Prices include shipping. Outside the U.S., add $8 to each book ordered.)

Mark in Istanbul, Turkey, June 2004; the posters behind him refer to an upcoming NATO summit, saying, "Bush stay away; we don't want you; we're warning you for the very last time."

MARK ANDERSEN is the coauthor of *Dance of Days: Two Decades of Punk in the Nation's Capital* (Akashic, 2003). He is a community organizer, advocate, and outreach worker with Emmaus Services for the Aging, a nonprofit that aids inner-city seniors in Washington, D.C. He is also active with Positive Force DC, the Washington Peace Center, Helping Individual Prostitutes Survive, and the Justice & Service Committee of St. Aloysius Catholic Church. He lives with his beloved Tulin Ozdeger, their cat Demo, and their snail Inkim in the Adams Morgan neighborhood of Washington, D.C.